Competing on the edge

Strategy as Structured Chaos

Gratis

Shona L. Brown and Kathleen M. Eisenhardt

HARVARD BUSINESS SCHOOL PRESS
Boston, Massachusetts

Library of Congress Cataloging-in-Publication Data

Brown, Shona L.
     Competing on the edge: strategy as structured chaos / Shona L.
Brown and Kathleen M. Eisenhardt.
     p.   cm.
     Includes index.
     ISBN 0-87584-754-4 (alk. paper)
     1. Strategic planning.   2. Organizational change.   3. Competition.
I. Eisenhardt, Kathleen M.   II. Title.
HD30.28.B7822   1998
658.4'012—dc21   97-41459
                                                          CIP

The paper used in this publication meets the requirements of the American National Standard for Permanence of Paper for Printed Library Materials Z39.49-1984.

To our parents, Marilyn and Richard Brown

and Marie and William Kennedy,

with love and thanks.

CONTENTS

PREFACE

This book began because of our interest in what is probably the most dynamic and fast-paced industry in the world—computing. This industry brings to mind the Internet, multimedia, video games, and networking. It has spawned a new vocabulary that includes terms like bandwidth and Internet time, a new way to conduct commerce, and the concept of the global village. When we started working together in the early 1990s, it was difficult not to be caught up in the energy and excitement of the hi-tech scene. Articles in publications from the *Wall Street Journal* and *Business Week* to *The Economist*, *Forbes*, and *Fortune* all tracked the industry's progress. Would Sun succeed with Java? What would Bill Gates do next? Could Netscape survive? Would IBM and DEC see a resurgence in their businesses? The players became larger than life and the wealth created was phenomenal. But just as significant, the industry was the harbinger of the tumultuous change that would affect many other industries as the decade progressed. Computing was the prototypical industry for the new reality of high-velocity, intensely competitive markets.

This book also began because of our interest in some of the most exciting science, the confluence of complexity and evolutionary theories. As we started working together, scholars from biologists to physicists to paleontologists were exploring the fundamental nature of change. These scientists were uncovering cracks in the fortress of Darwinian evolutionary theory. How could breaks in the fossil record be explained? Did creation reverse the second law of thermodynamics? What explains the tremendous surge of life in the Cambrian explosion? Why did the dinosaurs become extinct? On the physics side, a vocabulary of change arose around non-linearities, chaos, and strange attractors. It was difficult for us not to be excited by the momentum and fervor about the new thinking around evolution.

Our interest in the computer industry was pragmatic. To us, the managerial problems were unprecedented. How could executives manage in industries that were so fast-paced and highly competitive? Planning was unrealistic because the marketplace was so volatile. Reacting was not an option because managers were constantly playing catch-up. So, how did managers cope in an industry with slogans like "have lunch or be lunch," "snooze, you lose," and "only the paranoid survive"? In contrast, our interest in science was intellectual. In some ways, we were "science geeks" and found the ideas simply intriguing. But, more importantly, we were searching for new models to replace the mature paradigms that dominate strategy and organizational thinking.

Business and science converged when we undertook the research that forms the basis of this book. We gathered data on strategy and organizing in twelve businesses in Europe, Asia, and North America. Like true induction-ists, we built the ideas in this book from the data, which kept us pragmatic and close to the concerns of real managers. But the data also made us better theorists. As any inductionist knows, the data provide the intellectual hon-esty and the insights into truly new thinking. An important event occurred when we realized that our work was related to complexity and evolutionary theories. We realized that researchers in these traditions were also struggling to understand change, but in a way that was much different from our own approach. Yet, the frameworks that we were finding in our research resem-bled what they too were finding. "Have lunch or be lunch" turned out to look a lot like the "edge of chaos."

The tension in this book is between these two worlds: the very pragmatic and enormously challenging world of managing in rapidly changing and high-ly competitive markets, and the scientific world of complexity thinking, the nature of speed, and evolutionary theory. We wanted to write a book that had value for managers who not only create stock market miracles but also create companies and jobs. We don't envy the pressure of their world to succeed—not just for themselves, but also for those who work with them. Yet, we also wanted to write something for our academic colleagues that was theoretically relevant and pushed their thinking in new ways.

Balancing these tensions has been the hardest part of the writing—to say something to the pragmatist, the scientist, and to people who, like us, are intrigued by both. Ultimately balancing these tensions reflects our view that research, especially in professional schools, is about rigor and relevance, not as ends of a continuum, but rather as orthogonal dimensions. The very best research is as at home in *The Economist, Harvard Business Review*, and *Business Week* (with some jargon translation) as it is in major academic jour-nals. The risk is that we satisfy neither audience.

For scientists, we have tried to illustrate the way in which ideas like the edge of chaos, genetic algorithms, patching, semi-structures, self organization, and dissipative equilibrium play out in real firms. We wanted to show how these ideas are valuable and relevant to the pragmatic world of business. After all, fundamental principles of science may be universal, but they unfold in unique ways in each academic discipline. We have added our own take on complexity and evolutionary theories through, for example, definitions of complexity and edge of chaos that emerged from our data. Blindly copying someone else's theory would not help managers or theorists very much. Finally, we added some new thoughts around time pacing and experimentation.

For management researchers and consultants, we have tried to develop a dynamic view of strategy that makes sense in high-velocity, highly competitive industries, and highlight the power of field research to create insight. We have written a managerial book in part because we wanted to reach a broader audience. The style of this book is a response to the nudges we have felt, like Don Hambrick's presidential speech at the Academy of Management where he encouraged the profession to increase its impact beyond its own community.

Finally, this book is ultimately for managers. Although we have included some basic science for the interested reader, the purpose of this book is really to show managers how they might more effectively cope with the incredibly demanding, rapidly paced, and highly uncertain world that so many of them face. We have tried to capture effective strategy in this setting in a very pragmatic way. We highlight best practice and managerial traps—the specifics of what to do well and why.

We would like to acknowledge our intellectual debt to Karl Weick, whose notions of loose coupling foreshadow the edge of chaos, and whose wise thinking on evolutionary processes was a major source of insight for us; to Connie Gersick, whose work on time pacing and punctuated equilibrium was enormously important in our thinking; to Andy Van de Ven, for his thoughts on innovation, change, and of course, on prize-winning bulls, and to Henry Mintzberg, for his insights on emergent strategy. Kaye Schoonhoven gave us important early ideas on dynamic structures. Charlie Galunic's research was critical to our thinking on patching, while Anne Miner and Jo Hatch educated us about improvisation. We also learned from many other colleagues, including Robert Burgelman, Michael Cusumano, Rich D'Aveni, Jane Dutton, Sumantra Ghoshal, Gary Hamel, Rebecca Henderson, Dan Levinthal, Arie Lewin, Jim March, Bill McKelvey, C. K. Prahalad, Jitendra Singh, and Mike Tushman.

We want to thank the Alfred P. Sloan Foundation and in particular, Hirsh Cohen and Frank Mayadas, who very generously and patiently supported our research. We also appreciate the very generous support of our work by Cate Muther as part of her interest in entrepreneurial research by women in academics. We are also grateful for the support of the Stanford Computer Industry Project (SCIP) and our colleagues, Tim Bresnahan and Bill Miller. Marshall Meyer was a great help in our related academic writing. We also benefited from the support of the National Science Foundation and the National Science and Engineering Research Council of Canada.

We appreciate the heroic efforts of Linda Lakats, Melissa Graebner, and Carlo Pugnetti in assisting us with data collection. Laura Kopczak gave us some truly great insights and contributed half of the title. We also benefited from the insights of many people who took the time to read and comment on various parts of this book. We appreciate the helpful comments of Beth Bechky, Susan Burnett, Tom Byers, Russ Craig, Sam Felton, Ann Fletcher, Lee Fleming, Charlie Galunic, Andy Hargadon, Quintus Jett, Jean Kahwajy, Tom Kosnik, Mike Lyons, Joan Magretta, Heidi Neck, Gerardo Okhuysen, Tim Ruefli, Erik Strasser, Barbara Waugh, and Jeff Wong. Special thanks to The Neighborhood (Margaret, Tim, Dick, Pat, Sheryl, Lois, Richard, Nancy, Steve). We know that the book club will read it. Thanks for the thoughtful comments of friends at McKinsey: Richard Benson-Armer, Tom Copeland, Stephanie Coyles, Mike Dickstein, Stacey Grant-Thompson, Tsun-yan Hsieh, and Linda Mantia. Michael Cohen and Robert Axelrod helped to clarify our thinking while having a quick beer more than they probably realize. Colleagues at Harvard, Cal-Berkeley, UCLA, UBC, UT Austin, Duke, Oregon, Wharton, Colorado, and Michigan heard early versions of this material and gave terrific feedback that helped shape our ideas. We appreciate the patience of the IE270 students who helped us try out the material. We also appreciate the Fahey family and their baseball savvy. Of course, enormous thanks to many Stanford students, but most especially to Mike Chang, Eric Cielaszyk, Seema Gupta, and Yee Lee, who had the painful task of preparing many of the original graphics and the bibliography, and accomplished this in a cheerful and professional way.

There would be no book without the guidance of our editor, Marjorie Williams, and the rest of the people at Harvard Business School Press. They gave us great feedback, encouragement, and guidance throughout the process. They were wonderful on all dimensions.

We also would like to thank our friends and family for supporting us throughout this project, and for not continuing to ask when the book would really be completed.

Finally, we want to thank the many managers who took the time to talk with us, and allowed us to be voyeurs in their workplaces. The book is written for these managers who face the exhilaration and excitement of competing on the edge—a much more difficult job than our job of watching how they do it.

Competing on the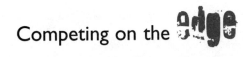

The only constant in our

business is that

everything is changing.

We have to take

advantage of change and

not let it take advantage

of us. We have to be

ahead of the game.

Michael Dell,

Dell Computer

Corporation

strategic challenge of change

DOWNSIZE. RIGHT-SIZE. REENGINEER. This has been the managerial mantra of the 1990s. But managers have begun to recognize that streamlining their businesses is just the first step. To prosper and grow, they are increasingly turning to the more fundamental issue of strategy. What is strategy? Basically, strategy is about two things: deciding where you want your business to go and figuring out how to get there.[1]

Traditional approaches to strategy focus on "where do you want to go?" They emphasize choosing an attractive market and picking a unique strategic positioning, a specific set of competences, or a particular vision for the future. Only then, if at all, does "how are you going to get there?" become germane. But traditional approaches to strategy often collapse in the face of rapidly and unpredictably changing industries. They collapse because they *over*emphasize the degree to which it is possible to predict which industries, competences, or strategic positions will be viable and for how long, and they *under*emphasize the importance and challenge of actually creating and then executing the strategy that is chosen. It is not that traditional strategies are wrong but rather that they are just not enough in industries with intense, high-velocity change.

We bring up the issue of change because change is *the* striking feature of contemporary business. Change is ubiquitous—in every industry, in every geography, in every firm. Change has reshaped drug discovery in pharmaceuticals, taken Nucor to the top of the U.S. steel industry, and altered the centrality of Asia to global business. From autos to telecommunications, from Santiago to Stockholm, constant change has become the norm.

Given the pervasiveness of change, the key strategic challenge is managing that change. The dilemma is how to do it. Should you focus on executing efficiently to reap the gains of current markets? Or should you be concerned with creatively adapting to the changing landscape? Do you plan ahead for expected shifts? Or should you stay flexible and ready to react? Should you focus on building a fit from past experiences? Or should you be more concerned about creating a fresh perspective? Whether you are running the company, managing a business, or shepherding a project team, the key strategic challenge remains the same. From the boardroom to the team room, that challenge is managing change. Given this challenge, what strategy is successful in rapidly and unpredictably changing industries?

The answer is a strategy that we term *competing on the edge*. Competing on the edge defines strategy as the creation of a relentless flow of competitive advantages that, taken together, form a semicoherent strategic direction. The key driver of superior performance is the ability to change. Success is measured by the ability to survive, to change, and ultimately to reinvent the firm constantly over time.

We grounded the ideas behind competing on the edge in very pragmatic lessons from twelve global businesses that we studied on site and in depth. We tied these lessons to fundamental thinking on change from complexity theory, the nature of speed, and time-paced evolution. The result is competing on the edge strategy and its five key building blocks: improvisation, coadaptation, regeneration, experimentation, and time pacing. At its heart, competing on the edge meets the strategic challenge of change by constantly reshaping competitive advantage even as the marketplace unpredictably and rapidly shifts. The goal is reinvention through a relentless flow of competitive advantages. In terms of strategy, competing on the edge ties "Where do you want to go?" intimately to "How are you going to get there?" The result is an unpredictable, uncontrollable, and even inefficient strategy that nonetheless . . . works.

Managing Change

If the central strategic challenge is managing change, what does it actually mean to manage change? At one level, managing change means reacting to it. For example, it means responding to a competitor's product move with a better product, adjusting to a new government policy by creating a novel service that exploits the change, or meeting unexpected customer demands with an innovative repackaging of existing products. Reaction is a defensive tactic. It is unlikely to create fresh opportunities, but it is clearly a necessary weapon in the arsenal of change.

But managing change also means anticipating it. By anticipation, we mean gaining insight into what is likely to occur and then positioning for that future. Anticipation means looking ahead to the needs of the global market and then lining up ahead of time the right resources, such as venture partners, crosscultural employees, and sophisticated currency trading skills. Or it could mean foreseeing the emergence of a new customer segment and developing the marketing channels to compete in it. Like reaction, anticipation is still defensive in that forces from outside of the firm, such as customers and competitors, are calling the shots. Anticipation, however, creates more new opportunities and so is a better way to change.

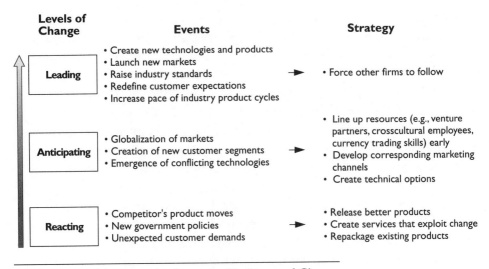

Levels of Change	Events	Strategy
Leading	• Create new technologies and products • Launch new markets • Raise industry standards • Redefine customer expectations • Increase pace of industry product cycles	• Force other firms to follow
Anticipating	• Globalization of markets • Creation of new customer segments • Emergence of conflicting technologies	• Line up resources (e.g., venture partners, crosscultural employees, currency trading skills) early • Develop corresponding marketing channels • Create technical options
Reacting	• Competitor's product moves • New government policies • Unexpected customer demands	• Release better products • Create services that exploit change • Repackage existing products

Figure 1.1 • Managing the Strategic Challenge of Change

Finally, at the highest level, managing change is about leading change. By this we mean creating the change to which others must react. It means launching a new market, raising the industry standard of service, redefining customer expectations, or increasing the pace of industry product cycles. It means being ahead of change or even changing the rules of the game. At the extreme, the best-performing firms consistently lead change in their industries. These firms dominate their markets. In fact, they *become* the environment for others. Not only do they lead change, but these firms also set the rhythm and pace of that change within their industries.

Inside Intel

The semiconductor giant Intel is an example of a company whose managers effectively blend all three levels of managing change. For instance, Intel executives sometimes react to change. Take the emergence of the network computer, an inexpensive alternative to the PC, as the gateway to Internet computing. Sun Microsystems, Oracle, and IBM pioneered this approach, which effectively "dumbs down" the desktop computer and reduces the need for the kind of sophisticated microprocessor "brains" that have been the mainstay of Intel's business. Were Intel managers surprised? Perhaps, but they responded quickly, initially by creating an Internet division and, more recently, by announcing plans for the development of the NetPC with Microsoft, a hybrid product targeted directly at the network computer market.

But reacting to change is not all that Intel executives do. They also anticipate change effectively. For instance, they foresaw the importance of the graphics and multimedia markets to their business. In the early 1990s, they launched anticipatory alliances with telecommunications, cable, and movie companies. These alliances included the development of an Internet server with MCI and the launch of a media lab with the Hollywood powerhouse Creative Artists Agency (CAA). In addition, Intel executives quietly invested more than half a billion dollars in more than fifty media, Internet, and graphics companies. Overall, Intel executives have positioned the company through a broad range of moves to take advantage of (and now create) the exploding multimedia and three-dimensional graphics market segments.

Finally, and most widely known, Intel leads change by setting the pace in the personal computing market. *Fortune* magazine proclaimed that Intel "aims to be the visionary leader for the entire computer industry."[2] Indeed, as the coarchitect with Microsoft of the Wintel (Windows plus Intel) standard, Intel sets the rhythm in multiple industries—computer hardware, software, and semiconductors—at a relentless pace with an array of products that has left clonemakers like AMD scrambling to catch up, and customers like Dell and complementers like the software maker Adobe marching to Intel's beat. Moreover, the power of Intel was never more obvious than during the Pentium chip recall in early 1995. Despite the significance of the product problem, Intel scarcely missed a beat. And the company's long-term success was never in doubt. At the moment, Intel not only commands market share but also leads its competitors and, to a very real degree, its buyers, complementers, and ultimately customers, through relentlessly driven change.

Complications of Change

But managing change is not easy. Managing change is difficult because managers cannot plan effectively. The direction of change is just too uncertain. Change can come from inside the firm or outside. It can emerge from outside the industry or within—from suppliers, customers, competitors, or complementers. In such situations, the future is too unpredictable for planning.

Managers cannot wait for the future to unfold either. If they do, they will surely be left behind in industries where it is almost impossible to catch up. Indeed, the faster the pace of change, the more difficult it is to keep up with that change and the more disastrous it becomes to fall behind. And so relying on a wait-and-see approach is not a viable strategic option.

Managing change is also difficult because of the fierce competition in most high-velocity industries. In such industries, managers cannot make major mistakes. Knowledgeable competitors are likely to exploit such mistakes quickly. A major false step or wrong move can set a firm back and make it impossible to recover.

Finally, managing change is complicated because managers cannot focus only on change. Short-term fiscal targets do not disappear just because change is rampant. Rather, managers must balance when and what to change with the demands for building and preserving current revenues and profits. Rather than focus on change per se, firms must manage change in a way that also meets the financial and social performance demands that every manager faces.

The strategic challenge in high-velocity, unpredictable industries is therefore to manage change by reacting when necessary, anticipating wherever possible, and leading change when the circumstances are right. Given this strategic challenge, an approach of competing on the edge makes sense.

Competing on the Edge

Competing on the edge contrasts with other approaches to strategy that assume clear industry boundaries, predictable competition, or a knowable future. As such, these other approaches are insightful for setting a broad strategic direction for markets in which change is slow enough that a sustainable advantage or defensible position can be identified as lasting for a long period, perhaps even "a decade or more."[3] A more dynamic approach, like game theory, gets closer to the competitive reality of fast-paced change that many firms face. It is incomplete, however, because it focuses on "where do you want to go?" and neglects the other half of strategy—"how are you going to get there?" In contrast, competing on the edge assumes that industries are rapidly and unpredictably changing and, therefore, that the central strategic challenge is managing change.

The underlying insight behind competing on the edge is that strategy is the result of a firm's organizing to change constantly and letting a semicoherent strategic direction emerge from that organization.[4] In other words, it is about combining the two parts of strategy by simultaneously addressing where you want to go and how you are going to get there. A semicoherent strategic direction is fundamentally different from what is traditionally called strategy. What is unique and even provocative about it? It is . . .

- UNPREDICTABLE. Competing on the edge is about surprise. It is not about planning an approach and knowing how it will

	Five Forces	Core Competence	Game Theory	Competing on the Edge
Assumptions	Stable industry structure	Firm as bundle of competences	Industry viewed as dynamic oligopoly	Industry in rapid, unpredictable change
Goal	Defensible position	Sustainable advantage	Temporary advantage	Continuous flow of advantages
Performance Driver	Industry structure	Unique firm competences	Right moves	Ability to change
Strategy	Pick an industry, pick a strategic position, fit the organization	Create a vision, build and exploit competences to realize vision	Make the "right" competitive and collaborative moves	Gain the "edges," time pace, shape semicoherent strategic direction
Success	Profits	Long-term dominance	Short-term win	Continual reinvention

Figure 1.2 • Models of Strategy

unfold. The future is too uncertain for such pin-point accuracy. It is more about making some moves, observing what happens, and continuing with the ones that seem to work. Although the past and future matter, the focus of attention is today.

- UNCONTROLLED. It is not about command and precision planning by senior executives. There is simply too much going on in rapidly changing industries for any single group to orchestrate every move. Rather, many people in the firm must make many moves on their own. Competing on the edge is about strategy-making centered at the business unit, not at corporate headquarters.

- INEFFICIENT. Competing on the edge is not necessarily efficient in the short term. It is about stumbling into the wrong markets, making mistakes, bouncing back, and falling into the right ones. It is about duplication, misfit, and error. Sometimes, it is even about adding randomness. Competing on the edge is not about being the most efficient firm or the most profitable firm at any particular time. It is not about creating fit. Rather it is about using change to relentlessly reinvent the business by discovering opportunities for growth and letting profits follow.

- PROACTIVE. Competing on the edge is not about passively watching for the occasional discontinuity or waiting for other

firms to move before taking action. It is about being early—
about trying to anticipate and, where possible, to lead change.

- CONTINUOUS. It is about a rhythm of moves over time; not a
set of disjointed actions. It does not comprise a few very large
moves, like massive corporate transformations or corporate
megamergers. Instead, it is about repeated, relentless change that
becomes endemic to the firm.

- DIVERSE. Finally, competing on the edge is about making a variety of moves with varying scale and risk. So the key to successful
performance is not a single generic strategy, a particular competence, or one startling move. Rather, it is about creating a robust
and diverse strategy. It is about making lots of moves. Some will
be brilliant, most will be good, and a few will be failures.

Strategy by Bill Gates

To much of the world, Microsoft CEO Bill Gates is the precocious mastermind of the stunningly brilliant and equally successful business strategy that
has propelled the firm to the top tier of global corporations. The popular
image is that Gates almost singlehandedly formulates the firm's strategy from
his Redmond enclave and then signals it to an eagerly waiting, well-disciplined
organization. Apparently combining insightful industry analyses with a cogent
grasp of Microsoft competences and a Machiavellian understanding of competitive moves, Gates seems to be the quintessential corporate strategist.

But is this image of a controlled, cerebral, and well-planned strategy accu-
rate? One observer has called recent Microsoft strategy "decisive, quick,
breathtaking," consistent with the popular image of planning, command, and
control. In contrast, others see the real story of Microsoft strategy as one of
coping with fast-paced and unrelenting change. Others have noted that "the
firm covers its bets and reconfigures strategy as it goes along."[5] Gates himself
claims, "Microsoft is a company that will never make any forecasts."[6] From
this perspective, strategy at Microsoft looks surprisingly like a semicoherent
strategic direction.

Microsoft's Internet strategy, for example is *unpredictable*. The initial strategy included an elaborate assault on America Online through the development
of a proprietary alternative. In part, this strategy reflected a belief among
senior Microsoft executives that it was not possible to make money on the
Internet because access was free. Microsoft executives ended up discarding this
formal strategy and joining the nonproprietary world. They embraced Sun's

Java, bought up Internet companies, and, ironically, became a close strategic partner of its one-time target, AOL. No one predicted this strategy.

Microsoft's strategy is *uncontrolled*. Indeed, much of the strategic thinking for the company's Internet products came from well below the senior echelon of the corporation. One manager visited Cornell University, observed students "hacking" on the Internet, and pressed for change within the corporation. A Microsoft renegade initially developed the first Internet server in an unsanctioned project. Only later did Microsoft's senior leadership announce the strategy that had emerged from below.

Microsoft's strategy is *inefficient*. The firm wasted resources on developing a proprietary version of the Microsoft Network, a misstep that ultimately cost millions. Money was spent on technologies that were later bought from other companies and on promoting products that were eventually dropped. The firm passed up acquisitions that later cost them much more, such as their licensing arrangement with Spyglass Inc., a Netscape rival.

Microsoft's strategy is *proactive*. Firm managers aggressively moved into a cable news channel and Web site produced with NBC; started *Slate*, a Web magazine; moved into information content with the film production company Dreamworks, and on and on. Of course, sometimes Microsoft is reactive, but more often the firm is aggressively proactive.

Microsoft's strategy is *continuous*. There was no one big move—no single acquisition, no major corporate restructuring, no single brilliant play. There were many moves, over several years, that coalesced into a strategy. For example, in 1993, work began on Marvel, an online service that became Microsoft Network. In 1994, Tiger, a video server for the Internet, was announced while Web page capability was added to Word, Microsoft's word-processing package, and a Web browser was included in Windows 95. In 1995, plans were made to coordinate with Sun's Java language. In 1996, Vermeer Technologies, maker of the FrontPage, a software tool for creating and managing Web documents, was acquired. And in 1997, WebTV was acquired.

Microsoft's strategy is *diverse*. It involves strategic partnerships, acquisitions, and in-house development of different scales and timeframes. It includes programs for video servers on interactive television, an online magazine, satellite communication, acquisition of information content, and an Internet gaming zone featuring multiplayer games, such as chess and bridge.

Ultimately, strategy at Microsoft does not look much like "do an industry analysis, pick a strategic position, and execute." It does not really resemble "examine our core competences and build off of them." It looks a lot more like a "creation of a relentless flow of competitive advantages" that are crafted together to form a semicoherent strategic direction. Indeed, Gates and

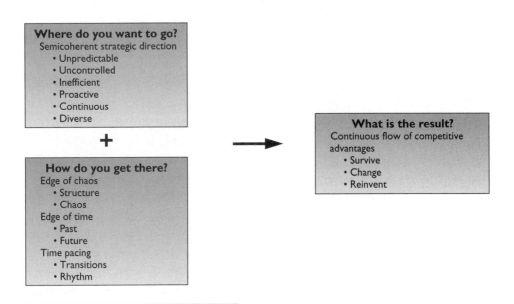

Figure 1.3 • Competing on the Edge

his colleagues apparently cobbled together Microsoft's Internet approach through a competing on the edge strategy. The result was that the company at times reacted (by striking alliances with Java and AOL), sometimes anticipated (all kinds of content moves), and increasingly led change (by challenging Netscape in Web browsers).

Core Concepts

If a semicoherent strategic direction is "where you want to go," the second strategy question is "how do you get there?" The answer lies in creating an organization that can continuously change and then allow a flow of competitive advantages to emerge that form a semicoherent direction. Three core concepts describe an organization that can change continuously: the edge of chaos, the edge of time, and time pacing.

The *edge of chaos* has been described as "a natural state between order and chaos, a grand compromise between structure and surprise."[7] In more concrete terms, being at the edge of chaos means being only partially structured.

The intuition behind the edge of chaos is that change occurs when strategies and their related organizations are sufficiently rigid so that change can be organized to happen but not so rigid that it cannot occur. On the one hand, too much chaos makes it difficult to coordinate change. There is no coherence. Confusion sets in. Competitive moves become random. Organizations fly apart. On the other hand, too much structure makes it hard for a firm to move. Strategies become brittle and prone to unexpected collapse. Centrally planned economies, like the former Soviet Union, are an illustration of this phenomenon. Businesses that are too tightly configured with their environment are another example.

In contrast to these two extremes, the edge of chaos lies in an intermediate zone where organizations never quite settle into a stable equilibrium but never quite fall apart, either. This intermediate zone is where systems of all types— biological, physical, economic, and social—are at their most vibrant, surprising, and flexible. The power of a few simple structures to generate enormously complex, adaptive behavior—whether flock behavior among birds, resilient government (as in democracy), or simply successful performance by major corporations—is at the heart of the edge of chaos. The edge of chaos captures the complicated, uncontrolled, unpredictable but yet adaptive (in technical terms, *self-organized*) behavior that occurs when there is some structure but not very much.[8] The critical managerial issue at the edge of chaos is to figure out what to structure, and as essential, what *not* to structure.

The second core concept is the *edge of time*. Change requires thinking simultaneously about multiple time horizons. Successful change involves relying partially on past experience, while staying focused on current execution, and still looking ahead to the future. This can be conceptualized as balancing on the edge of time—rooted in the present, yet aware of past and future. The edge of time recognizes the tendency to slip off the edge toward the past or the future, driving managers to focus too much on either. Mired in the past, managers quickly become over-dependent on it. Enamored with the future, managers waste time over-planning it. The challenge is to balance on the edge without falling off onto either side.

If there is too much attention paid to the past, strategies and organizations become locked into dated competitive models. Air France, for example, has

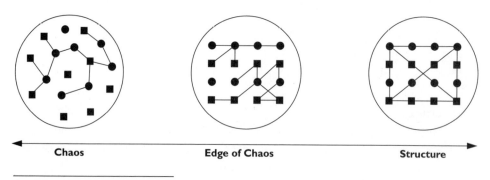

◄ Chaos
Edge of Chaos
Structure ►

Figure 1.4 · Edge of Chaos

been trapped by its past. This "symbol of Gallic inertia" has consistently lagged the airline industry in adopting innovations such as hub-and-spoke connections and baggage automation. Only government subsidies and domestic protection have kept the airline aloft. Yet if managers forget the past, then they fail to take advantage of experience. They are always starting from scratch, constantly repeating mistakes, and as a result, are slow to change. Effective change requires managers to balance on the edge—aware of the past but not trapped in it.

If there is too much attention paid to the future, strategies and organizations get too far ahead. Managers end up neglecting today's businesses. Silicon Graphics is one firm whose managers became entranced with the future. While SGI's managers were fantasizing about the future of products that could produce stunning *Jurassic Park*-type special effects, they were stumbling over day-to-day strategy and execution in their core computer businesses. Yet, if managers ignore the future, they end up reacting to the marketplace that other firms create. They are constantly playing catch-up rather than anticipating and leading change. Effective change requires managers to balance on the edge— aware of the future but not obsessed with it.

In more concrete terms, the edge of time is about focusing on today but never losing sight of the past or the future. The edge of time captures the complicated yet adaptive behavior that emerges at an intermediate zone where managers look backward to the past and forward into the future while concentrating on today. The critical management issue at the edge of time is how to manage all timeframes simultaneously without being trapped in any one.

The third core concept of competing on the edge is *time pacing*. Time pacing means that change is triggered by passage of time, rather than by the occurrence of events. For example, time pacing means launching a new product or service every six months, rather than whenever a competitive response is needed; entering a new market every third quarter, rather than whenever a

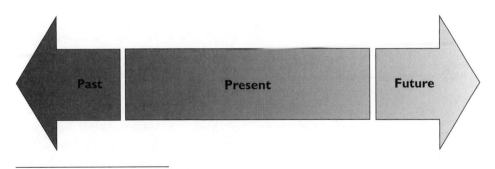

Figure 1.5 • Edge of Time

How Organizations Change

Our scientific understanding of how organizations (and systems, in general) change is itself changing. In disciplines ranging from physics and biology to economics and strategy, the new thinking is that change is the marriage of two processes. One process emphasizes the emergence of surprising and sometimes even abrupt change from partially linked systems called *complex adaptive systems*. This is *complexity theory*. The other describes the process of gradual change across time through variation, selection, and retention. This is *evolutionary theory*. Although distinct, both focus on how living things grow, adapt, and change.

Complexity theory is the newer perspective on change. It began with an interest in how order springs from chaos. According to complexity theory, adaptation is most effective in systems that are only partially connected. The argument is that too much structure creates gridlock, while too little structure creates chaos. A good example would be the traffic lights in a city. If there are no lights, traffic is chaotic. If there are too many lights, traffic stops. A moderate number of lights creates structure, but still allows drivers to adapt their routes in surprising ways in response to changing traffic conditions. Consequently, the key to effective change is to stay poised on this *edge of chaos*. Complexity theory focuses managerial thinking on the interrelationships among different parts of an organization and on the trade-off of less control for greater adaptation.

Evolutionary theory is the older, Darwinian view of how living things grow, adapt, and change. Systems evolve through *natural selection,* acting on inherited, genetic variation through successive generations over time. Variation is enhanced, making evolution more effective, by some randomness and inefficiency in the process. Moreover, systems evolve most effectively by gradually shedding what was useful in the past and adopting what will be useful in the future. The key is, therefore, to remain at the *edge of time* such that the past and future are connected. Evolutionary theory stretches managerial thinking across a longer time frame that includes past and future, and focuses thinking on randomness.

The fundamental argument of this book is that firms in rapidly changing industries are superior performers when they are able to combine these two change processes and continuously reinvent themselves. Complexity theory describes the quicker change process that happens as managers adapt their business to current conditions. Evolutionary theory describes a slower and more gradual change process that occurs over time. To this argument the notions of *time pacing*, the internal metronome that sets the pace of change within the firm, and *intentionality*, the belief that people can consciously affect both processes, are added.[9]

promising opportunity appears; refreshing a brand every three years, rather than waiting for market signals that indicate the brand is dated.

Generally speaking, time pacing is about creating an internal rhythm that drives the momentum for change. Managers who use time pacing—as distinct from speed—as a strategic weapon, understand the power of rhythm and the importance of transitions. A critical concept, time pacing is one of the least understood facets of strategy in unpredictable and high-velocity industries. The key management issues in time pacing are picking the right rhythm and choreographing transitions such as from product to product or market to market.

Poised on the Edges at 3M

Reflective guardrails. Sandpaper. Masking tape. Thinsulate. Post-its . . . . This array of products seems a little dull . . . . Yet these products are in the portfolio of a firm that has competed on the edge probably longer than any other major company. Launched in 1902 as Minnesota Mining and Manufacturing in frigid Two Harbors, Minnesota, 3M has constantly reinvented itself. In the early days, 3M managers switched from mining corundum to manufacturing sandpaper. Later, it was Scotch tape, and then Post-its. In a business world in which stagnant firms have been the norm, 3M managers have continuously reinvented the corporation through a parade of technologies that have allowed the corporation to remain a mainstay of the U.S. Fortune 500. These managers rarely make huge moves and rarely place risky bets; instead, they relentlessly change the company year after year.

Managers at 3M achieve superior financial performance through a strategy of competing on the edge. They organize the company on the edges of chaos and time and impose time pacing (the "how do you get there" part of strategy), allow a semicoherent strategic direction to emerge (the "where do you want to go" part), and achieve a continuous flow of competitive advantages.

Throughout its history, 3M has always been a bit bipolar, driven and orderly on the one hand and yet at the same time somewhat erratic. As *Fortune* describes, "The central secret of 3M: Beneath its orderly, AAA-rated Midwestern exterior, the place is dotty."[10] CEO Desi DeSimone called it "innovation and stability." We describe it as being poised at the *edge of chaos*. How do 3M managers do it? One way is through . . .

- CHAOS. In business units, which are often grouped together in ways that defy logic, scientists are free to spend 15 percent of their time on whatever they like. Businesses run with lots of freedom and loose planning so that they can pursue unexpected opportunities. Genesis grants are given by senior scientists for projects that are outside of the normal business system. Part of the culture is to circumvent the boss to pursue projects. A favorite story is that of Thinsulate, which was turned down five times by senior management (including the future CEO DeSimone) but kept reappearing. As one manager says, "We're managing chaos and that is the right way to do it."

But if 3M were only chaotic, it would hardly have a top-ranked performance, year-after-year. So it is also a firm with plenty of . . .

- STRUCTURE. There are sophisticated financial controls and information systems at 3M. One executive described 3M as a "money-making culture." Another senior executive observed, "You never see the productivity issue off the screen." Executives are held tightly accountable for financial performance. Each division is expected to hit specific quarterly profit, growth, and innovation targets. Priorities for the research portfolio are routinely assessed. CEO DeSimone says, "Just as important as our belief in flexible organization is our conviction that 3M's growth and profitability should come not from a few of our product lines, but from each and every 3M profit center around the world."

Although being poised at the edge of chaos is about how to manage change today, it is not the whole story. Managers at 3M have also poised the firm at the *edge of time*, to evolve yesterday's strategies smoothly to today's and on to tomorrow's. As one observer noted, 3M "sits on a foundation of extraordinary continuity from past to present and on to the future." Not surprisingly, then, 3M is firmly rooted in the . . .

- PAST. The firm has low turnover and is led by senior executives, most of whom have long histories there. An early president, William McKnight, is still revered throughout the corporation, and his wisdom about balancing freedom and structure is an integral part of the corporate culture. Scientists at 3M also routinely recombine past technologies. For example, its very successful microreplication business was built by linking several existing businesses to create a new one that has taken the firm into expanding markets. But 3M is not just about the past. What also matters is the . . .

- FUTURE. At 3M, support for leading-edge projects, basic research, and futurists is the norm. Company executives aggressively look to the future. They accelerate R&D projects across their thirty-five businesses by asking a simple question: Does the project have the potential to change the basis of competition for 3M? If the answer is "yes," the project gets accelerated funding. The idea is to ensure that every 3M business can reinvent itself periodically. Finally, 3M tightly links timeframes together through . . .

- TIME PACING. Change is triggered by a sacrosanct corporate edict that 25 percent of sales must come from products less than four years old. This simple rule sets the *rhythm* of change, from past to present to future, for the entire corporation. This relentless push for new products forces change at regular intervals and creates the rhythm and pace for the entire firm. And in the late 1990s, when CEO DeSimone needed to accelerate the pace to meet faster-changing markets, he ratcheted up the tempo for new product sales, from 25 percent to 30 percent.

  Taken together, time pacing and remaining poised on the edges of chaos and time has created a corporation that has a . . .

- SEMICOHERENT STRATEGIC DIRECTION. Strategy at 3M, which is based on constantly finding new products and new markets, can be hard to fathom, but unpredictable, uncontrolled, and inefficient strategies usually are. A *Fortune* writer even claimed that "3M has no strategy." But what this writer misunderstood was that 3M has a semicoherent strategic direction that is simply more complex than a "pick a strategy" point of view. At 3M, strategy is a loosely coherent direction focused on coating technologies and innovation that has emerged from a time-paced organization poised on the edges of chaos and time. As a result, 3M managers have achieved a . . .

- CONTINUOUS FLOW OF COMPETITIVE ADVANTAGES. 3M's performance speaks for itself. In 1996, 3M marked its thirty-eighth consecutive year of dividend increases. Sales increased nine percent, and income increased more than ten percent, while sales from products introduced within the past four years accounted for thirty percent of sales. The firm continuously reinvents itself, is perennially among the most-admired firms in the United States, and year after year is a strong global performer.

Intellectual Roots

Competing on the edge builds on an eclectic tradition of academic research on complex adaptive behavior, evolutionary change, and the origins of speed. This research addresses the fundamental nature of change and the elements that affect the speed, resilience, and efficacy of change. The metaphors that we have found useful for capturing these ideas include Formula One auto racing, space exploration, team cycling, and caribou hunting. In this book, we have combined our fieldwork in corporations around the globe with our and others' insights from complexity theory, the nature of speed, and time-paced evolution to create the competing on the edge approach to strategy.

Competing on the edge rests on the assumption that the marketplace is in constant flux. The assumption of static equilibrium no longer applies. Rather, the view is that competitors come and go. Markets emerge, close, shrink, split, collide, and grow. Today's collaborators are tomorrow's competitors . . . or both. Technology is constantly shifting. Getting to the market early matters. In com-

Complex Adaptive Systems

These systems are made up of multiple interacting *agents*. Agents may be molecules, birds, people, or companies. The number of agents must be greater than one. Agents must also be sufficiently different from each other that their behavior will not be exactly the same in all conditions. Systems of one or systems in which agents all behave exactly the same way exhibit predictable, not complex, behavior. An example is the textbook case of "perfect competition" in which companies are all assumed to act the same way.

These systems exhibit *complex* behavior—behavior that is "orderly enough to ensure stability, yet full of flexibility and surprise."[11] The behavior is *adaptive* because it adjusts to changes in the environment. Finally, the behavior is *emergent* because it arises from the system and can only be partly predicted.

Although the behavior that emerges is complex, the rules that guide it are necessarily simple. In fact, it is their simplicity that creates the freedom to behave in complicated, adaptive, and surprising ways. Further, the rules are associated with the system, not with any individual agent (i.e., there is no "lead" agent). Systems that exhibit this type of leaderless yet orderly behavior are said to be *self-organized* because the agents themselves figure out how to organize to change. This principle of self-organization governs change in complex adaptive systems.

Boids in Flight

A simple example that captures the behavior of complex adaptive systems is the simulation of a large number of autonomous, birdlike agents—or "boids"—interacting in an on-screen environment that has many obstacles. The behavior of each boid is governed by three simple rules:

1. Try to maintain a minimum distance from other objects in the environment, including other boids.

2. Try to match velocity of other boids in the vicinity.

3. Try to move toward the perceived center of mass of boids in the vicinity.

The intriguing result is that independent of the starting position of the boids on the screen, they always end up in a flock. These boids flock like birds and move fluidly around objects on the screen as the simulation continues. This behavior includes dividing and reforming again if necessary to maneuver around obstacles. Even if a boid mistakenly hits an obstacle, it recovers and then rushes to catch back up with the flock. This self-organized and complex behavior emerges despite the fact that there is no leader and no rule that says "form a flock." Yet "form a flock" is precisely what the boids do.[12]

plexity parlance, the marketplace is a *continuously deforming landscape*. The image of this kind of landscape is of a terrain richly contoured by peaks and valleys. And in this book, it is being continuously reshaped by warp-speed change.

The second assumption is that firms are composed of numerous parts or *agents*, in complexity parlance (or "businesses," in managerial terms). When these parts are linked together at the edges of chaos and time, they form complex adaptive systems. These systems are complex not because they are complicated. They are actually fairly simple. Rather, "complex" describes the complicated, innovative, and self-organized behavior that emerges from them. They are adaptive because they can change effectively. A classic illustration is a flock of birds in flight. Their ability to adjust to obstacles while flying together without an established leader can be simulated by a small number of simple rules like "always stay three feet from any obstacle and fly toward the center of the flock."

The key assertion of this book is that successful firms in fiercely competitive and unpredictably shifting industries pursue a competing on the edge strategy. The goal of this strategy is not efficiency or optimality in the usual sense. Rather, the goal is flexibility—that is, adaptation to current change and evolution over time, resilience in the face of setbacks, and the ability to locate the constantly changing sources of advantage. Ultimately, it means engaging in continual reinvention.

The constant change involved in competing on the edge contrasts with traditional thinking about how change occurs. For example, the popular business media—among them *Business Week*, the *Economist*, or *Fortune*—convey vivid descriptions of corporate change. But what kind of change? Often, it is massive, gut-wrenching corporate makeovers like the reorganization of AT&T, the realignment of Sony, the merger of Seagram and MCA, and the restructuring of Ford. It's the big move, the big bet, the big success . . . or the stunning failure. Whether the change involves the breakup of AT&T, revolution at Imperial Chemical Industries, or the rescue of Mazda, the traditional theme is the same. The change is dramatic, infrequent, and gut-wrenching. It is massive, perhaps with someone like "Chain Saw" Al Dunlop in command. In scientific terms, this paradigm of change is known as *punctuated equilibrium*.

But is this how the best corporations adapt to shifting circumstances? Is massive transformation the way that change happens in the best corporations? With such stellar firms as SAP in Europe, Toyota and Acer in Asia, or Wal-Mart, Gillette, and Merck in North America, does the notion of massive corporate transformation capture how these stunningly successful corporations change? In reality, the striking characteristic across these firms is the *absence* of massive transformation. Rather, in these firms, change is ongoing, relentless, and even endemic to the corporate culture. Massive transformations are signals of missed inflection points, not successes. Thus, the best firms change routinely, relentlessly, and even rhythmically over time.

Research Approach

The ideas behind competing on the edge emerged from our in-depth research study in Asia, Europe, and North America. We focused our primary research on the computer industry, because it is the prototypical illustration of a high-velocity industry for which managing change is a key competitive challenge. Moreover, conducting systematic and in-depth interviews of more than one hundred managers rather than relying on secondhand anecdotes from the business press allowed us to reach a level of candor and depth that is unavailable through other research methods. Although this intimate revelation means that these firms and managers necessarily remain anonymous, this level of frank and detailed insight about managing change is rare. We complemented this research with insights from our teaching and other research.

This book describes six pairs of businesses. One member of the pair is considered a dominant player within its segment of the industry by measures that

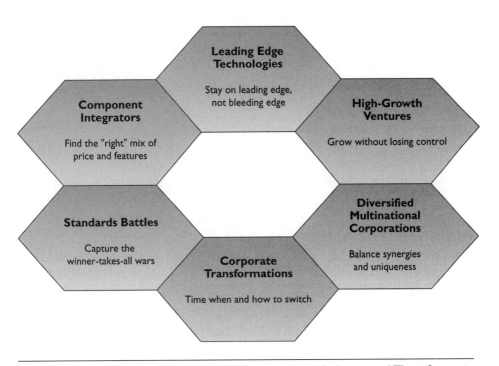

Figure 1.6 • Six Pairs of Businesses in the Computer Industry and Their Strategic Positions and Dilemmas

include profitability, growth, market share, and general industry reputation. That business is matched with a very good business but one that is not a segment leader. The dominant businesses showed an average revenue growth of approximately twenty percent per year during the 1990s. In contrast, the very good businesses paired with the dominant ones showed an average growth of only five percent over the same period. Although all of the businesses competed within the broadly defined computer industry, each pair faced unique strategic issues. The rationale behind this variety is to enhance the findings' applicability to many strategic contexts.

One of our colleagues asked whether managers in established firms like Kodak, Daimler-Benz, and Bethlehem Steel should read this book. After all, the computer industry is extraordinarily fast moving, and many managers are not on "Internet time" or pacing to the six-month product life cycle of computing. Our response is that even though the computer industry may be an extreme case, it is also the most visible industry in which many managers have learned to succeed in the face of relentless change. The dominant firms in computing are global exemplars for strategy in fast-moving, unpredictable, and highly competitive markets . . . the kind of markets that many managers are increasingly facing. So our view is that competing on the edge has insights for any manager (or would-be manager) for whom change is the critical strategic challenge—whether managing within a low tech or high tech firm, a fledgling venture, or a Fortune 500 giant. Competing on the edge provides a dynamic view of strategy.

In Chapter 2, the focus is on single businesses. Using edge-of-chaos thinking, we describe how successful managers rely on a few key rules to innovate adaptively while consistently executing products and services on time, on target, and on budget. These managers neither fall into rigid routines nor do they become chaotically undisciplined. Rather, they solve the dilemma of how to achieve adaptive innovation *and* consistent execution. Here *improvisation* is the first building block of competing on the edge.

In Chapter 3, we focus on managing multiple businesses within the same firm. The key managerial dilemma is how to balance collaborative synergies *and* individual success. Comparing corporations to competitive cycling teams, we observe how some managers are able to collaborate across these businesses and capture synergies without destroying their uniqueness or becoming trapped by endless politicking. Here *coadaptation* joins improvisation as a critical edge-of-chaos concept and a second building block of competing on the edge.

In Chapter 4, we explore the edge of time. Using an example drawn from caribou hunting, we examine how managers can use the past effectively. The dilemma involves exploitation of the old *and* exploration of the new. That is, how can businesses exploit the past without becoming trapped by it? Genetic algorithms, complexity and error catastrophes, and modularity form the underlying basis for the third building block of competing on the edge—*regeneration*.

Chapter 5 brings competing on the edge into the future. We sketch how managers in dominant businesses experiment with a wide variety of low-cost probes to gain insight and strategic flexibility. They solve the dilemma of commitment to *a* future and flexibility for *the* future. They neither lock into a single plan for the future, which would undoubtedly be naïve, nor play a reactive game that sentences them to constantly playing catch-up behind industry leaders. Options and learning are the central concepts that underlie the fourth building block of competing on the edge—*experimentation*.

In Chapter 6, we describe the critical concept of time pacing. Surprisingly, even the best managers often have only a vague awareness of the power of time pacing. Choreographed transitions and rhythm are the key. We explore the importance of transitions in the 4×100 relay and the advantages of rhythm in competitive tennis. Choreography, rhythm, and entrainment are the conceptual foundation for this fifth building block of competing on the edge—*time pacing*.

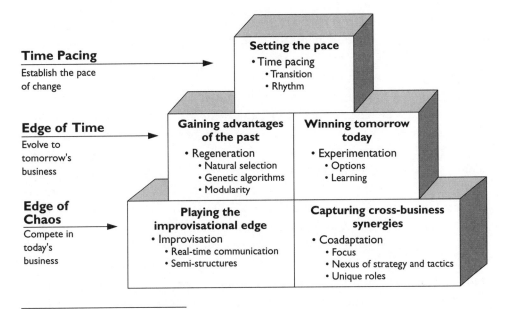

Time Pacing

Establish the pace
of change

Edge of Time

Evolve to
tomorrow's
business

**Edge of
Chaos**

Compete in
today's
business

Setting the pace
• Time pacing
    • Transition
    • Rhythm

**Gaining advantages
of the past**
• Regeneration
    • Natural selection
    • Genetic algorithms
    • Modularity

**Winning tomorrow
today**
• Experimentation
    • Options
    • Learning

**Playing the
improvisational edge**
• Improvisation
    • Real-time communication
    • Semi-structures

**Capturing cross-business
synergies**
• Coadaptation
    • Focus
    • Nexus of strategy and tactics
    • Unique roles

Figure 1.7 • Building Blocks

In Chapter 7, we focus on developing a competing-edge strategy. Using the metaphor of growing a prairie ecosystem, we emphasize that competing on the edge must be implemented at an explicit starting point, by relying on missing links and by following a specific sequence of steps. These characteristics also reveal why competing on the edge is so difficult to imitate.

In Chapter 8, we tackle sustaining the edge. Using an example from major league baseball, we describe three leadership roles. At the business-unit level is the key strategist. At the senior level is the synthesizer of strategy who channels, synthesizes, and articulates the semicoherent pattern of strategies. Finally, there is a mid-level patching role that focuses on constantly realigning businesses to match continually shifting market opportunities. The central concepts are modularity and patching.

In Chapter 9, we summarize the "laws" of competing on the edge in terms of strategy, organization, and leadership.

Conclusion

The premise of this book is that a broad swath of contemporary industries is characterized by high-velocity, unpredictable change. Change in customers, technologies, competitors, collaborators, regulation, suppliers, political conditions, and so on is the only constant in many industries. The fundamental strategic challenge is to manage this change.

Although a competing on the edge strategy is predictably unpredictable, uncontrolled, and at times inefficient, it is also effective in industries that experience relentless change. Competing on the edge, at a minimum, is about reacting responsively to change, anticipating change when possible, and at best, creating and even dictating the pace of change that others are forced to follow. Competing on the edge is about constant change, not just in rare corporate realignments but rather in unrelenting, day-after-day adjustment to a constantly shifting landscape. What are the rewards for competing on the edge? Like pinball, winning is about survival. But for the best firms, winning is an opportunity to seize the initiative, constantly change, and dominate an industry.

Competing on the edge is not about Silicon Valley fever, the success of Japanese behemoths, or newly nimble European firms. Rather, it is a set of transcendent themes that unite a group of dominant global businesses with diverse strategic issues. It intimately links together the two parts of strategy: "Where do you want to go?" and "How are you going to get there?" Rooted in the logics of complexity thinking, the nature of speed, and time-paced evolution, competing on the edge is a strategy and approach to organizing that some managers are mastering. Of course, competing on the edge is complicated and challenging. But it is also a strategy that works . . . when change is the name of the game.

I can't say that we had a

really smart strategy

going forward. We had a

strategy and when it

didn't work, we went

back and regrouped until

finally we hit on

something.

Phil Knight,

CEO, Nike

playing the improvisational

WHAT IMAGE COMES to mind when you think of Nike? A maverick? Yes. An innovator? Absolutely. Athletic footwear? Yes . . . well . . . but not exactly. Nike does dominate the athletic footwear business worldwide, but it is quickly becoming something more—a global sports and fitness company. Building on its strength in cutting-edge design and technology, company management has moved into sports accessories (sunglasses, swim goggles, golf gloves), apparel (Nike logo on all imaginable clothing), equipment (hockey sticks, soccer balls, in-line skates), and services (sports management, retailing).

One reason for Nike's success has been its extraordinary ability to compete for today's customers in its core businesses. The firm does it by keeping its immediate competitors off balance through innovation in its core area of performance—athletic footwear (progressing from Air, to Air Max, and then to Air Zoom technology). Nike also attacks strong niche players such as Speedo (swimwear) and Adidas (soccer shoes) with novel products. Not only does Nike out-innovate its competitors, the company also has a well-deserved reputation for acting flexibly and decisively to take advantage of unexpected opportunities, such as occasions to build brand image. Nike's very public support for the golf phenomenon Tiger Woods is one example.

Yet Nike is also about more than flexibility and innovation. The firm routinely produces competitively priced products that are on time to market and efficiently distributed on a global basis. Nike's well-known brand-building, retail/activity outlets (e.g., the elaborate Nike Town stores complete with climbing walls and basketball courts) and its equally impressive Futures inventory control system are further evidence of the firm's operational skills. Competitors observe that Nike has the best logistics system in the industry. This is a firm whose employees can both innovate and execute. With these competitive strengths, the company has moved one step closer to becoming a global household name in sports and fitness. Overall, Nike's innovative products and effective execution have enabled the firm to create an unpredictable, complex, and yet successful strategy.

Nike's experience illustrates, first, the importance of competing effectively in current businesses. In fast-paced and highly competitive markets, sage and successful competitors like Nike never forget that what matters most is *today*. Second and more significant, Nike's experience demonstrates that the fundamental

Attributes of the Edge of Chaos

The edge of chaos is a key concept in complexity theory that describes where systems can most effectively change. Systems with more structure than found at the edge of chaos are too rigid to move. Systems with less structure are too disorganized. Yet, the edge of chaos is not simply a bland balance of "not too hot and not too cold." Rather it is where . . .

1. Complicated behaviors (such as execution and innovation, but not just one or the other) occur. It describes, for example, improvisational music.

2. A few rules (like priorities) exist that are not arbitrary and not compromises between extreme values. They are specific rules that can create, for example, the flight of boids.

3. Work is required to maintain balance on the edge of chaos because it is a dissipative equilibrium. There is a constant tendency to fall into the attractors of structure and chaos.

4. Surprise exists. Expect the unexpected, because control is not tight and because the system is adapting in real time to unpredictable changes.

5. Mistakes occur because systems at the edge of chaos often slip off the edge. But there is also quick recovery and, like jazz musicians who play the wrong note, there is the chance to turn mistakes into advantages.

challenge in competing effectively in current businesses is to create exciting new products and services in the context of changing market conditions—and yet routinely produce them at the right time, for the right price, and for the right customers . . . time and time again. Simply put, the central dilemma of current business is how to achieve adaptive innovation and consistent execution.

The resolution of this dilemma is through an edge-of-chaos process, *improvisation*. Improvisation involves balancing the structure that is vital to meet budgets and schedules with flexibility that ensures the creation of innovative products and services that meet the needs of changing markets.[1] Too much structure leads to mundane products, predictable strategy, and missed market opportunities. For example, managers at the retail giant Sears elaborately structured their processes. (More than 29,000 pages of procedures have been reported.) Yet until the late 1990s, the firm had a record of lackluster innovation and failed strategic change. Too little structure leads to high costs, missed schedules, and confusion. The Hollywood movie industry is a notorious example. For instance, Arnold Schwarzenegger's action movie, *Eraser*, was great

Dissipative Equilibrium

When a system is driven to order by the constant flux of matter and energy, dissipative equilibrium occurs. The system is technically not in equilibrium, rather in orderly disequilibrium. Order arises from the persistent exchange of matter and energy. Simply, it takes work to maintain order. For example, when water comes out of a faucet at a rate that is fast enough to create a swirling pattern but not too fast to be chaotic, the water will flow down the drain in an "orderly disequilibrium." The orderly pattern of water flowing down the drain is a dissipative structure. Attractors are the stable equilibria to which dissipative structures are drawn.

In contrast, a system is in a low energy, or stable, equilibrium when its potential energy is minimized. Order arises from the lack of energy needed to maintain the constant state. For example, when a marble in a cup comes to rest in the bottom of the cup, no further energy is needed to keep it there.

fun for movie-goers who demand high-speed action and spectacular "shoot-em-up" footage. But the film exceeded its $70 million budget by $40 million. Confusion reportedly reigned on the set when, for example, extensive location shoots were arranged but never shot.

In contrast to these extremes, improvisation balances on the so-called edge of chaos. The underlying argument is that when systems of any kind (e.g., beehives, businesses, economies) are poised on the edge of chaos between too much structure and too little structure, they "self-organize" to produce complex adaptive behavior. If there were more structure, then these systems would be too rigid to move. If there were less structure, then they would fly chaotically apart.

Yet improvisation, like all edge-of-chaos processes, is challenging to achieve because it is so easy to err on either side—to slip into too much structure or too little. In complexity theory terms, improvisation is a *dissipative equilibrium*, an unstable edge between two *attractors* (i.e., structure and chaos) that tend to pull the system away from the edge of chaos toward the rigidity of too much structure or the confusion of too little structure. And yet, staying on that edge is essential because that is where systems of all kinds self-organize to create the most vibrant, adaptive, and complex behaviors. In more concrete terms, the edge is where businesses adaptively innovate *and* consistently execute. The result of remaining on the edge is a wider range of strategic options and a better sense of which option to choose.

In the case of Nike, the firm's innovative product line and its effective execution have enabled Nike to create an unpredictable and complicated strategy. Sometimes

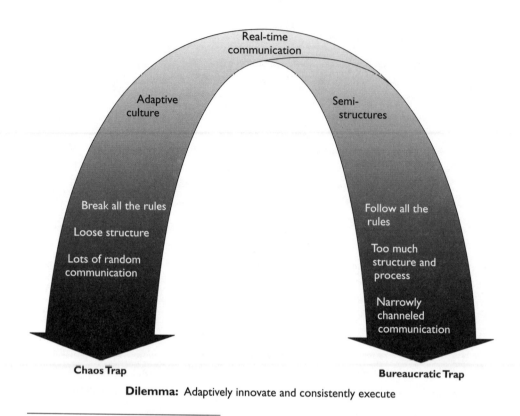

Dilemma: Adaptively innovate and consistently execute

Figure 2.1 • Improvisational Edge

that strategy has emphasized creative product leadership, sometimes it has stressed brand and image, and at other times it has focused on execution and cost. Yet this strategy has allowed Nike to average a 47 percent return on investment for its shareholders for a decade, and more significantly, to evolve from a group of runners with a terrific product to a consumer-focused marketer to a global retailer.

Survey Your Company

Where does your business fit? Take a pen and mark where your firm fits along each scale.

There are: no rules •••••••••••••••••••••••• many rules
Rules are created to be: followed •••••••••••••••••••••••• ignored
Processes are: undefined •••••••••••••••••••••••• lockstep

Change is:	expected ••••••••••••••••••••••	problematic
Responsibility is:	targeted •••••••••••••••••••••••••••	distributed widely
Everyone's focus is on:	end products •••••••••••••••••••	processes
Priorities are:	clear •••••••••••••••••••••••••••	ambiguous
Priorities drive resources:	always ••••••••••••••••••••••••	never
Communication is:	constant ••••••••••••••••••••••••••	infrequent
Communication is:	channeled ••••••••••••••••••••••	chaotic

Improvisation Basics

Imagine that it is 1972. The lights are dim, the air is smoky, and a band is in full swing in a shabby old theater in San Francisco. The full-capacity audience of 2,000 is on their feet. The young crowd is swaying from side to side, dancing in place, and tracing spider webs with their arms above their heads.

The energy increases as the crowd recognizes the beginning of a favorite song. The band responds in kind. But the crowd has never heard the song played quite this way before, and they couldn't have. Influenced by rock but grounded firmly in their jazz roots, this band never plays a song the same way twice. They improvise. The band members respond continuously to each other and to the crowd as they play. Yet the music is structured. For example, there is a band leader, the bass player has a specific role, and each musician knows which chords may be played.

Now jump ahead some twenty years to the mid-1990s. A crowd of all ages, shapes, and sizes fills an indoor stadium on the East Coast to its 20,000-seat capacity. The same band, its players now middle-aged, gray, and a bit overweight, is in full swing. They're having a great time, and so is the audience. As in the past, most are gyrating in some fashion to the music, twirling about and waving their arms.

Why is the audience still enjoying this music? For that matter, why is the band still enjoying this music? It's the same repertoire of familiar music. Why aren't they bored? Why doesn't the music seem stale? Why does anyone still come to these concerts? The answers lie in improvisation, which makes the music a fresh experience every time it is played. This explains why audiences still relish the concerts and why the band prefers to tour continuously and why it does relatively little studio recording. The musicians and the audience enjoy the spontaneous interaction with each other that defines performances by this band. Moreover, the band is well known for inviting surprise guest artists to

- At any given time in a performance, know who the leader (soloist) is and where you are in the piece.

- The soloist should listen to and build off of the work of other members of the band.

- Know the rules in order to know how and when to break them.

- Experiment as a group (e.g., by changing or eliminating structure) or as an individual (e.g., by overblowing or fiddling with your instrument).

- Expect occasional "trainwrecks." Recover and move on.

- Do not play the same solo over and over; practice new approaches and styles in familiar pieces. Incorporating the unexpected is the essence of great jazz.

Figure 2.2 • Rules for Jazz Improvisation

Source: Marc Sabatella, *A Whole Approach to Jazz Improvisation* (Lawndale, CA: ADG Publications, 1992) and Mary Jo Hatch, "Exploring the Empty Spaces of Organization," working paper, Cranfield School of Management, Cranfield, England, 1997.

perform with them. These famous guests know the rules (e.g., their role as a keyboard player, the legitimate chords, who plays first), but beyond that they do not practice with the band. The audience and the musicians enjoy the innovative and yet superior music that emerges from these spontaneous interactions.

The band, of course, is the Grateful Dead. It is a band that, until the death of its founder, Jerry Garcia, had been the music industry's top touring act and leader in touring revenues. The Grateful Dead created both a unique musical experience and an unusual business strategy. Unlike most rock bands, the Grateful Dead earned income predominantly from touring, not from sales of studio recordings. The band has, in fact, always encouraged fans to tape its concerts and has even provided a special taping section for the audience. The Grateful Dead was rock's premier improvisational band, and one of its biggest business successes.

Adaptive Innovation vs. Consistent Execution

What do corporate managers have in common with the Grateful Dead? In many ways, these musicians and managers face the same challenge. For the band, the challenge is how to create a fresh musical experience with changing musicians and audiences, while doing so at a particular time, with a limited repertoire, within a limited amount of space and budget, in concert after concert. This was the band's ongoing dilemma in what we might think of as its core business. For managers, the challenge is very similar: to master both adaptive innovation and consistent execution . . . again and again and again . . . in the context of relentless change.

The Grateful Dead, like many live bands, met this challenge through improvisation. Improvisation is popularly thought of as "winging it." But true improvisation is distinguished by two key properties. First, performers intensely communicate in real time with one another. They constantly stay aware of what others are doing through both listening and eye contact, neither looking ahead to the next note nor glancing back to what has already been played. They remain intently focused on what is happening at the moment within the group. What counts is "now."

Second, they rely on a few very specific rules, such as who plays first, what are the permitted chords, and who follows whom. Although the rules are few, they are absolutely essential to the performance and so are slavishly followed. This is because the structure provides an overarching framework within which the band can play. With too little structure, there are too many possible actions, which leads to either inaction (no music) or chaos (not music). With too much structure, the music loses its spontaneity (becomes boring) and originality (the same old thing). Intense communication allows the musicians to coordinate and adjust their playing with one another and adjust to the audience within this framework of a few very specific rules. In this way, improvisational bands can be both creative musicians and consistent performers, even as the audience and guest artists change.

The Grateful Dead Meet the Nike Jocks

Does this sound familiar? In the discussion of Nike, we've showed that what distinguishes the company is its ability consistently to create innovative products in the context of changing technologies and markets, yet still get the right products out, to the right people, at the right time. In the managerial situation, improvisation is about extensive, real-time communication in the context of a limited structure with a few sharply defined responsibilities, strict priorities, and targeted deadlines. Improvisation is what enables managers to continuously and creatively adjust to change and to consistently move products and services out the door.

To draw on the musical analogy, these managers improvise to create innovative products and services (they don't just endlessly replay the same old songs), even as the markets and technologies change (audiences and venues change, guest players come and go), yet they perform consistently well and on time (they routinely show up and play very well).

The success of Nike and the Grateful Dead, however, is not so easy to achieve. Many traps lie in wait on the way to successful improvisation.

Too Little Structure: Chaos Trap

Many managers wisely limit structure in situations in which innovation is critical to success, such as business start-ups or in businesses that are attacking new markets and technologies. Limiting structure is also wise in established companies attempting to revitalize a lethargic bureaucracy. Some managers limit structure simply because of their personal preference for nontraditional, nonhierarchical forms of organizing or because they employ creative professionals. The chaos trap arises when managers go too far and demonize structure as the anathema that stifles freedom, flexibility, and innovation.

These less structured businesses do tend to be truly creative environments. Indeed, they are *not* short of creative ideas. The best of them are even famous for their innovative strategies around unusual products and services. Not surprisingly, these businesses have reputations as fun places to work for designers, marketers, and other staffers. Sometimes these businesses are strong performers, especially when they lack competition. But more often, these same businesses are less skilled at making their creative strategies actually happen. They are often described by analysts as "inconsistent" or "never fulfilling their promise." And when they do have market successes, they may have difficulty following up with the next generation. Why? Because they are equally famous for poor or confused execution.

A good illustration is the ice-cream maker Ben & Jerry's. The firm was launched by New Agers Ben Cohen and Jerry Greenfield, in rural Vermont. The venture prospered by riding the wave of premium-priced, all-natural food products so much in demand in the United States in the 1980s. The company operated like a large family bonded together by their mission of socially responsible capitalism. By managerial choice, there were few rules at the company and no formal growth plans or budgets. There was little accountability for tangible goals like profitability or sales. The new product development process was haphazard, with co-founder Cohen frequently "cooking" up whatever flavors happened to appeal to him as he puttered in the kitchen.

Over the years, Ben & Jerry's has been truly innovative. The firm became renowned for its "anything but vanilla flavors," like Rainforest Crunch and Chubby Hubby. It was equally famous as a fun company to work for, with its self-described "joy gang," celebrations of Elvis, and values-led capitalism. But by the mid-1990s, the once fast-growing company was faltering. The financial performance of the firm declined as competition from companies like

Häagen-Dazs intensified. Ben & Jerry's stock price melted from a high of more than $30 to around $12 per share as the company was unable to control costs and was late to pursue important market trends such as the switch from fat-filled ice creams to nonfat sorbets. Consistent financial performance is difficult to achieve in the chaotic world of Ben & Jerry's.[2]

Another example is the financial services giant Fidelity Investments. This mutual fund pioneer long encouraged its individual fund managers to "take risks and defy conventional wisdom." Senior management cultivated a "fighter pilot" mentality among its fund managers and gave them broad freedom to run their funds "with guns blazing." But by the mid-1990s it appeared that this fighter pilot mentality had gone too far. One major business publication suggested that the firm had become inconsistent and undisciplined.[3] Several funds, including the approximately $50 billion Magellan fund, were possibly too massive to operate as free-form, "one-man shows." Seven current and former fund managers became targets of Securities and Exchange Commission investigations for extensive trading on personal accounts in 1996. There were also federal suits for stock price manipulation in the trading of Micron Technology stock. Both these situations contributed to Fidelity's image as having too little control over fund managers. Fidelity lost some opportunities to manage major pension portfolios, such as that of Minneapolis-based Toro Co., because "its funds were too erratic and unfocused." In 1996, its arch-rival, Vanguard, passed Fidelity in the inflow of new funds, and Fidelity's performance (the cumulative average total return across its funds) for the year left the firm tied for seventh place among the top ten equity fund companies.

How can managers determine whether their businesses are slipping into the chaos trap of too little structure? We have found three common traits that characterize these businesses. One trait is a rule-breaking culture. Businesses in this trap tend to have people who take the need for unfettered freedom to the extreme. It becomes not only acceptable but even preferable to break any rules that might exist.

A second sign is loose structure. Loose structure is manifested in unclear responsibilities for key, tangible goals such as profitability, or in the form of ambiguous priorities, missing deadlines, or blurred chains of command. Sometimes structures exist but are ignored. Sometimes they just do not exist . . . because no one has thought about them or no one wanted them.

A third trait of firms caught in this trap is random communication. Often there is abundant communication in these firms, but somehow no one quite knows what is really happening. Unlike the improvisational focus on real-time communication about what is happening "now," communication in the chaos

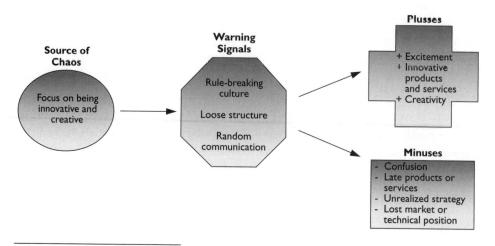

Figure 2.3 • The Chaos Trap

trap has no pattern. Conversations among random people chaotically drift to almost any topic, from last year's profits to bets on next year's hot markets.

Creating Chaos at Royal

One business that we studied, Royal (a pseudonym), was clearly floundering in the chaos trap. Royal has a long-established presence in traditional computing. It is a typical bureaucratic, vertically integrated corporation—the kind of business organization that is no longer very fashionable. The old Royal still exists (see Chapter 7), but along with its more traditional business model, Royal managers have embarked on a process of reinventing the corporation. Their approach is to create a new business model to attack the fresh market segment of multimedia computing. Our focus is on this new Royal, which is a quite different organization from the rest of the corporation. Indeed, corporate management has pledged to create a new business environment, one more in keeping with the multimedia computing opportunity that this business unit is pursuing and with what Royal managers perceive to be the successful North American business model. Yet Royal managers have taken their break from the stifling organization of the past too far in the other direction.

Rule-Breaking Culture

The old Royal is steeped in tradition. It has a clear status hierarchy and a rule for everything. The new Royal has the opposite—a "rulebreaking" culture.

Ignoring rules and procedures is expected and even encouraged. The focus of everyone's attention is on the creation of state-of-the-art technology that will dazzle customers. One manager described the focus as, "It's cool, it's hip, you want it." The organization is loose, fluid, and free form. In contrast to the old Royal, this world is one of truly creative ideas, of the pursuit of new concepts and new businesses at all costs, of finding that next hit product. Minimizing structure and violating rules is not only acceptable, it is expected. As one manager said, "It's part of the culture *not* to write things down."

Loose Structure

At a high level, the new Royal's structure did not appear dysfunctional. The business was routinely divided into fairly standard product groups, each run by a director. There were the usual trappings of bureaucracy, like planning and budgeting processes. Where structure broke down was at a lower level within the new Royal.

Product development, for example, was organized around particular projects, but day-to-day management of the projects was shared among hardware, graphics, and program managers. One manager obscurely termed the approach, "Well, it's something like a matrix." Despite (or perhaps because of) responsibilities being shared among all these managers, none was explicitly responsible for the financial performance (i.e., the ultimate profitability) of specific projects under development. Responsibility for product definition was ambiguous because two groups, hardware and graphics, both considered themselves in charge. Program management, the third group, was responsible for schedules. Managers in this group were supposed to combine graphics and hardware schedules into a coherent master schedule. However, they did not actually do this for two reasons. One was that the hardware and graphics people could never agree with one another. In fact, they were constantly battling. The other reason was that the nontechnical program managers never got the respect of their high-technology colleagues. As a manager recalled it, "Program managers are supposed to run the schedules, but no one pays attention."

So how were responsibilities organized at the new Royal? Both the hardware and graphics managers pushed their functional teams to be cutting edge. Their focus was on molding the best hardware designers and the best graphics developers. Yet no one was responsible for making sure that the technologies were aligned to create the desired finished product. Progress was often delayed because disputes between the two groups would have to "go two or three levels up before one person could resolve them," a manager told us. In the worst cases, the end products underperformed along both technological dimensions because graphics and hardware managers could not reach a compromise. Finally, the situation was further complicated by senior managers who tended to skip over middle managers to give direct advice to individual developers. Overall, no one was clearly responsible for key goals such as product profitability, product specifications, or schedule. Responsibilities were obscured in a maze of confusion.

Priorities fared no better. If a Royal manager was asked about priorities, he or she would answer but, in the next breath, quip, "They don't really matter." If any two people were asked, they probably would not agree. Priorities were not very well established or very central to life at Royal.

Resource allocation was equally vague. Consider product development. In theory, resources were given to the next projects due to market. As projects increasingly lagged their planned release dates, extra resources were allocated to them in an attempt to meet schedules. In practice, managers played a variety of games to grab resources. For example, some managers obscured resource allocations by creating "ghost" teams and fake projects to commandeer more. Others manipulated the schedules. A manager explained that "we have to show progress by doing things that the execs can see on our screens. So we do something quick for them, but we're really doing something else."

Chaotic Communication

"Hanging out" in the halls was a way of life at the new Royal. Everyone participated in the gossip of "hall talk." The feel was exciting—everyone on a double-espresso high—but without any structure, this hall talk flowed in every direction. It did not always bring the right people together. Further, it failed to keep people focused on current competition and real-time execution. Rather, hall talk drifted to industry gossip and discussions of "cool" new technologies among friends and officemates.

The shortcomings of hall talk were compounded by ineffective meetings. As one manager commented, "There is no organization of meetings as a form of communication. [You] never know what a meeting is going to be about; [you] never know when it is going to be." Moreover, project team members were compartmentalized by discipline. So graphic artists and hardware developers on the same team were often unaware of each other's progress. At the same time, several senior managers would constantly skip over multiple layers of management. The result was lots of talk, but little effective communication.

Business Implications

Some people thrived on the constant panic at the new Royal. They were energized by it and were excited by what they perceived as a Silicon Valley-style atmosphere at the company. One breathlessly described how much she relished the "who knows what's coming next?" feeling of trying to work at Royal.

But others agreed that the rule-breaking culture and the chaotic structures and processes were problematic. They created enormous confusion and much time was wasted. As one executive said, "This is a big, fun experiment, but the catch is we also need results." At the business level, there was little accountability for performance and no clear sense of the key operating variables. Frustration was rampant as well. A software manager explained that "we don't have a schedule; we don't exactly know what we're doing and what we're not doing. The approach is 'we sort of know what the product is going to be and design it on the fly.' It hasn't worked."

During the time that we spent with the new Royal, they were a success story with an exciting strategy of leading-edge technology and novel products. Although they were behind schedule in releasing their new product line, there was great optimism, both within the firm and in the marketplace, that the new Royal would continue to grow. A year later, the new Royal had not lived up to market expectations. As is typical of managers in this trap, the firm's managers were disorganized. They were unable to execute routine operations efficiently, get products to market quickly, or pounce on new opportunities. An early technology lead was squandered as Royal's competitors caught up. Royal ended up late to market with a strategy that it could not execute.

Warning Signals

There had been clear signals that Royal had too little structure:

1. *Rule-Breaking Culture.* Royalites celebrated their culture's lack of discipline—this was energizing and exciting for some people, but not an effective way to deliver products and services in a hotly competitive market.

2. *Loose Structure.* Ambiguity and argument shrouded unclear responsibilities. Game playing and panic dictated vague priorities. There were few milestones, measures, procedures, or rules.

3. *Random Communication.* There was lots of random talk—too much, in fact—about all kinds of topics.

Too Much Structure: The Bureaucratic Trap

The second trap occurs when companies become too structured. Managers in this trap often focus on hierarchy and disciplined processes—that is, reengineered and streamlined workflows in which products and services flow smoothly through the system. The emphasis is on schedules, planning milestones, and job descriptions. Often, however, scant attention is paid to the products and services themselves.

Initially, this focus on processes and structures may be sensible. For example, these processes may be the result of much-needed process reengineering that molds the business into competitive shape. Sometimes, they are carryovers from when the company competed at a much slower pace. Occasionally, they have been transferred from other parts of the corporation, where they are viewed as exemplary in established lines of business. These structures may be the result of cultural preferences for tight control. Often, process is a knee-jerk response to tough competition, in which head-to-head competitors take turns trying to outdo one another. Since the name of the game is to pump out a continuous flow of new products or services, the discipline of structure can be alluring in this kind of competition. Regardless of the source, the goal is efficiency . . . not flexibility.

Businesses in this trap may be steady performers. The best of them are respected for their reliability in consistently releasing competitive market offerings, possibly with targeted areas of innovation. Yet, more often, they fail to capture shifting strategic opportunities in new markets, products, or fresh business models. Especially in changing markets and technologies, extensive structure exacts a price. That price is stymied flexibility and stunted innovation. And so products and services get pushed through rigid systems, even when they may be the wrong ones, at the wrong time, and at the wrong price point. Efficiency and control dominate adaptation. As a result, these firms are often criticized for dated, predictable strategies that meet yesterday's, not today's, customer needs.

Consider the German luxury carmaker Daimler-Benz. In the 1990s, the company ran into trouble with its flagship Mercedes line. The firm was regarded by many as stuffy and its conception of automobiles inflexible. Mercedes-Benz was stuck in a bureaucratic gridlock of rigid hierarchy and rules. Between the board and the shop floor were six layers of management. The introduction of new models was rare and slow. For example, the decision to introduce the C-class took seven years, a glacial pace when compared with Japanese and U.S. automakers. Existing models were re-released annually, with only modest modifications. The big-selling E-class model, for example, was more than eight years old. On the manufacturing floor, strict hierarchy was the rule, despite an estimated 35 percent productivity gap between Mercedes and its Japanese competition. Overall, the stolid Mercedes image of comfort, safety, and longevity was no longer what many drivers were seeking. Although the company continued to pioneer some engineering innovations, their strategic position was "yesterday." The firm was stuck in a dated, predictable strategy of producing large, luxury sedans. As Mercedes stalled, its arch-rival BMW sped past in terms of total cars sold worldwide in the mid-1990s.

Another example is Campbell Soup. In the early 1990s, America's number-one soup maker was no longer simmering. The soup market had matured, and Campbell released mostly incremental changes to existing products. To many, the company was a lethargic bureaucracy in which, like its traditional red-and-white labels, nothing changed too much or too quickly. The product innovation process was regimented, with few attempts made to offer truly innovative products. Attempts to change strategic direction faltered as well. Even CEO David Johnson declared, "I want to rip out the bureaucracy."[4] Not surprisingly, earnings fell and the company's stock price hit an historic low. Campbell had particular difficulty in adjusting to U.S. consumers' growing penchant for eating out and for bringing home freshly prepared take-out food. Fresh strategies and innovative products were more likely to come from acquisitions like Pace, the salsa maker, than from the parent company.[5]

How can managers spot when their companies are slipping into the trap of too much structure? We have found that this trap is characterized by three common traits. The first is a rule-following culture. In these businesses, rule-following is often a source of pride among employees. Hierarchy and procedures are seen as signs of competence and effective discipline. Predictability and control are valued. Change is an annoyance because it upsets the rules.

A second trait is rigid structure. Often, structure takes the form of tightly choreographed processes, elaborate job descriptions, carefully crafted organization charts, and rules for every occasion. Process gates become critical checkpoints. Responsibilities are allocated for every step of the processes. Process definitions are often so clear that most employees can explain, step by step, overall procedures for such areas as quarterly strategic reviews, customer service, or product development.

A third common trait is channeled communication. Communication is typically directed along formal channels, such as the chain of command or the

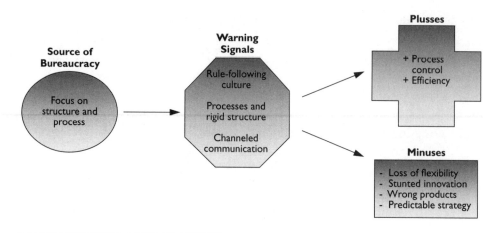

Figure 2.4 • The Bureaucratic Trap

steps of processes. If there is not a formal occasion for communication, then it is unlikely to happen.

Marching at Nautilus

One firm that was clearly caught in the overstructure trap was Nautilus (a pseudonym), a well-known global competitor in the extremely competitive consumer products segment of the computer industry. This is a tough oligopoly characterized by an intense rivalry in which the key firms play a rapid-fire, leapfrog game with one another.

How does the game work? One player introduces a new product, and then another player counters that product and beats it. Then another player tops that product, and the also-rans rush to catch up. The goal is to "one up" everyone else. How is Nautilus faring in the game? Not as well as corporate management would like. Nautilus managers launched a major reengineering effort that sharply tightened and streamlined key processes. But as we shall see, this was not a winning strategy in this very competitive, fast-paced market.

Rule-Following Culture

The culture at Nautilus thrives on regimentation. Rules are followed, and all of the rules are about process. The answer to any issue is a well-defined process. In any office at Nautilus you will find the walls plastered with detailed process descriptions and performance measures. Managers take great pride in executing these processes well. Some managers even regard their processes as a core competence. The culture is captured by an executive's comment: "What differentiates us from our competitors is our discipline." Rules, process, discipline—that's Nautilus.

Rigid Processes and Structure

Nautilus' approach to competing is to create very elaborate processes. For example, product development managers created a highly prescribed sequence of locksteps for moving from product concept to design and on to manufacturing. Projects were broken down into small tasks and then passed through a structured sequence of steps, from concept specification to pre-prototype, to prototype, and so on. The emphasis was on efficiency—that is, on designing products as quickly and efficiently as possible. The entire process was governed by specifications, procedures, and checkpoints. A project proceeded through a rigid sequence in which developers completed their tasks and then passed the project on. As each step was completed, the project passed through a checkpoint to the next step. The checkpoints were mostly concerned with whether the procedures were being followed properly (e.g., were the correct tests performed?). Finally, once a year, a master schedule with the timing, priority, workflow, and resources for all projects was set.

Yet, ironically, despite all this structure, two significant pieces of structure were curiously missing. One was the assignment of responsibility for major outcomes, such as overall product definition, the entire design schedule for a product, and the financial performance of a product. No single manager followed a product from concept to release, so no one had broad responsibility. Nautilus processes were about the "trees" . . . not the "forest."

The second missing structural feature was the setting of priorities once a year. After a project hit the development process, however, there was no strategic reassessment. No one reexamined whether the product was likely to be well positioned in the marketplace or whether its technology was at the appropriate state of the art. Nautilus' well-defined series of linear steps left little room for adjusting to changing markets and fresh technologies. Projects locked into the process, cranked through the new product machine, and emerged as completed products.

Channeled Communication

Communication follows process at Nautilus. The dominant processes are the product development cycle and order fulfillment. Not surprisingly, then, lines of communication are linear within these processes. Thus, managers are aware of issues related to their step in a process, but no more than that. The physical layout at Nautilus reinforces these formal communication patterns. In stark contrast to Royal, the halls are quiet. Security doors separate small groups of people who closely work with one another but not with others. Finally, since there are few formal processes for external communication with either customers or suppliers, the overall level of communication outside the firm is low as well.

Business Implications

The highly structured approach to current competition at Nautilus was a source of pride for many managers. They believed that disciplined processes were a key strength that gave them a competitive edge over less reliable and higher-cost competitors. One manager boasted, "I think that one of the things we can do is produce products quickly. . . . From that standpoint we're pretty leading edge." And he was partly right. Nautilus could certainly create products on time and on budget, and it could fulfill orders efficiently. These processes were probably wise management in slower-paced industries.

But other managers recognized the limitations of rigid structure, especially in the fast-paced and uncertain market in which Nautilus competed. For example, the product development process afforded little opportunity to adjust to changing conditions. The process blocked managers from backtracking or reshaping product specifications as circumstances changed. Reevaluation of product strategy often came too late . . . only *after* products were released. As one manager lamented, "By the time we figure out that there is a problem, it's already too late. We have no ability to react." The result was that Nautilus products often had the wrong combination of features.

Despite some technology strengths, Nautilus has primarily pursued a simple, low-cost strategy. Its most successful products appealed to the cost-sensitive buyers who wanted an inexpensive, fast "box." Nautilus managers tried cutting prices to take advantage of their favorable cost position and increase market share. But low prices did not compensate for poor product positioning. All that Nautilus managers accomplished was to lower margins for everyone in their segment of the industry. The business continues to trail its market segment leaders in growth, profitability, and market share.

Warning Signals

Nautilus' experience of becoming trapped in a process-bound organization was not a surprise. There were several warning signals that are characteristic of the bureaucratic trap:

1. *Rule-Following Culture.* There are rules for almost everything at Nautilus. But the most important rule is to follow all the other rules.

2. *Rigid Structure.* Lockstep processes, elaborate procedures, microscopically detailed organization charts, and rigid plans all constrained life at Nautilus. Yet, ironically, the plethora of detail obscured the absence of structure around significant issues like key responsibilities, critical operating measures, and overall priorities.

3. *Channeled Communication.* Informal talk at Nautilus was effective, but there was not enough of it or enough variety in it. The talk all centered on the major processes and was internally focused.

Navigating the Edge of Chaos

Although many managers fall into either the chaos or bureaucratic traps, others manage to avoid these pitfalls. They improvise. Like the Grateful Dead, they rely on a small amount of structure coupled with intense, real-time communication. These simple structures and extensive communication allow people to engage in much more complicated and adaptive behaviors than is possible with either more or less structure. Too much structure creates the rigidity seen at Nautilus, whereas too little structure leads to the confusion experienced at the new Royal. In contrast, limited structure combined with intense interaction creates enough flexibility for behavior to be fresh, surprising, and adaptive, and provides just enough structure for a business to deliver products and services on target and on time . . . time after time.

Improvisational businesses typically create products and services that are often successful but also somewhat unpredictable. Their strategies are usually more varied than those of the competition because they can shift their tactics quickly and can play on, for example, either cost or innovation advantages. They also typically excel at finding unexploited market niches and building competitive advantage. Overall, these businesses typically perform strongly in their current markets and are able to shift their strategy as conditions change.

An example is Putnam Mutual Funds. This fund management company stands out from the others. Across multiple measures, Putnam funds ranked first in one-year, three-year, and five-year total return among the top ten U.S. diversified fund families in the mid 1990s, and they consistently outperformed the S&P 500 during that period. The company's approach to money management is as distinctive as its performance. Rather than relying on a small group

---

Bulls' Coach Phil Jackson on Improvisation[6]

"You need structure to give your people a foundation so they aren't lost at sea."
Triangle offense puts three players in a particular place on the floor.

"But you have to make sure everyone has the freedom to act."
Cuts and passes are not programmed.

"You have to know instinctively where everyone else is going."
Jackson stresses full awareness on the floor.

"The players would often just take off on their own and use instincts to win games. I simply wasn't going to pull in the reins by telling them how to run the offense."
Jackson lets game strategy emerge.

---

of freewheeling "star" managers, the typical fund management model, Putnam relies on a more structured approach. The company uses an innovative and constantly updated quantitative approach to create a list of stock picks from which fund managers choose. The list typically has about 200 stocks, a much smaller number than the 5,000 or so stocks it is hypothetically possible to choose from. Further, rather than relying on a single individual who may pursue idiosyncratic hunches, teams of people work together to pick the stocks for a given fund within the constraints of the fund's goals. So conservative funds are conservative, while aggressive funds are aggressive. The range of stocks is restricted, responsibilities are assigned, and fund priorities are clear. But the specific strategy of the fund and the actual procedures for making the stock choices are left to the fund managers' discretion. As a result, fund managers have wide flexibility within the constraints. A few structures plus extensive communication among fund managers are the cornerstones of Putnam's improvisational approach to fund management. As a result, Putnam fund managers have made some surprising and yet high payoff moves, such as their backing of Xerox when the conglomerate appeared to be floundering. At the same time, they have also been consistent performers.

The airline titan British Airways (BA) is another example. BA is renowned within the airline industry for its superior and innovative services, particularly those aimed at business class travelers. The airline achieves this kind of service excellence by thoroughly schooling its employees in an intensive training program, in which they learn the nuts and bolts of BA's approach of pampering demanding travelers. But intense training is not the surprise. Rather, the surprise is that the BA training regimen also includes practice in when employees should deviate from standard BA procedures. Employees learn how to recognize occa-

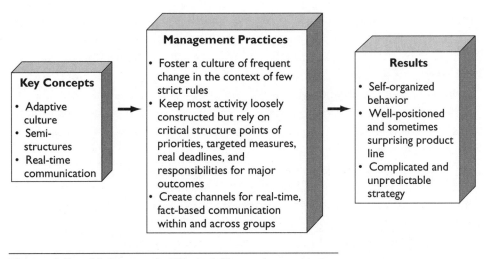

Figure 2.5 • Navigating the Edge of Chaos: Improvisation

sions when it makes sense to sidestep standard procedures, and they practice how to do it. In other words, BA executives not only encourage improvisation among their employees, but they also ensure that their employees know how to do it. The result is a service strategy that is both consistent and nonetheless personal.

Improvisational businesses have three traits in common. The first is an *adaptive culture*. Managers at these businesses expect change, so they anticipate the need to iterate, backtrack, and adjust what they are doing. Change is the norm, not the exception.

A second common trait is *semi-structures*. Although improvisational managers have few structures, they do rely on a small number of key structure points that are *never* violated. These structure points are priorities, deadlines, responsibilities for major outcomes, and targeted real-time measures.

A third trait is *real-time communication*. Improvisational businesses have a startling amount of communication throughout the entire organization. But this communication is not without boundaries. It is focused in real time, on the tasks at hand, such as manufacturing operations, customer complaints, and competitor moves.

Improvising at Cruising

Drive along a series of massive buildings in a region that was once the heart of the Industrial Revolution. They stand as placid reminders of an era that is long past. Pull into the parking lot. The scene is tranquil, a quiet retreat from today's hectic pace of business. But do not let the lush lawns and stately trees fool you—this is the home of Cruising Computing (a pseudonym), a company that competes, like Nautilus, in the highly competitive arena of consumer computer products. As noted earlier in this chapter, competition in this industry segment is a leapfrog game among a small number of smart competitors. Although all of the competitors would like to find the defensible niche that is the goal of traditional strategy, this objective is not very realistic in this rapidly and unpredictably changing market. A more realistic goal is constant reinvention through a series of temporary competitive advantages. Day in and day out, the strategic challenge is to gain an advantage by making the right trade-offs among product features, branding, channels, and new technologies in the context of a highly cost sensitive and competitive market. While Nautilus managers tightly engineered their structures and processes, managers at Cruising took a different tack. From the outside, it was obvious in the business press that Cruising managers executed a complex strategy that alternated its emphasis among brand, innovation, and low cost to become the top player in their market segment. But what was not so obvious is that they achieved that strategy through improvisation.

Adaptive Culture

A striking characteristic of Cruising is that *everyone* expects to change. For example, there is an expectation of "trade back and forth of what you can do and can't do" between marketing and engineering. This constant change, a manager said, goes "all the way up until the very end [of the product development cycle] dealing with the hardware stuff and then fiddling with the software benefits all the way up until the month prior to the announcement." This is all part of the self-described "fiddle" culture that exists at Cruising. Surprises from competitors are expected, too. As one manager described it, "We watch our competitors closely . . . and so if a competitor comes in and does something that we've not expected, we may end up stepping back, taking our strategy, and throwing it out the window." Throughout the organization, change is expected. According to another manager, "Our organizations, anybody will tell you, are temporary at best. I get a new office every six months!" The general manager at Cruising makes it very clear that "what he expects is continuous change."

Semi-Structures

Although constant change is a hallmark of Cruising, it occurs in the context of a few simple but very rigid rules. Cruising managers understand that creating innovative strategy that fits with changing customer needs requires flexibility, but flexibility in the context of a few rules or structure points that are never broken.

Table 2.1 • Improvisation at Cruising Computing

Structured	Product Level	Marketing was responsible for profit and definition
		Schedule belonged to engineering
		Strict priorities were communicated for each project
		Biweekly deadlines in engineering
	Business Level	GM was responsible for growth, share, and profit numbers, plus one other metric
		Performance bonus tied to numbers
		Weekly report of manufacturing, logistics, engineering milestones, sales by product, and channel metrics
Unstructured		Everything else
Extensive Real-Time Communication		Weekly review of competition
		Weekly product planning meeting
		Weekly cross-development project meeting
		Weekly business review
		Informal communication at coffee bars and cafeteria
Results	Self Organization	Product teams executed prototyping in their own ways
		Marketing groups used own approaches to focus groups
	Mistakes	Failed retail channel move
		Pen computing failure
	Unpredictable and Complicated Strategy	Initial price leadership, then technical innovation, later brand
Performance	Market Leader	Superior performance
		Created a lead in market share
		Produced growth rate in revenue of twenty percent—faster than overall market growth rate
		Maintained highest level of profitability in market segment, despite price-cutting in the market
		"Cruising is the player that everyone wants to be."

One of these structure points is priorities. Cruising managers all agreed that "the most difficult issue" in managing current businesses was setting priorities. The constantly changing marketplace makes it difficult to know what should be a priority at any given time. New opportunities arise continuously, tempting managers to take on too many attractive possibilities. Yet, like managers of other firms that handle strategy well, Cruising managers met the challenge of choosing priorities. They followed three steps for successfully managing priorities. The priorities for possible new product development projects illustrate how they did it.

First, managers relied on an explicit criterion for setting priorities among potential projects—estimated value creation with a minimum market size hurdle. Such a clear criterion let managers do a quick evaluation of opportunities, eliminate weak proposals, and set a rough priority list.

Second, the management team met on a regular basis to discuss and revise the priority list that contained, at any given time, many more potential programs than could be implemented. The priority-setting meetings were extraordinarily painful. A senior manager put it this way: "We go through a pretty excruciating process. We prioritize everything that we're doing. We draw a cut line and take a good hard look at it and take a big swallow. . . . If that one below the line is really a priority then you better be willing to kick something off the list. That's the gut check; it's really tough." Although the process was "really tough," the result was crystal-clear priorities that everyone understood. Indeed, a senior marketing manager observed, "We're well aware of where we sit in the priorities and we have a very specific priority list. You know your number; you know where you sit on that list." Although Cruising managers claimed that they were always looking for a better way to set priorities, they also observed that priorities were absolutely essential for getting focused on current business. It was their most significant task.

Third, this priority list was tied directly to resource allocation. This gave the priorities real impact. The priority list defined exactly which programs were active and their relative priority for resources. The executive team activated only as many programs as they could fully resource. This strategy reflected the often repeated philosophy at Cruising that "there are no resource problems, only priority problems." Except in rare circumstances, where there were strong signals that the team had made a mistake, no changes were made outside of the regular, priority-setting meeting.

A second structure point is deadlines. Managers set clear deadlines for a few tasks and then always hit them. Product release dates, for example, were carefully set based on the management team's collective assessment of the rate of new products that the marketplace could absorb. These dates were enforced strictly. So even though managers would constantly adjust the features and market positioning of their products, the release dates never changed.

Responsibility for a small number of major outcomes is the third key structure point. The general manager was responsible for market share growth and profits for the entire business. In product development, responsibility for a few critical goals was clearly assigned and split between the engineering and marketing functions. Engineering managers were responsible for product schedules. They were the catalysts who drove product programs and used their technical expertise to make the appropriate trade-offs in scheduling. Marketing managers were explicitly responsible for product definition and for product profitability. They treated their projects as small businesses, managing the bottom line to create the right products for the right markets.

Cruising managers also created some structure around communication (see below), as well as a handful of targeted measures of real-time operations that everyone watched constantly. These measures included bookings, short-term product development milestones, competitor pricing, customer returns, and manufacturing yields. These measures were always operational and real time—never accounting-based, historical measures.

Finally, although the structure was crucial, equally important was to understand what was *not* structured. A few, major responsibilities, priorities, operating measures, and deadlines were structured, but actual processes had little structure. Engineers could routinely modify timing and resource trade-offs on their own. Marketing managers could develop their own ways of working with focus groups. There were few of the lockstep, checkpoint procedures that typified companies like Nautilus. Rather, the three different product-line groups within Cruising self-organized into distinct ways of working, such as how they executed prototypes, met with customers, and handled interactions between marketing and engineering. These distinct patterns reflected differences in their product positioning (low-end products vs. premium-priced ones), markets and business models, and work style preferences. As one manager recalled, "Different programs just do things differently."

Similarly, Cruising had a loose hierarchical structure. Senior management was described as "peripheral" to many issues. A manager said that "we go in and say 'we want to do this' and they [senior management] say 'yes,' and then we say 'we want to change that' and they say 'yes.' " Senior management was involved only on a few issues, for example, in priority setting and the critical transition of product prototypes into volume production.

Real-Time Communication

At Cruising, the buzz of communication is everywhere. Executives at Cruising work hard to regularly reinforce, as one said, the importance of their "dramatic, tremendous, amount of communication." Communication is a self-described way of life at the company. "There's a tremendous grapevine within this company and, of course, we have a great e-mail system," a manager told us.

Communication begins with groups. Teams are built around core groups of people from marketing, engineering, and operations that meet frequently. "We may go out to lunch or go into the lab to look at displays and other things, think about trade-offs, and do models, form focus groups together, a lot of close work," a manager explained. One marketing manager spent so much time with engineering that she claimed that "engineering is my second language." Moreover, communication is centered on real-time execution. Plenty of time is spent on, for example, prototyping and on testing models and product concepts with consumers, coordinating materials logistics with product launch, and "watching very closely what our key competitors are doing," such that communication is grounded in what is happening now.

Equally striking, however, was cross-group communication, the focus of a recent improvement effort that rapidly was paying off. One manager said, "It used to be that it was a badge of honor not to use anybody else's ideas or to improve upon them. . . . Now everybody is borrowing everybody's stuff; the cycle is just so short and the pressure is so intense." Another said, "We encourage a lot of spreading the word back and forth across projects."

Much of this communication occurred in formal meetings. For example, there was a weekly, cross-project engineering meeting and a Thursday product planning meeting that was a cross-group review. These meetings provided opportunities for ideas to be shared across projects. Everyone actually looked forward to these meetings as a chance to discover what others were doing. A senior manager explained that, "the opportunities to trade insights across projects is just something we have to make time for." In addition to these formal occasions, there was also extensive informal communication in the cafeteria, in the hallways, and at conveniently located coffee bars.

Executives at Cruising have also worked hard at communication with external groups like consumers and suppliers. On the downstream side, marketing managers participated regularly in consumer focus groups to keep their understanding of consumers' perspective up to date. Engineers frequently went along. Upstream, engineering and manufacturing managers, together with operations managers, worked extensively with suppliers to assess the technical competence of suppliers. Since Cruising "pushes their suppliers to their limits," engineering managers were vigilant about this communication channel. Overall, one manager summarized, "Communication is the way the company is built."

Business Implications

Cruising's approach to strategy is to improvise. Its managers establish a few structural elements, create lots of communication, and then let strategy emerge. One result was the self-organized behavior that we described above. More important was the impact on product strategy. Since managers could adapt to changing competition, technology, and customer needs very late into the development cycle, their products were typically on target. Yet with fixed deadlines and sharp responsibilities for profits, timeliness to market and cost effectiveness were part of the Cruising equation as well. A major business publication noted, "they control costs and quality better than anyone and still get innovation out to the market faster."

At the same time, as in musical improvisation, there was often an element of surprise and unpredictability. Indeed, from the point of view of the popular business press, Cruising's key to success was a more complex and less predictable strategy than others in its market segment. Sometimes Cruising managers cut cost and then price; sometimes they innovated with new technology features; and sometimes they moved into a new market niche or emphasized brand. And they were able to execute each strategy. In contrast, Nautilus played a simple strategy of churning out products quickly, and their successes came primarily at the low end of the market, where price was the primary factor. To use a baseball analogy, Nautilus was a one-pitch pitcher. That pitch was sometimes very successful, but it was also predictable and often not enough. More chaotic opponents, like the new Royal, were like knuckle-ballers. They were effective when they could control the pitch, but they threw a lot of balls in the dirt. In contrast, Cruising was more like a versatile Cy Young award winner, the year's best pitcher in major league baseball. They had more varied pitches, could change pitches in different situations, and yet could hit the strike zone.

Overall, Cruising is number-one in its very competitive market. As one analyst observed, "Cruising is the player that everyone wants to be."

Key Signals

To summarize, the Cruising example highlights several key signals of effective, improvisational management of current businesses:

1. *Adaptive Culture.* Cruising managers foster a culture in which people expect to adjust as conditions shift. Cruising managers even look for change.

2. *Semi-structure.* Managers rely on key structure points, including "owner-ship" of a few major outcomes, a few deadlines, tracking key operating variables, and sharp, well-defined priorities. But they kept much of their activity unstructured, ad hoc, and flowing. They let strategy emerge.

3. *Real-time Communication.* Communication was wide-ranging and focused on concrete, real-time operating information. It was both formal and informal, internal and external.

Implementing Improvisation

Here is the survey you completed at the beginning of this chapter. Below we have filled in the responses for Royal (R), Nautilus (N), and Cruising (C).

There are:	no rules ••••••••••••••••••••••••• many rules	R C N
Rules are created to be:	followed •••••••••••••••••••••• ignored	N, C R
Processes are:	undefined ••••••••••••••••••••• lockstep	R C N
Change is:	expected ••••••••••••••••••••• problematic	R, C N
Responsibility is:	targeted •••••••••••••••••••••• distributed	C R, N widely
Everyone's focus is on:	end products ••••••••••••••••• processes	C R N
Priorities are:	clear •••••••••••••••••••••••• ambiguous	C R, N
Priorities drive resources:	always •••••••••••••••••••••• never	C R, N
Communication is:	constant •••••••••••••••••••• infrequent	R, C N
Communication is:	channeled •••••••••••••••••••• chaotic	N C R

Look again at your answers to the survey. The comparison with our case studies should give you an idea of the next steps to take. Consider each of the traits in turn. The first is culture. If your business is primarily built on strict rule-following, like Nautilus, then you need to work at giving your people a fresh outlook about change. Change needs to be seen as the norm, not the exception. Training in dramatic or musical improvisation is a concrete way to reassure reluctant people that reducing structure can be beneficial and, more important, that they can succeed in a less structured, change-oriented environment. A related tactic is to follow the lead of British Airways and develop training drills that allow people to practice their responses to unexpected situations. If your business resembles the new Royal, then your task is to convince people that some structure can actually improve their creativity. It can be helpful to remind everyone that seemingly disorganized but highly creative groups, such as the Grateful Dead or Chicago's theater improvisation group, Second City, are actually tightly structured in a small number of critical ways. Here, too, training in dramatic or musical improvisation can help people experience its value in a business setting.

Although a shift in perspective is essential, improvement is often accelerated when preceded by shifts in structure. If your business is more like Royal, then you need to add accountability for a few key areas of responsibility and deadlines for a few major activities. Also add some operating performance measures. The most critical step is follow-up: ensure that everyone understands that the new structures are real, not a passing fancy. Keep in mind that just a few simple structures may be enough to have a major impact.

If your business is more like Nautilus, dismantle some of your structure. Eliminate it, especially around checkpoints and responsibilities for minor goals. Then add a focus on end products and services by assigning a few key responsibilities and deadlines. Most managers find dismantling structure quickly rather than slowly is more effective because it forces people to confront change. If this approach seems too risky for your business, start with dramatic change in one part of the organization and then move to others.

Whether your business is like Nautilus or like Royal, your toughest job is priorities, because invariably there will be more opportunities than you have resources. Nonetheless, cut the number of activities to fit the resources and then set priorities tied to those resources. Given the sensitivity of priorities, priority setting should involve employees throughout the organization. That way everyone understands what they have to do, even if they do not all agree.

Finally, what should you do if your firm is like Cruising? Congratulate yourself on having found the elusive edge between order and chaos. But bear in mind that successful improvisers, from the Grateful Dead to Cruising, know that constant vigilance is required to stay on the edge. Most businesses tend to veer in one direction or another. Usually, you will know your weakness. The key to staying on the edge is to test the limits. If too much structure is damaging to your firm, try reassessing which rules you really need by violating them or by imagining what would happen without the structure. Do the same experiment in the reverse if chaos is your weakness. You have to keep testing the edge to ensure that you are still on it. If your industry pace is slowing, then you probably want to push toward structure. If it is accelerating or you have a leading-edge technology strategy, push more toward chaos.

A Final Note on Changing the Rules of the Game

Strategies that change the rules of the game (also known as home runs or "killer" strategies) are alluring, but in highly competitive and fast-moving industries, such strategies are difficult to find. If they were simple and obvious, then someone would already be executing them. Any observer can spot the killer strategy of a company like Wal-Mart, Intel, or Ikea—once it has been executed. The real question is: How do managers actually find killer strategies?

Perhaps incredible strategic planning by a senior executive or a prolific brainstorming session can lead to a rule-changing killer strategy. But equally as often, such a strategy comes from an improvisational approach. It comes from quickly spotting the temporary advantage provided by the confluence of strategy and luck, acting rapidly to take advantage of the competitive opening created, and building from this advantage a platform for combining advantages into a rule-breaking killer strategy.

Executing a strategy is integral to innovating it. Moreover, changing the game redefines the playing field for all the players, and only the best companies with the best execution can change the game and still win it. In Nike's case, the Air Jordan shoe was the lucky hit of Nike's improvisational managers and became the platform from which they executed their rule-changing image athlete strategy. At Cruising, managers made a couple of price cutting moves based on their cost advantage, added some innovative products, layered on brand, and ultimately created and executed a business model that not only changed the rules of the game in their segment of computing, but made Cruising the winner of that game. Cruising's managers improvised a killer strategy through a series of small, unanticipated moves and became "the player that everybody wants to be."

They [Chicago Bulls] play
as a team. There's no
evidence of ego . . . .
When they come in[to
the game], the guys on
the floor bring them right
into the game and get
shots for them. They all
know their roles, and they
all can fill their roles.

Jack Ramsay,

ESPN analyst

capturing cross-business

SPUN OFF FROM two icons of U.S. publishing in 1961, Time Life Books swiftly became known for its in-depth series, such as the *Time Life Nature Library* and *The Second World War*. These series became mass-appeal staples throughout the United States. In the 1980s, music and video businesses were added to the company's burgeoning media empire. In the 1990s, multimedia publishing businesses were launched. Along the way, "Books" was dropped from the name, and the company became simply Time Life.[1]

The Time Life media empire actually comprises several distinct businesses. Each of these businesses is unique. Each has its own business culture, individual customer demographics, and distinctive creative approach. For example, the book division is the mature business. It is dominated by older employees and has a culture of editorial integrity and respect for facts. Precision, detail, and accuracy—these matter in the book business. Although no longer fast-growing, the books segment nonetheless is a very significant portion of overall corporate revenue. In contrast, video and television are smaller businesses but are growing faster and are more profitable. Their cultures are fast-paced and freewheeling. Success turns on attracting and keeping top creative people, and on networking into the relationships-driven broadcast industry. These distinctions mean that it makes sense to run the businesses independently.

At the same time, there are numerous opportunities for synergy. The businesses all share the well-established and valuable Time Life brand. They all rely on mailing lists, distribution facilities, and editorial research staff. They all have opportunities for cross-business selling, such as producing books that are tied to video and music releases. There are also opportunities to share the best ideas from each. For example, innovations in the music business, like single releases of past hits, could be adopted by other businesses. These opportunities for synergies suggest that collaboration would enable the various businesses to save time, to save money, and to learn from one another.

The uniqueness of each business and the opportunities for synergies across businesses create a dilemma at Time Life that is more than an abstract problem. Day after day, a tension surfaces around all kinds of decisions: If the company creates a more contemporary image, how does this affect the traditional books business? Should television be allowed to pay higher salaries than books? If mailing lists are shared, who gets first access? Should editorial research dollars be spent on topics that favor video over music? Should an Internet business be launched through books or music, or through neither? Should the television business be allowed to go its own way? The tension is a dynamic one, complicated by rampant change and heated competition within the media industry.

The Time Life dilemma highlights the fundamental challenge of competing across multiple businesses. That challenge is to take advantage of the synergies that exist across these businesses and yet maintain enough independence so that managers can address successfully the unique and changing needs of their particular businesses. Simply put, the dilemma involves achieving collaborative synergies *and* individual success.

The solution to this dilemma is another edge-of-chaos process—*coadaptation*. Like improvisation, coadaptation is poised on an edge between structure and chaos. Too much interlocking structure across businesses creates excessive coordination, politicking, and indistinct products and services that are poorly adapted to their markets. In this atmosphere, strategy becomes compromised. Too little connection among businesses results in isolated fiefdoms, duplication of efforts, uncoordinated products and services, diminished ability to learn from one another, and disconnected strategies.[2] In contrast, coadaptation focuses collaboration on a few areas of mutual gain but not on every possible gain. This coadaptive edge is where the most complicated and yet effective collaborative behavior emerges from a few simple rules. Yet like all the edge-of-chaos processes, coadaptation is a dissipative equilibrium and so requires constant managerial attention to stay poised on the edge.

Coadaptation

Coadaptation is the process whereby systems of related agents take mutual advantage of each other in order to change more effectively, yet still be adaptive in each agent's particular situation. For example, any particular animal in a species can adapt to its own surroundings, but it can also learn from other animals in its species and coordinate with them in mutually beneficial activities—like hunting in packs. The result is complicated yet successful behavior. As in any edge-of-chaos process, coadaptation is most effective when poised on the edge of chaos between too much and too little structure.

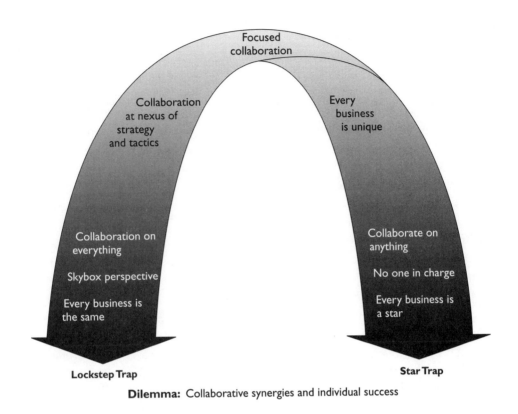

Figure 3.1 • Coadaptive Edge

Survey Your Company

Take a few moments to answer the following questions. At your business . . .

Cross-business collaboration is:	frequent ••••••••••••••••	rare
Cross-business collaboration decisions made by:	corporate management •••••••••••••	low-level management
Roles for different businesses are:	clear ••••••••••••••••••	undefined
The culture rewards:	team play ••••••••••••••••	individual win
Reinventing the wheel is:	common ••••••••••••••••	rare

Coadaptation Basics

The Tour de France is cycling's premier event and showcases one of the most popular sports on the globe. The route begins in Paris, winds to the south of France, turns up into the Alps, and finishes at the foot of the Champs Élysées at the Place de la Concorde. Thousands of miles (or kilometers, if you prefer), all kinds of terrain, and the July heat combine to make this an ultimate test of athletic skill and endurance.

Race progress is monitored closely in the media. Newspapers, radio, and television all describe the terrain, critique the cyclists' tactics, and track the competition. Even in countries like the United States, where the sport is not a national passion, the Tour de France is daily news. The leader at each point in the race is unmistakable because he wears the distinctive yellow jersey that symbolizes the frontrunner. The lead often switches, and when it does, the jersey is passed to the new leader. Often, the eventual winner takes command in the Alps, where several days of grueling effort string out the pack. Winners become the royalty of bike racing—names like Indurain and LeMond come to mind. They become sports heroes and even legends. Throughout Europe and much of the world, people know who won the Tour de France.

Yet behind each winner is a team, because the Tour de France is both a team *and* an individual event. Team members can share sponsors, equipment, mechanics, tools, and training. Although the top rider on the team is the one whom everyone knows, other team members are essential. They draft one another, a key strategy in which one cyclist leads while the others conserve energy by following in his slipstream. Team members pace the race to play to one another's strengths and to mitigate weaknesses. They pick up the pace on flats or hills that favor their team, and slow it down where they are less strong. They muscle and block to protect teammates from passing moves by competitors. And they do all of this in the context of one of the fastest-moving team sports on earth.

Lessons from the Tour de France

The key to a successful outing at the Tour de France is effective collaboration within the team. But how should team members compete? Should they simply compete for themselves, sharing sponsorship and little else? Probably not, because no one on the team is likely to win; no one has the stamina to win as an individual. If the team does not collaborate, no team member, no matter how strong, can win.

Blocking:	When riders try to slow the pace of the pack when one or more of their teammates is leading a breakaway.
Breakaway:	A rider or group of riders is able to advance away from the main field of riders during the course of a race.
Bridging the gap:	When a rider is able to come up from the main field of riders to catch a breakaway.
Chase group:	A group of riders trying to catch a breakaway. If a chase group is to be successful, all of the riders in the group need to be willing to work together. If a rider refuses to take his turn in the front, he will affect the whole group. If a teammate of a breakaway rider is in the chase group, he will work against the group to help his teammate retain the lead.
Domestique:	The "work horses" of the team. They sacrifice personal performance to help a designated team leader who has proven himself as a top competitor in the sport. If the team leader crashes or has a mechanical failure, it is the domestique's job to help the leader catch up to the main field of riders and then to bridge the gap by allowing the leader to draft behind. This is to make sure that the team leader is not forced to waste unnecessary energy. The domestique also helps in team strategies like blocking if the team leader is involved in a breakaway. Why sacrifice? More money for the winner means more for the team, and not all riders have the same ability to win.
Lead-out:	When one rider helps a teammate get in a better position for a sprint by picking up his pace before the last 200 meters of the race with a teammate drafting behind him. This helps the teammate pick up speed faster before jumping out of the slipstream. A lead-out often surprises the other competing riders and allows the sprinter to sneak around the outside of a pack. Competitors are often forced to react without the help of a teammate.
Support Crew:	Vehicles accompanying the riders that give aid such as food, drink, and mechanical assistance. In addition, team managers, "director sportifs," provide strategy and coaching.

Figure 3.2 • Glossary of Cycling Terms

Source: E.I. du Pont de Nemours and Company (1995), www.dupont.com/tourdupont/terms.html.

Should the team collaborate equally? This is not an effective strategy, either, because while the team as a whole may do well, no individual member is likely to capture the yellow jersey. This is because no one will be able to gain sufficient advantage over the field to secure the victory. Yet at the Tour de France, the glory and the money are in the individual win. What matters is capturing the yellow jersey.

How, then, should the team collaborate? The best approach is through coadaptation. Coadaptation involves collaboration in which each member of the team has a role. Some are domestiques, others are hill specialists, and the best all-around rider is typically the lead rider. The team captain (and sometimes one or two others) assign roles to the other team members. Neither the team sponsor nor the individual cyclists make those choices. Coadaptation also involves focusing collaboration around particular moves like drafting, breakaways, and bridging the gap. Rather than collaboration on all facets of the race, the goal is to collaborate in specific situations using particular tactics.

Finally, the collaboration is dynamic. Coadaptive cycling teams understand that the race that is planned and the race that is ridden are often quite different. A flat tire, heat problems, an unexpected breakaway by competitors, and rain are just some of the unforeseen events that can change a team's approach mid-race. Coadaptive team members dynamically adjust their collaboration and sometimes even their roles as the race unfolds.

The result of coadaptation is a complicated collaboration that involves an unpredictable blend of tactics that depends on the weather, the performance of team members, and the competition. It also takes advantage of chance. Yet, this kind of collaboration improves the chances of a team member winning the yellow jersey and the rest doing well.

Cyclists Meet Editors

We mention the Tour de France because team cycling is a powerful metaphor for business, in that it highlights the importance of complicated and dynamic collaboration. As in cycling, managers have many ways in which they can cooperate, such as sharing technologies, distribution channels, customers, and manufacturing facilities. This variety of collaborative opportunities makes it more difficult to figure out how to collaborate. A fast pace complicates the situation.

Team cycling is a powerful metaphor also because businesses within a company are not alike in their ability to create an extraordinary win. Some businesses have better strategic positions within their markets. Some possess technologies with more inherent potential. Some compete in markets with greater likelihood of profits or growth. The opportunities to win, especially to win in an extraordinary fashion, are not distributed equally across the various businesses.

Most important, team cycling, unlike most team sports, emphasizes the individual win, not just the collective outcome. Yet the dynamic of the individual win is particularly powerful for businesses, especially in rapidly changing markets. These markets create destabilizing opportunities that can have major payoffs. The extraordinary win of an individual business is thus often more crucial to the success of the entire company than is simply good performance by every business. Indeed, the story of some of the most successful corporations, like Sony with its Walkman line of products, Monsanto's Round-Up weed killer, Microsoft and its operating systems, Nokia with cellular phones, Hewlett-Packard in printers, and NBC with its hit show *Seinfeld*, is about capturing the extraordinary win and letting that win carry the rest.

Finally, team cycling captures the emotion of cross-business collaboration. Most people find collaboration to be frustrating and time consuming. These emotions are exacerbated by asking people to adopt procedures, technologies, and other resources from other businesses. Most people prefer their own, "home-grown" solutions, especially when someone else's solution does not fit the focal business as well. Collaboration often involves compromising on products and services when people really prefer their own way. These emotional issues are exacerbated because the individual win is enormously important to most managers, and yet in the most effective collaborations, many of them will be asked to make sacrifices that help someone else to win. There is a very real tension when the collaborating managers would all like to be the top rider—the one who gets the shot at the yellow jersey. At their roots, both team cycling and business are unique team sports because particular individuals are often the biggest winners, but the team (in a very real sense) made him or her so.

Too Much Collaboration: The Lockstep Trap

Many otherwise excellent businesses stumble into the lockstep trap of too much collaboration. Sometimes these businesses lack resources or are under intense competitive pressure. In these situations, cross-business collaboration can seem like an inspired way to save time and money by sharing common resources, such as manufacturing facilities or technical expertise. Sometimes managers become devotees of core competence and, in their zeal to deploy specific competences, apply these competences to numerous products or services—whether they fit or not. Often, the architects of overcollaboration are senior executives who do not understand the nuances of different businesses. But regardless of source, managers who overcollaborate begin to gloss over the drawbacks of collaboration and focus only on the benefits.

These businesses typically do gain some synergies. These synergies come at a price, however. Coordination time increases as managers struggle with excessive sharing across businesses. Politicking is heightened as rival groups bicker over who will compromise and how. Products and services lose distinctiveness in their own markets. Sometimes managers realize that they are attempting too much collaboration and then backtrack. It is more serious when managers continue to overcollaborate to the point of losing important capabilities to others within the company. These losses create overdependence on others and make it difficult to reverse overcollaboration. Ultimately, the business pays the price in terms of rigidity to change and poor financial performance.

An example of a company beset by overcollaboration is Snapple, the Long Island-based maker of iced-tea and fruit drinks. Founded in 1972 as a supplier to health food stores, Snapple prospered through close relationships with distributors, a smart product concept, and a quirky advertising approach that featured the Brooklynite and Snapple employee Wendy Kaufman in a series of uniquely humorous commercials reminiscent of home movies. After Quaker snapped up the wildly successful company in a headline-making $1.7 billion acquisition, senior managers at Quaker sought synergies between Snapple and their other businesses, such as Gatorade. They attempted to switch Snapple's distribution to existing Quaker channels to save money and to create better collaboration across the related product lines. They jettisoned Wendy and attempted to create a consistent corporate image across Snapple and other products. In making these and other choices, senior managers did not appear to understand the nuances of Snapple's business and did not heed the advice of Lenny Marsh, the Snapple cofounder who was retained by Quaker. Marsh claims to have believed that Quaker should have kept Snapple more independent. Under Quaker's stewardship, Snapple sales fell, direct losses totaled more than $100 million over three years, and the acquisition "surely stands as one of the decade's worst."[3] There may have been synergies between Snapple and the rest of Quaker, but Quaker senior executives did not find them. In 1997, Quaker sold Snapple for just $300 million.

Another example is British Petroleum. BP executives made a bold bid to diversify the company into minerals extraction. On the surface, there were many opportunities to be gained from collaboration across the existing oil and the new minerals businesses. Like oil, minerals extraction involves high-risk exploration, complex extraction processes, and sensitive government relationships. But the senior executives who architected the collaboration among the businesses were apparently not familiar with key specifics of the minerals business model. Although these seemingly intimately related businesses rely on geology as a base, subtle distinctions in the economics and market structure of minerals led to major differences in optimal exploration strategy. For example, minerals profitability is much more sensitive to supply and demand than is oil. Ultimately, BP sold off its minerals holdings.

How can managers recognize when they are overcollaborating? Several common traits signal this trap. One is the skybox perspective. Businesses in which there is overcollaboration place the choice of how to collaborate with senior-level managers who do not understand the compromises involved or who have only one or two of the relevant perspectives. These people see collaboration as easier to accomplish than it is.

A second trait is collaboration on everything. Managers in this trap typically try to capture most of the possibilities for collaboration. They do not focus their quest on the best opportunities.

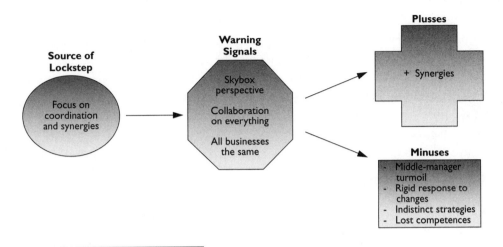

Figure 3.3 • The Lockstep Trap

A third trait is treating all businesses as the same. Like parents with children, these managers tend to place equal importance on all businesses. But businesses are not children, nor are senior executives their parents. These managers fail to make distinctions among their businesses regarding differences in their potential for profitability and growth. As a result, these collaborations do not take advantage of differential opportunities for success.

Locking Together at Jupiter

Jupiter (a pseudonym) is a global brand, a household name around the world. A classic "generalist" company, Jupiter's products range from personal computers to workstations, from servers to mid-range and high-performance computers, and from Internet to multimedia applications. They include software offerings as well as hardware. If the market is computing, then Jupiter is in it. Jupiter's headquarters fits the image of a global giant. It is a multistory supertower, sleek, with lots of glass and steel construction. Inside is a sea of cubicles, whose occupants orchestrate the far-flung Jupiter businesses.

People at Jupiter are intense and focused, and they have to be. Product cycles are very fast. The competition is voracious. People at Jupiter pour out a lot of new products—a new one every six months in some businesses—because this is what the market demands. This kind of product flow is the price of admission into these brutal product markets. When we studied Jupiter, the goal of the senior management team was to beat the competition . . . at every price point . . . with better performance . . . up and down the product line.

The strategic challenge at Jupiter is to create synergies across the businesses. In particular, senior executives were convinced that creating core competences across their diverse businesses was the way to prosper in their relentlessly changing and competitive businesses. They saw this collaboration as a way to save time and money. But as this chapter shows, Jupiter managers collaborated more than they should have, and as a result lost the distinctiveness of their business.

Lockstep Traits in Action

Skybox Perspective

One architect of Jupiter's collaborative strategy was a high-level executive, Art. He was the mastermind for several divisions whose product mix and positioning were driven by his "business sense." Art's charge was to catapult his divisions from mediocre players to dominant ones, and his strategy for doing this was a core competence strategy.

In many ways, Art was a great executive, but not when it came to collaborating. His focus was strategic (and appropriately so), not tactical. Therefore, he did not grasp the intricacies of the operating issues at the level of detail necessary to implement sharing across businesses effectively. Although he understood the critical success factors in each business at a conceptual level, he was too distant from day-to-day operations to have an intimate feel for these factors. Not surprisingly, Art glossed over the challenges to effective collaboration.

Effective collaboration was further hampered by Art's marketing emphasis. A marketing pro, Art walked, talked, ate, and breathed marketing. His world was product families, branding, pricing, channels, and positioning. He easily recognized the marketing case for collaboration surrounding the power of the brand and the importance of compatibility across product lines for easy upgrade sales. But he was less informed about technical possibilities. Art misunderstood and even dismissed the technical and manufacturing intricacies of collaboration. Nonetheless, he pushed to develop common technology across several businesses.

In the Europa project, for example, (Europa was the code name for a major corporate effort to leapfrog competitors in several computer hardware markets), the idea was to create a family of computers from a single platform design that would be developed jointly by several of the businesses. Each business would then use the common platform to create products for its particular market segment.

Although the Europa strategy had several advantages, such as building con-sistency throughout the product lines and spreading development costs over more products, there were some critical disadvantages. Notably, the platform design had to be viable for many products. But servers require strong commu-nication capabilities and robust reliability. Workstations demand faster comput-ing power and graphics. Desktop computers need to be produced in high volume and at low cost. Multimedia home computers have still other demands. So, major technical design trade-offs emerged—communications vs. computing power vs. high-volume manufacturability. The technical challenges were exacer-bated further when geographically distant business units were forced to collab-orate. Unfortunately, the technical challenges inherent in these design trade-offs and distance relationships were not recognized when Art decided on the collab-oration. He simply did not know (or perhaps care) much about technology. The result was that Jupiter managers ended up overcollaborating.

Collaboration on Everything

Executives at Jupiter adopted a core competence approach, but they lost sight of the "core." They tried to collaborate on everything. One manager described their approach in these terms: "If some technology or concept is already out there, we use it. . . . We try to collaborate as much as possible." As a result, Jupiter managers had no focus to their collaborative effort and thus did not distinguish extraordinary opportunities for synergies from the ones that were not worth the time needed to find them.

Every Business Is the Same

Earlier in the chapter, we noted that one of the things that makes team cycling such an unusual sport is the amount of team effort needed to produce a single winner. Cycling competitions such as the Tour de France demand a unique form of collaboration in which the role of some riders is to sacrifice their own opportunities to win so that teammates can. Figuring out the strengths of team members (and who can realistically win) is key.

Yet at Jupiter, every business was considered the same. There was little recog-nition that some businesses had distinct strengths (or weaknesses) that affected what they could bring to any collaborative effort. Further, there was also little recognition that some businesses had greater opportunities for success than oth-ers. For example, there was no shared sense that multimedia home computing might be more attractive than commercial computing or that servers might offer greater growth potential than personal computers. One manager lamented, "Right now we have no real good way of prioritizing the businesses."

The "every business is the same" mentality went even further. Managers at Jupiter did not recognize that there could be much greater payoffs to collaboration and, ultimately, corporate success if focused efforts were made to help particularly well-positioned businesses. As one manager said, "I am not thinking about how to help the manager of another business. We are all about the same, and so mostly I am thinking of how to help me." Although the businesses may have been equals in the corporation, this was not the case in the marketplace.

Again, the Europa strategy provides a good illustration. As we noted earlier, there was a fundamental design trade-off that put several businesses into conflict. But conflict per se was not the problem. After all, such conflict is inherent in most collaborative situations. Rather, the problem was that Jupiter managers had not come to grips with the differences in market potential of the various businesses. Without any business priorities, personalities and lobbying skill came to play a larger role in the collaboration strategy than did strategic position and market opportunity. As one manager related, "We all had different parameters of performance and so we all lobbied to get it [Europa design] to favor our own needs." The results were often suboptimal because Europa's collaboration strategy depended more on political skills than on exploiting business opportunities.

Business Implications

If you could walk in, sit down, and spend just fifteen minutes with any middle manager at Jupiter, the job would seem ideal. . . . That is, if endless coordination, rampant frustration, conflict, and politics are your idea of perfection. These overworked executives encounter seemingly endless obstacles. They spend hour upon hour coordinating with one another. A manager described to us how "his 'bandwidth' was consumed by coordinating with everybody— always." Others described coordination as their "number one" management task. The result was that managers spent more time coordinating and less time tending to their businesses.

Frustration was rampant among managers, who had to deal with many businesses in many locations. As one manager lamented, "There is so much frustration. . . . I can't get my work done . . . and it's worse because the other people aren't here and I just can't talk to them." Conflict was a way of life at Jupiter. A Europa manager had warned us, "There are conflicts all over the place with respect to trying to create a common set of chips, a common technology that is used throughout Jupiter." Particularly controversial were decisions concerning which businesses would develop which core competences. Some technical competences were regarded as state of the art. Managers intensely fought to land these "plums" for their respective design groups.

Political infighting was a major feature of life at Jupiter, too. Currying favor and playing influence games were the way to resolve collaboration problems. One manager complained, "They [another business] are trying to influence things to benefit them, and we are trying to influence to do things that will benefit us. It's suboptimal for both of us."

In the short run, excessive collaboration damaged marketplace distinctions within the product line. For example, Europa's collaborative design was too expensive for a viable low-end product. A manager commented, "The reason that we don't do a good job at the low-end is that the common technology is too expensive to build cost-effective low-end systems." Yet the low end was critical for Jupiter's strategic positioning within a key market segment. Moreover, since Art was so busy and collaboration often involved several different businesses, he was very slow to adjust collaborations to changing market circumstances.

In the long run, excessive collaboration increasingly trapped Jupiter. As individual businesses ceded key competitive skills to others in the company, these competences were no longer easily available to the focal business. This loss of skills made it increasingly difficult to reverse the excesses of overcollaboration. Individual businesses no longer possessed the key competences to be successful on their own. The lockstep trap steadily became more pernicious.

Overall, Jupiter has been a good performer within the computer industry. Its record is one of solid but unspectacular performance. Its businesses have had difficulty shaping distinctive strategies for specific markets. Despite the emphasis on collaboration at Jupiter, the company's businesses lag behind the industry leaders.

Warning Signals

There were clear warning signals at Jupiter that overcollaborating might have been occurring:

1. *Skybox Perspective.* Senior executives, especially those with a particular functional bias, often miss details and end up believing that collaboration is far easier than it is. So, like Art, they collaborate more than they should.

2. *Collaboration on Everything.* Jupiter's executives tried to collaborate wherever possible. The result was too much collaboration with an often time-consuming focus on low payoff opportunities.

3. *Every Business Is the Same.* Jupiter's executives did not distinguish among their businesses. Although such evenhandedness might make sense for raising children, it leads to poor collaborations and lost

opportunities where highly competitive situations demand that a company mobilize resources quickly.

Too Little Collaboration: The Star Trap

Overcollaboration is the well-known trap, but undercollaboration is probably more the norm. Undercollaboration is especially likely to occur in companies with powerful "barons" or whose cultures across businesses are very distinct. It is common in businesses with a strong market position. Here, there is not a lot of pressure to share, from either time or cost perspectives. So managers often end up exaggerating the coordination problems, the need for creative freedom, and the politicking that can accompany collaboration. Undercollaboration is exacerbated by individualistic cultures or by the need for "hit" products or services. Undercollaboration is sometimes the result of managers' being too busy. They believe that they simply do not have the time to collaborate.

Businesses in this trap may have some individually strong members. But like competitors in the Tour de France, they may not perform as well as expected because they do not gain the synergies of collaboration. These businesses frequently deliver products or services that awkwardly mesh together, have high cost structures, or are difficult to manufacture easily because they lack common parts. More subtly, these businesses miss opportunities for new revenue: they overlook economies of scale and are unaware of collaborative opportunities that may emerge in another business. Over the long run, fiefdoms naturally result as people who never work together become increasingly isolated from one another. These fiefdoms make it progressively more difficult to reverse undercollaboration, because people lock into often negative stereotypes about different businesses.

Time Warner found itself in the undercollaboration trap. The merger of Turner Broadcasting System with Time Warner (itself the progeny of the 1989 Time and Warner coupling) created a media colossus but one that makes little sense together so far. A few key Turner executives were charged with creating some sense of the merger. As one observer noted, "The more difficult part of the mission is to make Time Warner more than just the sum of its parts—to force feuding baronies, which often feel more loyalty to their 'talent' [such as Madonna and Clint Eastwood] than they do to Mr. Levin [head of Time Warner], to work together."[4] An excellent opportunity for synergies is in the area of copyrights, which are the exclusive right to exploit creative products across the publishing, music, and movie studio operations of Time Warner. Yet

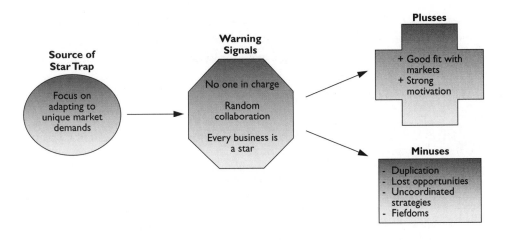

Figure 3.4 • The Star Trap

thus far, "these gems have, in general, been locked up in those powerful baronies." In part, these "barons" are correct in resisting corporate pressures to collaborate. *Gone with the Wind*'s Scarlett O'Hara may have little crossover to *Sports Illustrated*. At the same time, there are probably significant opportunities for synergies and competitors like Disney, as well as Turner Broadcasting, have exploited these masterfully.

Businesses that undercollaborate share several common traits. One trait is that no one is in charge. Managers of businesses in this trap rarely recognize that collaboration is something to be managed. As a result, collaboration becomes an individual effort by particular people who happen to spot opportunities.

A second trait is collaboration on anything. These businesses have no focus to their collaborative efforts. There is no particular interest in promoting collaboration. If it happens, it happens. . . . Collaboration is a random event.

A third trait is that every business is a star—or at least is trying to be a star. Protecting turf or even just individuals' pushing for their own "brass ring" is typical of these businesses. The informal culture and the formal reward system usually favor achieving for the individual, not the group.

Becoming a Star at Galaxy

At Galaxy, you're instantly hit with technospeak from the employees of this high-flying software firm. Galaxy (a pseudonym) is populated by smart, hip, twenty- and thirtysomethings who were chosen for their brains and their attitude. Tour Galaxy and you'll be struck by the collegelike atmosphere. One developer said that "every week is like finals week." Another called Galaxy "a family where all the kids are smart and competitive." Late nights and crash schedules to create some of the market's hottest software are the norm. Coming in on the weekends is not only encouraged, but, we were told, Galaxy tries to hire only people who would *choose* to work weekends. Galaxy's dual career ladder of technical and managerial tracks is one more indication that the firm is run so that top developers can retain their status as the royalty of the firm. Fun and pranks get top billing, too.

Landing a job at Galaxy is hard. The screening process is intense. It takes many interviews with lots of people to get that coveted Galaxy job offer. Managers grill prospective candidates and coordinate among themselves to keep the interview process tough for prospective employees. They want only the brightest and the most innovative. As one manager described, "We hire extremely talented people and spend as much time as it takes to hire them and then spend time up front so that they know our expectations."

Once hired, the Galaxy philosophy is to let people "do their own thing." It is a deliberately hands-off management strategy. Even newly hired employees have enormous freedom. The belief is that if people are good enough to be at Galaxy, then they can figure out on their own how to go out and make things happen.

The strategic challenge is to create individual "hit" products or "killer apps," in industry parlance, like TurboTax, Pagemaker, Excel, and Quicken, that can dominate an applications category. On the surface, there are lots of collaboration opportunities at Galaxy. There are many complementary products and common features across products, such as graphics and word recognition, that could be shared. The suite concept of packaging groups of programs together, pioneered by Microsoft and Lotus, makes collaborating across products particularly attractive from a marketing standpoint as well. Yet few people collaborate across products and businesses.

No One in Charge

Galaxy's system of promoting "hit" products and "star" developers has significant plusses. People stay focused, very busy, dedicated, and even obsessive about making their software run. Managers give their people the freedom to manage their work. The result is that people are energized.

But cross-business collaboration is an afterthought. Collaboration is left to the vast, informal network in which somebody knows somebody who knows somebody. . . . As one manager described this system, "A lot of it is personal or informal. You know someone on another project who you see occasionally

Titmouse and Red Robin

Coadaptation is most effective when poised between too much and too little structure. The comparison of the structure of social interaction between the titmouse and red robin illustrates this central idea of coadaptation.

In the early 1900s, milk was delivered to homes in the United Kingdom in bottles without caps. Two bird species, the titmouse and the red robin, learned to drink the cream that floated to the tops of the bottles. Eventually, dairy distributors began putting aluminum seals on the bottles to solve this problem. In about twenty years, the population of titmice (about 1 million birds) learned how to pierce the seals. In contrast, the red robins did not. Occasionally, one robin would discover how to pierce the seal, but that knowledge never spread. What is the explanation?

Titmice are social. They travel in flocks of about eight to ten birds for two to three months per year. They communicate some of the time, but not always, and their flocks vary in membership. In contrast, the red robins are territorial. A male robin will exclude others from his territory. They rarely communicate, and when they do, it is usually antagonistic.

Generally, related agents adapt most effectively when they partially interact with one another. If related agents are always together, then they adapt quickly. However, they have too little diversity to cope with sudden change. If they are never together, the population of agents adapts very slowly to change and may ultimately evolve into a different species that cannot communicate.[5]

---

and this is how you find out what is going on there." Sharing software code, coordinating marketing approaches, and collaborating in other ways are not discouraged explicitly. People are just not very interested, and collaboration is not very organized. As one manager said, "The biggest way that sharing happens is [that] people who used to work together get together every so often to compare notes and sometimes they find ways to cooperate."

Sometimes, the "no one in charge" approach to collaboration works well. This happened in one of the businesses. A low-level software developer from another part of the corporation transferred into this business. While she was working on her part of the project, she recognized the opportunity for the rest of the group to collaborate with her old business unit on writing a major piece of software code. The collaboration was successful, and both businesses saved time and resources. As one of the managers recalled, "Within our group, we had one person who is very strong in registers and text layout code. She came over from the publishing group. . . . It was just a really good idea to collaborate. . . . So the fact that she understood that code well enough was pretty valuable to us."

But "no one in charge" collaboration does not always work. Sometimes the other side does not pay attention. For example, a manager discussed trying to collaborate (unsuccessfully) with a much larger business: "We need to have more cooperation with them, but we are like a little gnat to them. We're nothing." Sometimes the other side sees no incentive to collaborate. One manager described an opportunity to collaborate that he thought would have worked well for both sides. But the other side did not agree. As he recalled, "We asked, 'Will you do it for us?' and they said, 'Not until somebody tells us that it is strategically important. . . . We've got too many things on our plate.'"

Collaboration on Anything

At Galaxy, whenever a few people anywhere in the corporation wanted to collaborate, they would simply do so. There were no guidelines to follow nor any overall logic for collaboration. A typical manager told us, "I think about collaboration case by case. I don't have any generalizations."

An example was a collaboration on a common graphical user interface (GUI) for several products. There were no corporate mandates to share, but rather a couple of software developers on their own saw an opportunity to collaborate. They worked together for several months to create common software code that accelerated each other's development cycle. Was this project a wise choice for collaboration? Were there better choices? Could other businesses have used the same interface? Would these developers have been better off collaborating with someone else, on something else? No one really knew.

Everyone Is a Star

The Tour de France example highlighted how effective coadaptation requires that some people limit their own chances to win by helping others who are better positioned for success. Yet this kind of behavior was hardly part of Galaxy's culture.

Everyone wanted to be the star. Galaxy intentionally hired this kind of person—extremely competitive and achievement oriented. Said one manager, "There is competition between the managers to be the coolest, to have the best stuff, to be in Sandy's [the boss] favor." But being a star meant being dazzling, and clearly, using someone else's work was not dazzling. As a consequence, there were no real incentives to collaborate.

The effects of the star system were bolstered by the accounting system. As one manager explained, "There is no way of getting credit for contributions in the sense that if I give something to the pot, I get something for it." If one business group helped another, there was no way to get credit for the resources that were devoted to the other group's success. Managers who helped others were penalized. Not surprisingly, then, managers shied away from collaboration because the "system" could not figure out how to give them equitable credit for their efforts. In the minds of many managers, there had to be an immediate balancing of effort across groups, something that was difficult to accomplish. Otherwise, how could someone be a star?

Business Implications

Too little collaboration led to rampant reinventing of the wheel at Galaxy. One manager was surprised by the "incredible duplication of effort." Another said, "Everybody is reinventing the wheel around this entire friggin' company," and a third, "you hear about three different people doing the same thing all the time." The result was slowed product development time and higher costs that particularly damaged Galaxy's competitiveness in its fast-paced markets.

Too little collaboration also created bundles of products that did not work together very well. Customers expected that products from the same company would have similarities, and it was confusing for them when Galaxy's products did not mesh well. Galaxy had complementary products with often poor interfaces and nonstandard "looks." One manager lamented, "We could be so well-aligned [across products], but we're not."

More subtly, undercollaboration led to lost opportunities for new revenue. Galaxy managers were late to capitalize on growth opportunities. Managers in one business would spot new markets, but they did not share these insights with others in different businesses. New opportunities were therefore sometimes underexploited or developed too slowly. One executive complained that, "each product group acts on its own. What is happening is that we have this great opportunity, and if we could get our act together we could really take the market by storm. As opposed to each product group deciding which businesses to be in and which technologies to be in." Economics of scale were often lost as well. For example, we were told that sometimes it was hard to justify creating particular features for a single project, and so these features were dropped. Yet the expense could have been justified if it were spread across a broader revenue base.

In the long run, collaboration was becoming increasingly difficult at Galaxy because undercollaboration created competitive fiefdoms. People were not familiar with one another. There were signs of "Not Invented Here" and negative stereotyping cropping up. One manager described managers in another business as "arrogant." Another said, "I would never work with them." It was becoming more, not less, difficult to collaborate at Galaxy.

Overall, Galaxy was in good financial shape and had great people. But the firm was living off of one set of unusually successful products from another part of the corporation, whereas the rest of the businesses were much more modest performers.

Warning Signals

The Galaxy example suggests several warning signals of too little collaboration:

1. *No One in Charge.* Collaboration is an afterthought that is mostly the province of low-level people. Although these people often understand the details, they have little vision about high-impact collaboration possibilities. Their collaboration reflects friendship and happenstance, not a deep understanding of collaborative possibilities.

2. *Collaboration on Anything.* Anything was a candidate for collaboration at Galaxy. Sometimes managers made wise choices about opportunities to collaborate, but sometimes they did not. There was no coherent way to sort through these random possibilities.

3. *Everyone Is a Star.* When career ladders or business processes like accounting do not support collaboration (or, even worse, penalize it), no one collaborates very much. This was the case at Galaxy.

Coadaptation at the Edge of Chaos

Whereas managers at Jupiter were locked into the rigidity of too much collaboration and those at Galaxy fell into the chaos of too little collaboration, managers at some other firms are able to balance synergistic collaboration and individual success. Like the Tour de France cycling teams, they coadapt. That is, they focus on a few key tactics for mutual gain, but not every gain. They yield the decisions about how (if at all) to collaborate to middle managers who understand both the strategic and the tactical issues of collaboration. They assign distinctive roles to individual businesses. Within this limited structure, they then let collaborative behavior emerge in unpredictable, dynamic (*self-organized*), and yet effective ways, creating strategy that is both unique and synergistic.

Coadaptive businesses often consistently do well in individual markets, are particularly strong in very attractive ones, and excel overall. Like the top Tour de France teams, these businesses frequently are collectively a strong team *and* have one or two members who wear the yellow jerseys in their market segments.

Disney is a superb illustration of effective multibusiness collaboration. A global symbol of U.S. culture, Disney has excelled in businesses ranging from retail stores to cable television and cruise lines. In a few businesses, such as theme parks and animated movies, Disney is widely seen as *the* global leader. By almost any financial measure, the corporation is a pace-setting performer, with growth on the order of 20 percent per year for the past decade. A major reason for that success is collaboration across businesses. Best known is the sharing of hit movie characters like Pocahontas and the Lion King across music, video, merchandising, and other businesses. CEO Michael Eisner dubs it "the multiplier effect," in which the Disney brand name flashes into the collective global consciousness millions of times per day. But what is less well known is that Disney does not share the Disney image across all of its businesses. For example, Disney enterprises such as Touchstone Pictures and Miramax Films, the independent film studio behind such adult movies as *The Crying Game* and *Pulp Fiction*, avoid the Disney brand. Rather, these businesses capture different synergies within the corporation. Disney managers collaborate, but not everywhere in a rigidly standard way nor chaotically, either. Business strategies are unique, and yet collectively take advantage of Disney's strengths.

Another example is Banc One. Smart collaboration across its various banks is one reason why this midwestern giant was a top U.S. firm in the early nineties. How did Banc One businesses collaborate? Rather than putting collaboration choices with senior corporate executives or not managing the process at all, Banc One corporate management left collaboration decisions to the heads of the banks. These middle-level managers had both a strategic view and knowledge of the operating details and the local nuances of their respective banks. These managers were on the line to meet the operating performance numbers. Cross-bank collaboration was focused on a set of common products from which these bank heads could choose. This meant that Banc One affiliates in Indianapolis could carry one set of products while the affiliates in Columbus might offer a different set. The collaborative opportunities were focused but the actual choices were not determined by corporate headquarters. Collaboration was further enhanced by comprehensive monthly reports. These cross-bank scorecards opened the door to collaboration by providing bank heads with the incentive to collaborate (no one likes to be last) and the information (other banks with similar issues) about how to do it. As one Banc One executive observed, "If you see that you are the worst, you pick a better bank and see what is happening there."[6] Ironi-

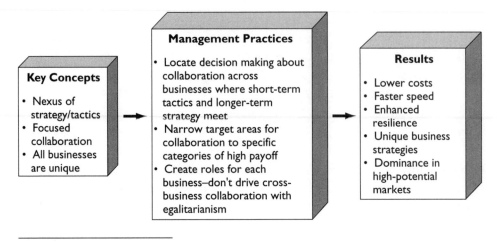

Figure 3.5 • Coadaptation

cally, Banc One has apparently since switched to more centralized control of collaboration and has not performed as well later in the decade.

We have found that managers who have mastered coadaptation share several common traits. The first is placing collaboration decisions with the managers of businesses or product lines. These people are at the nexus of strategy and tactics. At this middle management level, executives tackle both day-to-day business and long-term strategic direction. They can therefore readily formulate a broad strategic view of collaboration while maintaining a grasp of operating detail such that their choices are not naïve.

The second trait is focused collaboration. Managers who balance effectively between too much and too little collaboration focus their attention on a small number of high-payoff areas—usually about 20–30 percent of all possible collaborative opportunities. These managers do not try to capture all possible synergies. This would be too time consuming and would constrain learning opportunities. But these same managers do not leave collaboration to chance, because major opportunities for synergy might be missed.

The third trait is that every business is unique. In these firms, managers have a sharp sense of the opportunity that each business presents. Just as cycling teams recognize that not all cyclists have an equal shot at the yellow jersey, so too do the managers in these businesses understand that not all opportunities are the same. As a result, collaboration is often unequal.

Collaborating at Tai-pan

Downtown, in the heart of a sprawling city is the headquarters of Tai-pan, the flagship business of a premier global computing firm. Tai-pan (a pseudonym) sells a broad line of the best known computing products in the world. The firm competes across a band of very competitive and fast-paced oligopolistic markets like workstations, networking, and Internet software, whose boundaries are blurring daily. Continuous jockeying with tough, global competitors is the only constant. One manager described the environment as "opportunistic chaos." Speed and cost matter. Continuous improvement matters. Creating new markets as mature ones die matters. The impetus to collaborate is strong—on the marketing side, through branding and common distribution channels; in product development, through standard designs, components, and subassemblies; and in manufacturing, in common assembly lines, purchasing, and logistics. Not surprisingly, Tai-pan managers see collaboration as one of the most critical aspects of strategy.

Nexus of Strategy and Tactics

At Tai-pan, collaboration is orchestrated by the middle managers who run the key businesses and product lines within the company. These managers live operating details. They sit in on product design reviews and product planning meetings. They review the results of market focus groups. They get to the shop floor as well. They know inventory numbers, bookings, and the latest products from competitors. Like the improvisational managers described in Chapter 2, these middle managers are deeply involved with their businesses, and they "own" profit and loss responsibility for them.

Yet they also grapple with strategic issues affecting their businesses. They are the prime strategists for their businesses, shaping the vision of their businesses for the future. They play a critical role in overall corporate strategy. Together with the top corporate officers, these managers form the corporate-wide Strategy Forum. This group meets every four weeks to shape corporate strategic direction. At these meetings, each business is reviewed in order to create a common strategic view of the corporation as a whole. The meetings also give these managers an opportunity to get to know each other and to exchange information so that they can collaborate with one another where it makes sense.

Focused Collaboration

Most companies have many opportunities for collaboration. Branding, distribution channels, logistics, product design, and core technologies just scratch the surface of the possibilities. But Tai-pan's managers are not concerned about all of these possibilities. These busy executives focus their attention on specific high-potential areas of collaboration and simply ignore the rest.

For example, Tai-pan's strategy involved collaboration in the use of common product parts across businesses. But managers did not examine every possibility for using common parts. Rather, they explicitly centered their attention on the approximately 20 percent of product components that represented 60–85 percent of the cost of the product, depending upon the business.

There were several advantages to increasing the volume of these critical parts. The most obvious was that Tai-pan could cut deals for more attractive pricing by purchasing in volume. But the collaborative advantages went well beyond price. Tai-pan's volume of business made it attractive for suppliers to give the firm preference on prototypes. Tai-pan engineers received early versions of new components that they integrated into new designs, well ahead of the competition. Tai-pan also received more reliable deliveries. So even though parts shortages frequently beset other companies, they rarely affected Tai-pan.

There may have been better collaborative opportunities within Tai-pan, but in Tai-pan's high-velocity markets, there is no time to check every possibility. In effect, managers simplify their collaboration. Moreover, by not collaborating on everything, managers leave some room for serendipity. Sometimes this pays off. For example, engineers in one business used a new digitizing technology instead of collaborating with sister divisions on an alternative technology. Although this specific product was unsuccessful, the technology proved to be much more robust than anyone imagined. Other businesses adopted the technology in subsequent products.

Every Business Is Unique

Cycling team members differ from one another. Some are hill climbers, others are great sprinters, some excel on downhills, and some are just better than the others. Coadaptive cycling teams create distinct roles to use these differences to their advantage. Tai-pan managers do the same.

In Tai-pan's portfolio of businesses, some compete in extraordinarily cost-competitive markets. Some focus on home consumers, whereas others target Fortune 500 corporations. Some have high-growth potential. Like cycling teams, Tai-pan's businesses are not all the same. And like top cycling teams, Tai-pan managers create roles to reflect this uniqueness.

An example is their "golden goose" business. When we visited Tai-pan, this part of the corporation was in an exploding growth market. The business accounted for approximately 20 percent of corporate revenue and a much higher percentage of profits. It also claimed the number one market share position.

Managers of the "golden goose" borrowed extensively from other Tai-pan businesses so that they could better keep up with the pace in their market. For example, they borrowed some engineering designs, manufacturing processes, and key marketing people from their sister divisions. But these managers did

Table 3.1 • Coadaptation at Tai-pan

Focus of collaboration	Twenty percent of product components that represent 60% to 85% of product cost. Assembly lines in two manufacturing facilities for three of five businesses. Centralized logistics. Television brand advertising.
Primary decision makers	General managers of Tai-pan's five businesses meet monthly at a strategy forum to discuss collaborative possibilities and collective strategies. These meetings begin with real-time operating information.
Roles of businesses	
Golden goose	Win in the most attractive market (defined by growth rate and size) in which company participates
Work horse	Be competitive in a large, moderately growing market with steadily decreasing margins
	Develop procedures such as rapid ramp up to volume production for other businesses to use
	Protect other businesses from low-end competitors
	Provide intelligence on moves by low-end competitors
Scout	Attack a new market
	Look out for opportunities for growing other businesses
	Form strategic alliances to preempt competitors and learn more about the market
Closer	Get the most out of a dying product line
	Learn from Scout businesses
	Provide low-risk training ground for new managers
Complementer	Provide complementary products to flesh out product line
	Add to economies of scale for purchasing and logistics
	Keep competitors busy on this front
Common goal	"Get rich together"
Results	Golden goose holds number one position
	Top three market segment performance for others

not share much in return. They just worried about their own needs and did not even try to share. Like a cycling team's number one rider, the "golden goose's" only job is to win.

Contrast the "golden goose" business with a second business. This business is in a low-end market with a modest potential for profit. The strategic role of this business, as one manager explained, is "to protect the 'golden goose' and other high-margin businesses from competitors approaching from the low end." To use cycling terms, this is one of Tai-pan's domestiques. Their role involves providing market intelligence on the upmarket moves of low-end competitors and designing business processes that all businesses use, such as the ramp up to volume production. Although this business is expected to perform well in its market, no one expects that any business in this segment of the industry can perform like Tai-pan's "golden goose."

Business Implications

Tai-pan managers take a coadaptive approach to collaboration. That is, they structure some aspects of the process like targeted areas for collaboration, fixing decision making on collaboration at the business manager level and roles for the various businesses, but then they let collaboration unfold. The result is collaborative behavior that is attuned to changing conditions, complicated, and realistic about whether a particular collaboration will be effective (unlike Jupiter) as well as targeted toward high payoff opportunities for synergies (unlike Galaxy).

A key result from this collaboration is that Tai-pan has scale economies among their shared components that give them some of the lowest product costs in the industry. Tai-pan also has an enviable record of fast product development time because of the targeted sharing of designs. These cost and speed advantages have given Tai-pan a strategic flexibility that other firms cannot match.

In contrast, Tai-pan's strategy of not collaborating on everything has provided the firm with several distinct business models that make sense in specific markets. For example, while businesses collaborate on some product parts, some aspects of manufacturing are kept distinct from one another, due to the differing quality and volume demands in respective markets. More subtly, Tai-pan's approach of *not* collaborating on everything has given the firm enhanced resilience. Leaving some things unique within each business broadens the opportunity for serendipitous learning, such as in the case of the digitizing technology mentioned above. Partial linkage across businesses means that Tai-pan managers are more likely to spot trends early in one market and then spread information throughout the corporation. Both too much and too little connection between businesses would stymie this process.

Overall, Tai-pan's managers have balanced synergistic collaboration with individual success. Tai-pan's "golden goose" has the number one position in the highest-margin and one of the fastest-growing segments of the industry. This success has buoyed the entire company. Tai-pan's other businesses are typically among the top three in their markets. From the outside, Tai-pan's strategy is one of competition in many markets, with particular emphasis on booming ones. From the inside, their strategy emerges from coadaptation. As one major business publication observed, Tai-pan is "the king of global computing."

Key Signals

The Tai-pan example suggests several key signals of coadaptation across multibusinesses.

1. *Nexus of Strategy and Tactics*. Tai-pan managers locate decision making about when to collaborate with middle managers who understand both short-term tactics and long-term vision. They get the right compromise between what is realistic and what is wise.

2. *Focused Collaboration*. Tai-pan managers focus on particular targets for collaboration, even if it means missing good opportunities. They recognize that they do not have time to examine every possible alternative. The side benefit of focus is unexpected surprise and learning.

3. *Every Business Is Unique*. Tai-pan managers know that not every business is the same. So they create different roles for different businesses, and they do not feel obligated to share equally.

Creating Coadaptation

Here is the survey that led off this chapter, completed for our case illustrations of Jupiter (J), Galaxy (G), and Tai-pan (T).

Cross-business collaboration is:	frequent	⟶	rare	
		J ··· T ··· G		
Cross-business collaboration decisions made by:	corporate management	⟶	low-level management	
		J ·· T ··· G		
Roles for different businesses are:	clear	⟶	undefined	
		T ········· J, G		
The culture rewards:	team play	⟶	individual win	
		J ··· T ··· G		
Reinventing the wheel is:	common	⟶	rare	
		G ··· T ··· J		

If your firm is more like Jupiter, then you need to refresh your approach to collaboration across businesses. At the top of the change agenda should be adjusting (typically lowering) the level of decision making on collaboration. Usually, this adjustment is to the business unit or product line level. You should also ensure that all relevant functional or geographic perspectives are represented in the decision process. In addition, be sure to address obvious problems in collaboration, like trying to coordinate too many businesses or businesses in distant locations. If these collaborations are necessary, budget for "face to face" time or excellent video conferencing facilities. Also, you should focus your collaborative efforts. No one has time to pursue every collaborative opportunity. Know why each unit is successful and what role each plays. Remember that if you have overcollaborated for some time, then you may have to rebuild competences in particular businesses.

If your firm is more like Galaxy, you need to ensure that your formal and informal reward systems are not blocking effective collaboration. With that done, revise your incentive system for reward sharing and question why more of it is not happening. It is also smart to inventory the competences and capabilities within your organization and then evaluate which have the greatest strategic potential for collaboration. Also, think carefully about what aspects of your products and services or business processes make the most sense to share. Overall, put the onus for thinking about collaboration with middle managers at the business or product line level. Don't leave it to chance encounters by lower-level people.

If your company is like Tai-pan, then you are poised on an edge from which even the best managers sometimes slip. Ensure that you keep your processes simple and focused only on the highest-payoff opportunities for collaboration.

Receiver-Based Communication

U.S. Air Force pilots sometimes coordinate with one another when no ground control is available. One way they do this is through **receiver-based communication**. In this process, each pilot briefly broadcasts information about what is happening in his air space. Then each pilot decides with whom to coordinate. Each then preferentially contacts the pilots who possess particular information each needs. In other words, the receivers, not the senders, of information decide the pattern of coordination. They coordinate with some while they ignore others. In this way, a group of pilots without a leader can cope effectively with a rapidly changing landscape. Managers at Tai-pan use this communication pattern to coordinate their collaboration efforts.[7]

Manage the collaboration of important and challenging technology particularly carefully. Also, keep in mind that when change and pace are critical, it is better to undercollaborate than overcollaborate in order to stay flexible. Finally, reassess your approach frequently.

A Final Note on Collaboration

In the 1970s, the Boston Consulting Group developed a popular approach for analyzing a company's portfolio of businesses that emphasized cross-business capital allocations based on market share and product life cycle. More recently, the core competence view has emphasized sharing competences across businesses and contrasted the view of companies as portfolios of competences with companies as portfolios of businesses.

Coadaptation takes the intermediate position that companies are collections of unique businesses, but that internal collaboration is also valuable. Moreover, coadaptation suggests that collaboration possibilities are more numerous than those that arise through simply transferring capital or sharing competences. Collaborations as diverse as exchanging intelligence on the moves of competitors, gaining economies of scale in purchasing, sharing a distribution channel, or cooperating on a one-time product development project can be valuable. Coadaptation is more dynamic than earlier models, and shifts the decision point for collaboration from corporate headquarters to the offices of middle managers. Indeed, the heart of coadaptation is the group of middle managers who actively run their own businesses, even as they collectively create strategy around the portfolio of businesses.

The key to making coadaptation work is to maintain a palpable tension between the collective and the individual win. This means clear accountability and reward for meeting individual business goals, as well as transforming groups of individuals into teams. But, beyond the obvious incentives such as stock options and promotion policies that favor successful individuals who are also team players, how do companies encourage middle managers from different businesses to work together as a team? We have seen several tactics that seem to be effective.

One such tactic is to arrange for managers to meet often as a group. Once a month meetings are the minimum frequency that is necessary for people to get to know each other well, become comfortable with one another, and deal with real issues. At Tai-pan, the Strategy Forum created frequent interaction among managers. This monthly gathering of the heads of businesses became the main way through which managers developed a mutual understanding of one another and their collective businesses.

A second tactic for making these groups effective is creating a common goal that highlights managers' opportunities for collective success. Sometimes a common goal is created by emphasizing competition. For example, during the software wars between Lotus and Microsoft, the Lotus cafeteria featured a famous Army recruiting poster, with Bill Gates replacing the finger-pointing Uncle Sam. The doctored poster read, "This man wants your lunch!" Another way to create a common goal is through a rallying cry or slogan that conveys a general sense of threat, as Intel's slogan of "only the paranoid survive" did. A common goal can also be emphasized through a positive slogan like Tai-pan's "let's get rich together!" The slogan should emphasize the importance of the collective success of meeting the group's goal and serve as an emotional rallying point.

Another tactic is to be slavishly focused on concrete, real-time information about the various businesses and the competition. At Tai-pan, the Strategy Forum centered managers' attention on each business's key operating numbers, as well as field intelligence on competitors and customers. This focus on concrete data and multiple decision alternatives signaled the importance of collective problem solving rather than politicking. This style of communication (technically termed *receiver-based communication*) also alerted managers to the possibilities for collaboration.

Finally, coadaptation may involve managers' sacrificing their own opportunities for the success of someone else. Managers will do this only if they believe that someday they may get the opportunity to manage a golden goose.

89

I don't program

contemporary works

with a deeply serious

sense of responsibility,

but as something . . . that

is exciting and expands

your conception of what

music can be. So when

you come back to the

traditional pieces, you

play them in a way that

presents something new

about the piece, or at

least reaffirms the sense

of wonder the music had

when it was first heard.

Michael Tilson Thomas,

Music Director,

San Francisco

Symphony

gaining the advantages of the

INDUSTRIES ARE CHANGING shape rapidly. New firms are entering and markets are opening up, even as old ones are transforming or maturing. Major technological changes, such as the Internet phenomenon and biotechnology miracles, have become commonplace. New opportunities abound in managed healthcare, pan-European products, and Asian markets. As firms vigorously compete in today's businesses and diversify into tomorrow's, the past is becoming irrelevant. Or is it?

The investment banking firm D. E. Shaw & Company was launched by David Shaw in 1988. Since that time, the firm has joined the ranks of the top securities companies in the United States. In a decade, the payroll expanded to include more than 400 employees, the firm amassed roughly $800 million in capital, and its annual returns averaged more than 20 percent. On a busy day, D. E. Shaw & Co. may account for about 5 percent of the total shares traded on the New York Stock Exchange.

What is behind Shaw's success? Known as the most mysterious firm on Wall Street, Shaw began as a hedge fund managed from an unlikely location—a loft over a communist bookstore in Greenwich Village. Shaw's particular hedge was algorithmic trading, which exploits tiny, short-lived price differences among multiple markets. For example, if the stock of Cummins Engine is selling for fifty cents less in New York than in Tokyo; algorithmic trading exploits this kind of market inefficiency by buying low in New York and selling high in Tokyo. More generally, these market-beating algorithms are targeted at complex relationships among unusual investments across a wide range of international financial markets. These relationships can be unearthed only through repeated experimentation and sophisticated modeling that uses superior computational skills. In fact, David Shaw and his bevy of mathematicians, computer scientists, and other bona fide "quant jocks" have spent more than $100 million to create their closely guarded proprietary software.

What is more significant, Shaw managers have leveraged their software and expertise in byzantine financial transactions into a series of successful new businesses. By building on this original hedging business, firm managers have adeptly moved into the "third market"—that is, automated off-exchange trading of listed stocks as well as obscure, complicated financial instruments like Japanese warrants and convertible bonds.

More recently, the firm's growing notoriety comes from its longer-term diversification—as it moves from its computational base in finance into various products and services that further eliminate intermediaries from financial markets. CEO Shaw claims that the matching of buyers and sellers—the fundamental role that is played by financial intermediaries—can be done by computers alone. And he is betting that the Internet is the marketplace where this will happen. To this end, the company launched Juno Online Services in April 1996, which by year's end provided free e-mail to 700,000 subscribers. The service is free, but just as in network television, customers will be advertising targets. The company has also launched a subsidiary, FarSight Financial Services, to offer an integrated package of services that includes both Shaw's traditional financial products and services, plus credit card, bill paying, and other new services. The ultimate goal is a revolutionary concept in online, one-stop financial services. But as in all of their businesses, managers at D. E. Shaw are drawing on their unique computational software, which few can duplicate. So rather than being irrelevant, for D. E. Shaw, the past has been anything but.

Capturing the gains of the past, however, is not easy. There is an ongoing tension between the old and the new. Should Shaw stay close to its algorithmic trading past, or is it time to branch out to new areas of computational modeling? How aggressively should Shaw expand into the Internet? How much (or little) should the firm rely on its core business of algorithmic trading as its entry point into electronic commerce? Would the firm be better off with a new breed of employee, or are mathematicians and computer scientists the right choice? Ultimately, the dilemma that managers such as those at Shaw face is how to take advantage of their past while moving into new opportunities—that is, how to exploit the old *and* explore the new.[1]

Cosmopolitan, a hip magazine for under-forty women, is an excellent example of the tension between old and new. The publishing icon Helen Gurley Brown served as *Cosmo*'s editor for more than thirty years until her retirement in 1997. The new editor, Bonnie Fuller, has begun to place her own stamp on the magazine. Under Fuller, readers can expect more emphasis on fashion and fitness. Articles about relationships are more explicit than under Brown; graphics have a more airy cast. The photos, the features, and the look—all have greater "attitude." But Fuller has not jettisoned the past. She says, "My philosophy echoes Helen's: I believe in a young woman who wants to have it all . . . and have fun doing it." She also promises, "You're not going to see revolutionary changes in the magazine. We're not going to change the whole reason for the magazine. I feel it's very important to build on the strengths and to bring some freshness to it, to make readers enjoy it even more."[2]

For established businesses like *Cosmopolitan*, building on the past is crucial for creating competitive advantage over new firms. The ability to exploit a brand image, distribution channels, past product designs, and other assets is *the* primary advantage that established firms have over newcomers. For example, Sony managers have been particularly adept at exploiting their long-established global brand, their experience in retail channels, and their expertise in miniaturization into a seemingly endless succession of consumer electronics products.

For younger firms such as Shaw, building on the past is equally vital. The ability to keep an early lead over competitors depends significantly on their using the company's short but successful past to economize on resources, save time, reduce mistakes, and ultimately outrun bigger, richer, and more established competitors. For example, the ability of Amazon.com., the upstart Internet bookseller, to maintain its torrid pace of growth and keep traditional players like Barnes & Noble at bay is closely related to the firm's wise use of its intricate website, and its close ties with book distributors around the United States.

The solution to the dilemma of exploiting the old while creating something new is an edge of time process, *regeneration*. Regeneration involves a set of evolutionary tactics that rely on the past to allow a business to evolve faster and more effectively into new businesses than the competition. These regener-

Table 4.1 • Regeneration in Symphony Orchestras

	San Francisco	New York
Music director	Michael Tilson Thomas	Kurt Mazur
Programming	Mix of modern and classical music	Classical music
Rationale	Draw new audiences to the symphony with contemporary music and refreshed interpretation of the classics	Draw audiences who are looking for the comfort of familiar music
Attendance as percent of capacity	90%	94%
However …		
Audience	Includes a range of ages with 60% under 35 years old	Older audience of long-time supporters
Change	Evolving	Static

Source: Anthony Tommasini, "West Coast Symphonies Defy Tradition," <u>San Jose Mercury News</u>, 22 June 1997, 86.

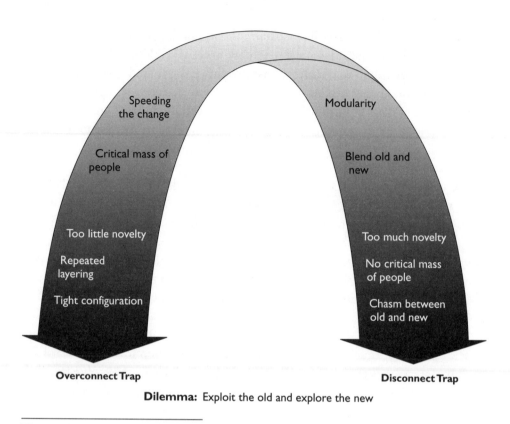

Figure 4.1 • Regenerative Edge

ation tactics involve a few, simple rules that strike a balance between the old (what is well known, comfortable, and often very profitable, especially in the short run) and the new (where the risk is greater but so, too, are the opportunities for reinvention and growth). Moreover, when managers poise on the edge between the past and the future, the complicated and adaptive behaviors of simultaneously using the old to evolve into new businesses and using the new businesses to refresh the older ones emerge.

Survey Your Company

This simple quiz should help you to begin grappling with how well you are capitalizing on the past. We will return to these questions at the end of the chapter.

To what extent do new businesses, products, or services reuse past concepts?

0 % • 100%

How old are your principal business, service, or product concepts?

Less than I year   I to 3 years   3 to 5 years   More than 5 years

To what extent do your business, product, or service teams blend experienced and new members?

Extensively • Not at all

To what extent have your new businesses, products, or services refreshed your established ones?

Extensively • Not at all

Regeneration Basics

When most of us think of magic, we think of some sort of primitive hocus pocus. Magic is something that ancient people may have used, but it is certainly not something that is very realistic or acceptable in today's corporations. So why do some people believe in it? Is there a valid contrarian view? Does magic have any kind of utility?

The northern region of eastern Labrador, one of the coldest and most desolate locations on earth, is home to the Naskapi people, an example called to our attention by a colleague, Karl Weick. Traditionally, the Naskapi lived a nomadic existence, traveling in small bands and tracking animals. Theirs was a subsistence living in a brutally cold and isolated world. The Naskapi relied on the relentless pursuit of game, day after day, during startlingly brief hunting seasons. When they found animals, they feasted. When they didn't, they scrimped and sometimes starved.

The mainstay of Naskapi life was caribou hunting. During the spring and fall, large numbers of caribou migrated through Naskapi lands. Driven on by swarms of insects, the caribou traveled at a very fast pace, covering almost forty miles in a day, over tundra that humans could barely negotiate. The key to successful hunting during the spring and fall migrations was anticipation of the migration route, because the hunters had no hope of overtaking the caribou herds otherwise. But in winter, the Naskapi hunting tactics were quite different. There were fewer caribou, and they were dispersed more widely. They moved much more slowly through the snow, and they favored the woods over the tundra. In winter, the pursuit of caribou demanded a much different strategy. Summer called for yet another approach. Since there were almost no caribou during that season, the Naskapi instead hunted beaver, fish, and other game.

How did the Naskapi cope with these harsh conditions? Essential to their success was an immense store of knowledge about terrain, weather conditions, and animal behavior. This knowledge, accumulated slowly over time, was carefully passed down from one generation of Naskapi to the next, through precise rituals, myths, and apprenticeship. This experience was vital to the Naskapi's survival in a cold and brutal environment. Experience, then, was a treasured resource.

But the Naskapi also were ambivalent about their experience because the past was both something to be retained and something to be forgotten. On any particular hunt, there was always a combination of events that the Naskapi had seen many times before, plus circumstances that were unique to that hunt. In one sense, then, each hunt was like every other: the standard elements—the hunter, the quarry, tracks, and the weather—were always there. Experience mattered. But every hunt was also unique in that the weather was different, the composition of the hunting party changed, the caribou herds were more or less wily, and so on. From this perspective, experience mattered less.

Given their ambivalence about the past, how did the Naskapi make the continuously recurring choice of "where do we hunt today?" Most days, the Naskapi relied on the experience of senior hunters in the band. But in times of high uncertainty, when game had been particularly scarce, the Naskapi set aside their experience and turned to magic.

Caribou magic centered on burning bones to reveal the location of game. Charred caribou bones were the medium through which the Naskapi communicated with their hunting gods. The ritual began with a sweat bath and drumming to induce a chosen Naskapi hunter to dream. Progress was made once the hunter-dreamer began to visualize capturing caribou. But his dream would be too vague to actually pinpoint the location of the caribou. So the hunter-dreamer cradled a shoulder blade from a long-dead caribou, attached it to a stick, and put it over the campfire. The band patiently waited for cracks to appear and then hunted in the direction of the cracks.

From a modern perspective, finding caribou by following the cracks in a charred shoulder blade seems ridiculous. Yet the Naskapi prospered in their harsh environment while following this seemingly useless ritual with caribou bones and similar magic involving the pelvis of beavers, skinned otters, and the jaws of fish. Was their magic smart? And what did these rituals really accomplish?

The answer is that the rituals provided novelty. These rituals mixed freshness with experience in the hunting process. They blended the old with the new. In

Natural Selection

Natural selection is the process whereby change occurs through inherited genetic variation, selection of the variations best adjusted to the environment, and perpetuation (or retention) of the genetic qualities best suited to a particular environment. It is through this process that systems are able to gradually change over a period of time in a Darwinian evolutionary pattern.

Mutations are critical to natural selection because they keep the system from converging too quickly on suboptimal characteristics. Mutations may introduce completely random variations that add freshness and novelty. Mutations may also reintroduce characteristics that were dropped, but are needed again. Mutations may persistently reintroduce characteristics that are harmful in the short term, but helpful in the long term.

particular, they affected the success of the hunt in several ways. First, they introduced an element of randomness into the inevitably patterned actions by which the hunters' tactics became too predictable to the hunted and too locked into a set pattern. They helped the Naskapi to avoid overhunting, what we would call "success-induced failure." Second, by following these random patterns, the Naskapi were much more likely to explore new hunting grounds that could yield new ways to hunt caribou and perhaps even new game. Finally, the shoulder blade ritual was an inexpensive insurance policy. Maybe their hunting gods really did exist!

The use of magic in caribou hunting holds several lessons for managers. First is that the past is critical. If caribou hunters fail to use past experience in the hunt, they in effect start from scratch, make errors, and miss capitalizing on the knowledge that was gained from their ancestors. Much of the success of the hunt relies on accumulating wisdom about the past, selecting the best of it, and exploiting it (technically termed *natural selection*). The same is true of executives. Effective diversification involves accumulating experience, selecting the most relevant parts of that experience, and exploiting it to create new businesses.

The second lesson is the importance of having a critical mass of people to carry forward the experience. People are the DNA of the process. Without a critical mass of apprenticeship and personal contact, the Naskapi would typically forfeit the gains of the past.

The final lesson is that novelty and even randomness (technically termed *mutation*) are critical to success, especially in times of rapid and unpredictable change. Without novelty and randomness, hunters will be slow to spot change and will uncover few opportunities to find new game or to hunt the old game in new ways. Novelty breaks the frame of the past. The same is true of managers who become stuck in routines and trapped by tightly configured business models. Whereas the Naskapi create this freshness by following random cracks in charred caribou bones, contemporary managers can do so by pursuing new opportunities in unexpected and possibly even random ways. Blending the old and new, however, is not easy. There are traps along the way that prevent effective regeneration.

Stuck in the Past: The Overconnect Trap

Many managers use the past wisely. But sometimes these managers are fooled by their success. They may skillfully craft strong business models but neglect to change them even after competitors have launched more attractive ways of competing. Other likely victims are managers whose businesses are caught in intensely competitive markets. These managers become so wrapped up in gaining the efficiencies that the past can bring to today's competition that they forget the relevance of novelty for reinvention and growth.

The best of these businesses have tightly synergistic value propositions that attack particular market niches. They are effective because few others can match their efficiencies. They have clearly defensible positions. But they are not so effective when the market changes. Although some managers recognize early on that their strategies are static, others do not. Ironically, tight interconnections within their businesses can make it increasingly difficult to extricate from the past because there is so much to refresh. If they wait too long, managers may end up without the time or financial resources to catch competitors as they sprint by. The worst outcome is the *complexity catastrophe*, in which a business collapses under the weight of its own ponderous past.

One example is Toyota, which has dominated the Japanese automotive market for years. In 1996, the company came close to dropping below 40 percent market share for the first time in fifteen years. One reason was that Toyota executives were focused on producing sedans, the type of car that had made the company so successful in the past. But middle-class Japanese families were switching to minivans, station wagons, and sport utility vehicles. Rival automaker Honda was the main beneficiary of Toyota's outmoded mindset. Honda launched a series of extremely successful products, among them the Odyssey minivan and the CR-V sport utility vehicle, which have enabled the firm to grow at more than 20 percent annually in Japan and capture domestic market share. Toyota was forced to play catch-up as managers attempted to regain share through a blitz of new products, such as the Ipsum minivan and Prado land cruiser, and through saturation advertising. As an executive admitted, "We didn't read market changes. We put too much emphasis on sedans."[3]

Although Toyota managers were quick to launch a recovery, McDonald's managers have had more difficulty escaping their past, especially in the mature North American market. Over the years, McDonald's managers created a tightly synergistic business model around a low-wage workforce, tight control of food supplies, image advertising, and efficient cooking techniques. But as consumer preferences shifted to better-tasting hamburgers like those at Wendy's and Burger King, and to alternative foods like tacos and pizza, McDonald's growth slowed. In 1996, for example, average store sales fell, market share dropped from 42.3 percent to 41.9 percent, and its stock returned a disappointing 1.2 percent. Although McDonald's managers attempted to adjust to the change through various menu innovations like the Arch Deluxe burger and pricing moves such as Campaign 55, they have not been particularly successful. McDonald's seems limited to a static strategy by its traditional hamburger image and cooking techniques that restrict menu offerings. As one observer noted, "McDonald's got obsoleted on their food . . . now America wants taste."[4]

What are the signs that managers are relying too much on their companies' past? We found three common traits. The first is too little novelty. Managers who are caught in this trap continually rely on the same people, the same strategies, the same markets, the same internal processes, and the same technologies.

A second characteristic trait is repeated layering. Managers often create new businesses, products, or services by simply piling additional features or capabilities onto old ones. Similar to the infamous Elizabethans, who, it is claimed, never bathed but just kept adding layer after layer of makeup to their faces, these managers just keep adding to the practices of the past. What is new is just piled on top of the old.

A third trait is tight configuration. Especially in the extreme cases, managers develop tight fits among different parts of their business models. Sometimes these tight connections are among the different technologies that make up a product. Or a particular sales approach is closely interwoven with manufacturing, or strategy is linked intimately to a particular market image.

Lingering in the Past at Fable

On the surface, Fable (a pseudonym) resembles a lot of companies. There is the de rigeur campuslike setting, the suburban location, and the usual tilt-up

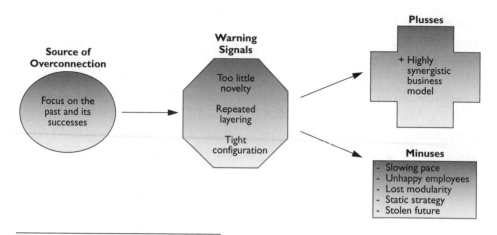

Figure 4.2 • The Overconnect Trap

buildings that have become an intrinsic part of the North American high-technology company "look." The reality is that Fable Software is one of the world's leading packaged software companies. Although the exterior of the building may signal the ordinary, the interior is filled with top-notch software developers who spend most of their waking hours crafting some of the best-known software in the world.

Fable competes in the brutally competitive packaged software industry. This is a "positive feedback" industry. In other words, the more people who use Fable software today, the more new people are likely to use it tomorrow because everyone wants to be compatible with everyone else. Profits are about being first and about making the right bets on hardware platforms, operating systems, and product features that consumers will value. The goal is to become the industry standard. To stay in the race, firms have to keep up with change.

Fable has often been the winner in the software wars. Early on, Fable managers capitalized heavily on past experience to sprint past competitors with more quickly developed products. In doing so, they captured market share and gained a strong brand image. But Fable ran into trouble when its managers exploited the past too much. They made several mistakes.

Too Little Novelty

Suppose that the Naskapi always hunted in the same place, at the same time, and in the same way. That would be foolish, yet Fable managers stayed in the same core business and just kept doing the same thing. Their strategy never changed. In this products-driven industry, their approach was to "see what the competition is doing in terms of product features and price, match them, and add something slightly better." The target market was always the same. The product line was always the same. There was little mix of people from other parts of the firm into Fable. There was no thoughtful sorting of what to continue from the past and what to drop.

Repeated Layering

What few changes Fable made were added to past practices. Managers would add a marketing or distribution channel or would add features to products without taking anything away. There was no selectivity about what to keep. Fable managers just kept everything.

An example of this layering occurred with Fable's flagship product, Aesop. Managers of the project historically relied on past designs to gain speed and cost advantages over the competition. On any given product generation, fully 85 percent of the software code was reused from previous products. For seven generations of products, the drill was the same: take the current version of the product, match competitors' features by piling new code on top of the old base, and leapfrog the competition by layering still more features on top.

At first, repeated layering was a choice. Moreover, it was a wise choice because it enabled engineers to develop the product faster and less expensively than the competition. But eventually layering was a necessity because Aesop became so convoluted that no one really understood it anymore. One manager explained, "Say someone touches the code over here and it breaks over there. No one really knows why. There are lines of code that no one has any idea why they are there. . . . It is known as the House of Cards." Developers could not change Aesop because no one fully understood its design. Yet the pace of their business did not give managers time to rewrite Aesop from scratch. Another manager said, "A restart is an impossible job because there is just so much that goes into a product of this complexity that [we] would never catch up. The competition would always be ahead." The only competitive option was to add to layer upon layer.

Tight Configuration

Fable managers tightly integrated different parts of the business. From the outside, customers expected a particular "look" from Fable products, a particular pricing strategy, and a particular distribution approach. Fable products were matched to one another. From the inside, Fable's products took advantage of synergies among hardware platforms and operating systems.

Complexity Catastrophe

Natural selection can fail when too little variation exists. Without variation a system stagnates and slowly becomes less fit for the changing landscape. In the extreme, the system becomes gridlocked by too many interconnections. These ties constrain the system and prevent adaptation. The result is a **complexity catastrophe**. Its striking property is its often very sudden and catastrophic onset, as in Fable's death march.

Again, the experience with Aesop provides a telling illustration of this tight configuration. In designing Aesop, Fable's developers closely integrated the software operating system, business application technologies, and hardware features. Initially, this produced a product that easily outperformed the competition because it took advantage of complementary features that could be exploited by tightly intertwining the technologies. For example, tricks that relied on the specifics of the hardware could be exploited by the software. And because Aesop took advantage of unique hardware features, it was initially a faster and more feature-rich product than the competition. But this tight fit among the different technologies made the product more difficult to change. When one technology changed, the entire product had to be changed.

Business Implications

Initially, Fable moved quickly in the marketplace. But as products such as Aesop became increasingly complicated and interconnected, product development times became slower and slower. They stretched from nine months to a year to eighteen months and then to two years. The increase was gradual, but the results were clear. Fable went from having products in the market early to being chronically late.

What happened to the once-efficient Fable product machine was that repeated layering in its software products created a huge, indecipherable mess that its creators called the "House of Cards." But that was not all. The technology for microprocessor platforms, operating systems, and application interfaces began to evolve at different rates. But because these technologies were configured so tightly in the products, managers were forced to update entire products at the rate of the fastest-changing technology. When one technology changed, the entire product had to be changed. "Each time we try to release a new product," one manager complained, "we have to rewrite a large part of the internal applications." That takes time.

In addition, many people became frustrated working with the same old products. They were dissatisfied with the low quality that they felt was inevitable given the repeated layering approach to development. And so Fable's fate became tied to products that people hated to work on and no longer understood. The loss of control over these mammoth products created disgruntled employees who became increasingly angry, apathetic, and anxious. Many drifted away from the company. Those who stayed were the weakest people, the ones who could not figure out how to leave.

Ultimately, Fable collapsed under the weight of its complicated, layered products. In technical terms, Fable experienced a complexity catastrophe, which occurs when there is so much interconnection that a business, product, or process suddenly collapses from too many conflicting demands. A manager explained it this way: "At the start it was not going to be a real ambitious project: we were just going to get it out the door. I kept having to add people along the way and it became really hard and intense hours, and then it became a death march."

The death march was the "effort from hell." Employees would work 70 to 80 hours a week or more, every week for months, with no time for family or friends. They barely had time to go home. Executives were getting fired for missing targets, and developers were burned out trying to meet them. Many of the managers with whom we spoke believed that they barely survived the death march. One said that "It was a complete management failure. . . . We worked for months and months and months with no vacation and working nights and weekends."

Fable made it through the death march but not without pain. A manager told us that "everybody worked really, really hard and was very, very tired . . . and [the new product] flopped. It was horrible. We had terrible press, we had terrible quality, and we weren't selling anything. Everything bad that could happen, happened." Many people left the company. The resulting products were poorly received in the market and were late. Key features were badly implemented and overly complicated. Brand image was damaged by these awkward products and strategy stalled. Worst of all, the death march stole the future. Managers had stripped people and dollars from new strategic initiatives to feed the death march, and Fable was stuck with feeding the increasingly voracious appetite of its decaying business model. What was once a strategic choice was now a vicious cycle of downward performance. Fable's managers were trapped, unable to lead new initiatives and unable to set or even keep up with the pace of the industry. The business was like an aging, overweight boxer gasping to stay in the ring with younger, faster, more fit opponents. It could last a few more rounds, but the eventual outcome was hardly in doubt.

To the outside world, Fable went from being a star to being a mediocre performer. And inside the firm? There was a nagging, gnawing feeling that the future was gone and that there was no escape from the "House of Cards."

Warning Signals

There had been clear warning signals that Fable was exploiting the past too much:

1. *Too Little Novelty*. Fable lacked freshness—in people, strategy, market, customers, or products. The result was short-run success but long-run stagnation and missed opportunities for new products growth.

2. *Repeated Layering*. What did pass for new at Fable was really just layered on top of the old. The old was always there and never really went away.

3. *Tight Configuration*. Fable managers created a very tightly configured business model around products that initially created superior performance but later harmed the company's ability to change.

Ignoring the Past: The Disconnect Trap

Just as some managers rely too much on the old, others are enamored with the new. Some managers believe that their business model is so hopelessly locked in the past that a drastic leap into new businesses is their only option. Other managers may be so mesmerized by the lure of exciting new technologies or markets that they are blind to the advantages of the past. Inexperienced managers and those with leading-edge strategies are especially vulnerable here. Occasionally, these managers just want to protect existing business from disruption and so launch new businesses with few links to the past. But regardless of why the past is ignored, managers begin to see the past as the problem and the future as the hope. They gloss over the risks of the unknown even as they dismiss the value of experience.

Companies that leave their pasts behind occasionally perform extremely well in their new businesses. Breaking the shackles of the past can be a plus. Unfortunately, when this happens, the rest of the organization is left behind because there is little transfer back to the older parts of the company. The connections are just not there. More frequently, managers who disconnect from the past make mistakes that could have been avoided. It can be increasingly difficult to reconnect with the past as the cultures of the old and new become increasingly distant. The worst outcome is an error catastrophe which occurs when a new business fails because it has too few connections with the past

An excellent illustration of disconnection with the past is Apple's personal digital assistant (PDA), the Newton. Virtually everything was new about the Newton. For example, the product concept was really a new product category. In the words of former Apple CEO John Sculley, the Newton was conceived of as a "friend"—a product concept that was very distant from the mainstream concept of a computer as a tool. The Newton relied on state-of-the-art technologies, including handwriting recognition, that had little do with existing Apple expertise. The Newton's target market was consumer electronics, where Apple had no experience. Lacking connection to Apple's experience base, managers spent a lot of money to develop the product, took a lot of time to do it, and made a lot of errors, including basic ones around pricing (too high) and product positioning (too much emphasis on handwriting recognition, too little on communication capabilities). Ultimately, the product was a commercial disaster, took resources away from more mainstream businesses, and damaged the image of the firm. An observer noted that it was "a humiliating experience with the over-hyped but disappointing Newton."[5] The Newton has since been repositioned as the more familiar "business tool."

Another example is General Motors' Saturn venture. Although part of GM, Saturn was launched as an all-new car company with its own greenfields factory in Tennessee and a unique labor relationship with the United Auto Workers. A brand-new dealership network and a new sales philosophy were also part of the Saturn vision. GM managers, in fact, took almost nothing from the past in their creation of Saturn. But GM may not have had to disconnect from the past so completely. Toyota, for example, was able to introduce their new Lexus line much more quickly and with much less investment than the reported $3 billion invested in Saturn. Some observers believe that GM will never recoup its Saturn investment. Perhaps most ironically, although the car line is now profitable, the weak connection to the rest of GM means that Saturn innovations have not reinvigorated the rest of the automotive giant. As an industry analyst observed, "There is no doubt that if you are a consumer the car is a great success . . . [but] it is difficult to prove that Saturn has helped GM as a corporation."[6]

We found three surprisingly simple traits that characterize firms in the disconnect trap. One is too much novelty. Managers who fall into this trap typically jump into new strategies or businesses with a "blank slate" or greenfields approach.

A second trait is no critical mass of people from the past. Managers who slip into this trap launch new opportunities with people who usually have rele-

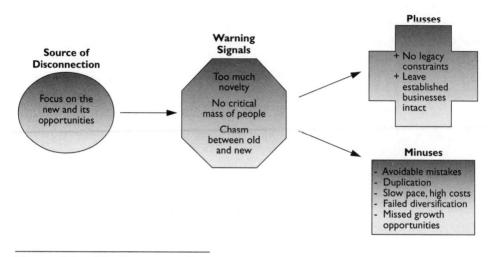

Figure 4.3 • The Disconnect Trap

vant skills for the future but lack a connection to the past. Although the new people often plan to learn from the more experienced employees, both sets of people are often swamped by the realities of daily competition.

A third trait is a chasm between old and new. Often, experienced people have no incentive to link with the new, while the new people have little incentive to connect with the old.

Erasing the Past at NewWave

How can we capture NewWave (a pseudonym)? It's young, hip, and on the frontier of the growing Internet marketplace. The average age is no more than 30. Typical clothing? Casual, of course. The typical workday? Far too long. The corporate culture? It is best described as a kind of global Euro-North American blend. And who wants to work at NewWave? Almost anyone who wants to be at the forefront of the latest technology and the newest markets. NewWave is always at the frontiers of technology, always pursuing the newest and the "coolest." Its latest Internet products will be the coolest yet.

NewWave's aggressive leading-edge strategy has paid off in a stellar and even outrageous market capitalization. The firm was early to the Internet with products that were technically impressive and market-wise. Managers stayed on the leading edge very successfully. They placed the right big bets on technology and on key collaborating firms. But NewWave is still an upstart. Despite its high market capitalization, the firm has limited resources, especially in comparison to the Microsofts and Oracles competing in its market segment. And so capitalizing on gains from the past would seem to be a smart way to conserve resources, avoid mistakes, and save time when competing against tough, established players. But the past holds little attraction for the managers at NewWave.

Too Much Novelty

For their latest venture, a foray software product to exploit the Internet's next goldmine, the NewWave management team had several options. They could play it safe and restrict themselves to ventures within the scope of current products and strategies. Another option was to take a few risks and blend old technology with some fresh concepts to create a new strategy. A third option was for NewWave managers to take big risks and lead with cutting-edge technology. Their choice was the third option. NewWave's managers decided to make a clean break and use almost nothing from the company's past. Rather, the strategy was to go into a new market with all-new technology. So they designed the new products and marketing strategy from scratch.

No Critical Mass of People

NewWave managers staffed their latest venture with fresh hires who were extraordinarily enamored with the Internet. These people knew about novel markets and the latest technologies. They were top-notch graphics, hardware, and software people who came to NewWave to work on the newest things. These people were very centered on now—on what's happening today. Indeed, the excitement of "now" was the appeal. They were attracted to the "clean slate" opportunity that the NewWave venture had offered. Old products and market concepts held no appeal for them. The fewer constraints, the better.

At the time, the rest of NewWave was booming, and so experienced NewWavers were caught up in running the core businesses of the corporation. It seemed to everyone involved that the best thing to do was to keep most of the NewWave veterans involved in the existing business. After all, the new people would simply ask for advice when they needed it.

Chasm between the Old and New

NewWave's plan was to have the old and the new people work together as needed. The reality was that the two groups did not know each other. Although the experienced NewWavers worked one building away and so were physically close, they were psychologically distant. Perhaps most important, these just-hired NewWavers were not very interested in the past. They found nothing to draw from it and little to learn. For example, a manager within the old business said, "Their managers [of the new business] were given information, but they chose not to use it."

The experienced NewWavers shared the same lack of interest in contact. They were supposed to answer questions and give advice. They were only an e-mail away. But the reality was that they were too busy running the existing business, too preoccupied with building the business that was providing current cash flow and growth. Further, no one had bothered to provide incentives for the experienced NewWavers to work on the new business. The incentives were to make their own business even more successful. Any time spent in the new areas by these more experienced people was time taken from their own business and their own rewards. They saw the new move as an intriguing experiment but not a crucial one. From their perspective, the new venture was more a hobby than a business. One manager recalled, "The [old business] managers were supposed to help out, but they don't see any personal benefit." The result was a chasm between the old and the new. As an executive told us, "Each group feels like a separate company within the company."

Business Implications

The greenfields approach to change had plusses. Managers could take advantage of new opportunities without being constrained by company legacies. They could also leave intact the older businesses. These businesses were the source of current profits, and shifting people to the new venture might have hurt their performance. So a greenfields approach made it possible for the company to move into the new market opportunity without hurting current revenue. Another plus was that NewWave was able to lure top-notch hires to the firm with the prospect of creating their own greenfields business. These people added to NewWave's stable of talent. Despite these benefits, the drawbacks were substantially greater.

One problem was schedule slippage. Before this venture, NewWave managers had released products to market in a timely fashion. They had to, because as a new firm, they had to meet and better yet beat competitive products to the marketplace. In contrast to these earlier products, products in the new venture slipped behind schedule. Some schedule slip was to be expected with such an aggressive, leading-edge strategy, but this was worse than anyone had imagined. For example, in one portfolio of six projects, developers fell behind schedule on every project almost immediately. The schedules were

Error Catastrophe

Natural selection also fails due to too much variation, as is the case when too many mistakes occur. As the errors build up, the system cannot adapt well because it cannot distinguish useful variants from errors. Eventually, the system cannot change at all because too many errors prevent its parts from coordinating with one another and functioning properly. The result is an **error catastrophe**. The NewWave venture failure is an example of this type of catastrophe.

never caught up. First, developers were a month behind, then two months, and then more. The combined challenge of using all-new technology, fresh hires, and a brand-new market was just too difficult.

A second problem was duplication of what existed elsewhere in NewWave. For example, a manager described how he "struggled for months to build this capability. . . . All along they had this really cool solution already in our own backyard." In another example, NewWave managers learned at an industry trade show that they had just spent months developing a feature that consumers did not value and that this was well known by the experienced NewWavers. Not only was this duplication frustrating, but it robbed NewWave developers of precious time and money that, if the venture were really to dazzle consumers, was better spent on the truly new. Finally, the new venture's products ended up with a look and feel that conflicted with existing products and confused customers.

NewWave managers eventually recognized their hubris. But by the time they figured this out, it was too late. The novice managers in the new venture had made too many errors that had taken too much time. They had lost their early market position. There was no good option for the NewWave management team. Ultimately, the new venture was closed.

Warning Signals

At NewWave there were clear warning signals of the disconnect trap:

1. *Too Much Novelty.* The firm's management failed to see the value of reusing lessons learned from past experiences to save time, save money, and avoid mistakes. Instead, they reinvented virtually everything from scratch. This was a slow and mistake-prone process.

2. *No Critical Mass of People.* NewWave management assumed that by asking the old and the new people to coordinate, they would. In reality, they didn't.

3. *Chasm between Old and New.* There were no incentives for coordination at NewWave. The result was the creation of two companies within the company.

Regeneration on the Edge of Time

Fable and NewWave took completely different approaches to the past. Yet, ironically, they both ended up in the same place. Although Fable managers were trapped in the past and NewWave managers dug a chasm between old and new, both teams of managers were unable to move effectively into new opportunities.

Two Patterns of Failed Change

Complexity catastrophe

Fable
Too little novelty initially led to fast product introduction but later led to dated products and slow change.

Layering on the past was initially quick, but later led to slow change and products no one understood.

Tight configuration initially led to superior products, but later retarded change because it meant that any change involved all connections.

Stolen future resulted because so many resources were required to keep old business going.

Error catastrophe

NewWave
Too much novelty initially attracted strong talent, but later slowed change because of too many errors.

Too much novelty took time away from creating new business.

A lack of a critical mass of experienced people allowed the company to focus on current activities, but later slowed change due to many errors.

Even if the venture had been successful, no tie was in place to improve old businesses.

Common result
Failure to evolve to new businesses.

In contrast, other managers who have taken a more successful approach to the past regenerate their businesses by wisely exploiting (with *genetic algorithms*) the best of the past (*selection*), adding something new (*mutation*), and mixing their blend of old and new with the not-quite-new (*recombination*). As a result, these managers often effectively evolve their businesses into new market opportunities and simultaneously extend the longevity (and profitability) of existing lines of business by blending insights from the new businesses back into their older ones. By being poised on the edge of time, between the past and future, these managers are able to achieve this more complicated and adaptive behavior.

A terrific illustration is Nintendo. Although this once-pacesetting Japanese firm lost its lead in the video-game industry to Sega and Sony in the early 1990s, Nintendo is back. In Japan, the entire first production of its stunning N64 machine sold out in two hours. When the first shipment of 500,000 machines was delivered to U.S. stores, half were sold as soon as they hit the shelves. One retailer reported the good news—185 units of the $200 toy were sold in seven minutes—and the bad news—that was all the stock he could get. A youthful aficionado enthused, "The 3-D capabilities are unbelievable. I've never seen anything like this."[7] His grade for the N64? A+.

What has made the N64 such a winner? Nintendo took a gamble with the very latest in 64-bit microprocessor electronics, sound, and graphics from Silicon Graphics, the company behind such movie marvels as *Jurassic Park* and *Lost World*. Also part of the N64 package is a state-of-the-art joystick that even rival companies call a superb innovation. As a result, the N64 has taken game play to unprecedented levels of speed, complexity, and 3-D visualization. But at the same time, Nintendo played it safe by relying on its classic hit character Super Mario. The mustachioed hero's latest adventure, Super Mario 64, headlines the game titles for the N64. Proven cartridge technology and a continued focus on the company's traditional and very loyal market segment—young males—were further ties to the past.

Another illustration is Gap, Inc., the jeans emporium turned global retailer. Like Nintendo, Gap slumped in the early 1990s. Sales growth in stores open for more than a year (a crucial success measure in retail) dropped to 1 percent per year, down from 12 percent in previous years. But like Nintendo, Gap is back. Existing store sales jumped in 1996, while total sales rose more than 20 percent. Stock price soared 46 percent (compared to 18 percent for retail as a whole and 22 percent for the market). How did Gap managers do it?

Gap managers regenerated their businesses by aggressively blending the old, the new, and the not quite new. For example, they mixed the original Gap concept with unusual new store locations, such as airports, and they integrated the well-known Gap brand with new products as varied as nail polish, watches, sunglasses, and Barbie dolls. They created their hit Old Navy stores from a combination of Gap's world-class prowess in sourcing and logistics, which underlies all Gap, Inc. stores, plus fresh merchandise, a new name, new store locations, and a distinctive warehouse shopping experience that appealed to the price-conscious consumers whom the Gap had neglected. Old Navy rapidly transformed itself from a fledging diversification effort to a profitable piece of the Gap retail empire. In just three years, Old Navy accounted for a billion dollars in annual sales and close to 25 percent of the firm's total retail space.

Gap managers also relied on not-quite-new tactics for their recovery. For example, they "rearchitected" the upscale Banana Republic division by redecorating the stores and repositioning the merchandise. They kept the chain intact but upgraded its inelegant jungle motif to leather furniture and subdued fabrics, consciously creating an ambience of "where you would like to live." Sales climbed

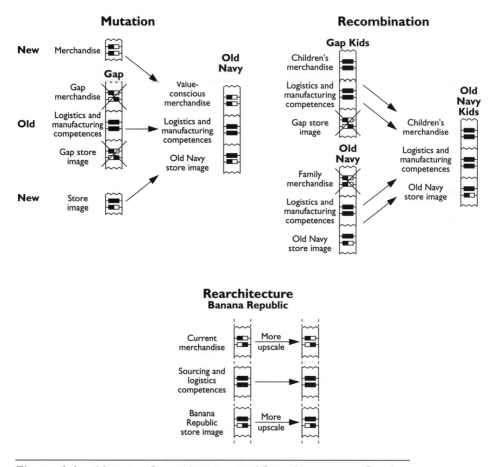

Figure 4.4 • Mutation, Recombination, and Rearchitecture at Gap, Inc.

18 percent. Gap managers also recombined two old ideas in a new way. They took two existing concepts, Old Navy and Gap Kids, to create Old Navy Kids.

Yet as in all edge processes, balancing Gap's established past with the new was tricky. Gap executives were concerned about straying too far from the essence of the firm. As one executive pledged, "We never want to have a customer say 'You have nice sunglasses, but I can't find jeans in my size.'"[8]

Firms whose managers effectively manage the past share several common traits. First, they always blend the old and the new. Whether staying close to existing markets or diversifying into new ones, they always select some relevant part of their past and blend it with something that is new.

A related trait is a critical mass of people. Managers who leverage effectively always bring along a critical mass of people as the DNA of that past experience. They recognize that in transmitting the past, meetings, e-mail, and documentation are no substitute for people.

Genetic Algorithms

Natural selection is gradual and blind. **Recombination** speeds up natural selection by mixing up the gene pool. For example, in sexual reproduction two parents provide genes and the offspring has greater variety. Recombination allows the adapting population to make use of large scale features of the landscape, and as a result make larger changes and adapt more quickly. Recombination is also intelligent (not blind) when it combines parents who are known to have the desired properties. Cross-breeding of horses or of crops are examples of such engineered recombinations.

Genetic algorithms further enhance the speed and intelligence of natural selection by relying on variation through both recombination and mutation, and selection proportional to fitness. These algorithms take the best of multiple populations plus some mutation, making it more likely that the next generation will scale the highest peaks in the fitness landscape. The resulting evolutionary process encourages the rapid spread of desired traits throughout the population, as well as innovation through the creation of new combinations from previously successful traits.

Genetic algorithms have primarily been applied to systems where performance (i.e., fitness) is easy to measure, like the performance of painting robots in auto plants. When robots are programmed to combine approaches that work and discard those that don't, they "learn" the optimal painting algorithm faster than simply waiting for random errors to occur and correcting them. The ideas behind these algorithms, however, can also be applied to managing businesses, as we have done.

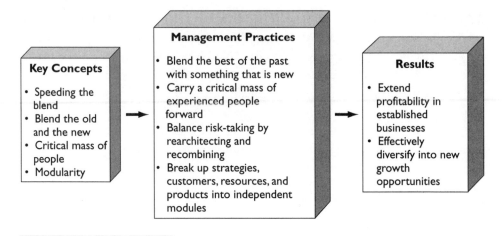

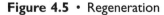

Figure 4.5 • Regeneration

A third trait is speeding the blend. To do this managers depend on tactics that accelerate the evolution of their businesses by adding in the not quite new. One such tactic is *rearchitecture*. Much like the way auto mechanics rebuild car transmissions, rearchitecture involves refurbishing some of the past. The result is not a new "engine," but it is not really an old one, either. It is something in between. A second speeding tactic is *recombination*. Recombination refers to mixing or synthesizing different pieces of the past in fresh ways to create something that is almost new . . . but not quite.

A final trait is modularity. Managers who effectively leverage the past keep pieces of their businesses, such as delivery systems or product features, distinct from one another. This creates the flexibility to change pieces of the mix at different rates. It also enables managers to use the speeding tactics of rearchitecture and recombination.

Midas Touch

If you were to trudge up the subway stairs, turn right, wander past the newspaper kiosk, and walk into Midas (a pseudonym), you would instantly know that you have entered a unique corporation. The lobby design is what strikes a visitor first. Spectacular demonstrations of Midas' latest products are set about like pieces of sculpture in a gallery. If you were to step into a cubicle and peer at a developer's screen, what you would likely see is an impressive display of leading-edge computer technology. If you talked with a few employees, these seemingly geeky engineers would dazzle you with fervently messianic descriptions of their creations.

Midas' strategy is to use leading-edge technology all the way. Managers have crafted an aggressive, pioneering strategy that relies on state-of-the-art technology to make that strategy happen. But Midas does more than that: it defines the state of the art. The firm is typically first to the market, and often even creates the market, with the best technology in the world and with products that everyone wants. The products are so good that Midas' customers clamor for what they believe is the best computing on the planet. A senior executive claimed, "Our customers want to do what no one else can do."

The primary strategic challenge at Midas is to hang onto the leading edge without slipping onto the so-called bleeding edge of too-new technology. This strategy is tough to execute, as NewWave found out, but Midas managers have done it. The big surprise is that capitalizing on the past is a major reason that Midas managers have been so successful. Capturing the gains of the past gives these managers more time and resources to diversify into new products and markets, and ultimately to reinvent their business strategy. But the real question is how Midas managers do it.

Combine the Old and the New

Midas managers depend on a blend of the old and the new in both their core businesses and their diversification ventures. In their core business, Midas managers rely on the past by building from a clear set of specific technology competences in multimedia and semi-custom semiconductor chip design. Managers claim to have an extraordinarily "strong understanding" of their key technologies. They also draw on a core group of customers to test new products and they exploit well-established distribution channels. In addition, Midas managers rely on a cadre of highly experienced product developers. Since these developers typically have worked on several generations of Midas products, their understanding of Midas' very state-of-the-art products gives the firm an advantage over the usual computer firm in which there is significantly more employee turnover.

Second, Midas managers always add something new to their strategic mix. In product development staffing, for example, no matter how incremental the product, *every* product development project has some people with fresh perspective assigned to it. These people are either new to the company or are veterans coming off projects from other parts of the company. The newcomers provide fresh perspective from either the latest in academic thinking or from other firms. The veterans bring fresh perspectives from other parts of the company. People who come from internal research projects are particularly valuable. They bring a window into the latest technical thinking at the company (and, indeed, in the world) back to their core product development projects. In addition, every new product always contains features targeted to new customers or new markets. So even though Midas managers emphasize the past in their core business, they always add something new, even in the most incremental efforts.

In contrast to their core business, where the blend leans toward the old, diversification moves rely more on what is novel. Like the Naskapi, who depend more heavily on magic in times of high uncertainty, so too do Midas executives. They loosen their link to the past when they diversify into attractive but typically uncertain opportunities for growth.

A telling illustration is Midas' entry into the Internet market. This new opportunity brought with it high growth potential but also high uncertainty. This venture would require significant pieces of new technology and fresh thinking about marketing, as well as a departure from Midas' experience base. As a result, Midas managers decided to go with more "new" in the blend. They lured an executive from outside the firm to shepherd the business, added to her top management team several members from outside the firm, and included product and market developers who were hired from outside Midas' traditional industry segment.

But although the diversification into the Internet was primarily new, Midas managers simultaneously blended in a bit of the old. Every diversification move at Midas, no matter how large, also contains some elements of the past. In this case, Midas managers drew on selected features of existing products to create new ones. Although the products were new, they also had carefully selected components that were well known from past products. The overall balance in the Internet initiative was toward the new, but there were still clear links to the old.

Critical Mass of People

The philosophy that people are the carriers or DNA of the past pervades Midas. In contrast to NewWave, whose Internet venture was staffed exclusively by newcomers to the firm, every significant new initiative at Midas, including their Internet initiative, is staffed by at least a few people with significant experience at the firm. Typically, managers retain a core of very experienced people who remain with particular businesses for multiple product generations. As one person explained, "They are much more in tune with what is going on." Another agreed, saying that "low turnover really helps. . . . Many people have worked on at least one generation of the products." No matter how significantly new the growth opportunity is, Midas always relies on a critical mass of old staffers who know how to turn silicon into gold.

Speeding the Blend

Regeneration at Midas also relied on rearchitecture and recombination tactics to speed the evolution of old to new. Although rearchitecture can apply to services, marketing concepts, and overall strategy, a good illustration at Midas is their Mercury product. Like Fable's Aesop, Mercury is huge and complicated, but Midas was able to avoid the crisis Fable experienced. The difference is in layering (Fable) vs. rearchitecture (Midas). Midas engineers systematically refurbish Mercury on a regular basis, according to a set schedule. On each generation of the product, a particular portion of the design is reworked. On a subsequent generation, another segment is tackled, and so forth. The exact schedule depends on such issues as the pace of technical change and competitor actions, but most pieces of the product are rebuilt. As a result, every product contains parts that are not really new, but also not really old. Rather, they are cleaned up, rebuilt . . . rearchitected.

Drawing an analogy with a clothes closet helps to illustrate the process. In Imelda Marcos fashion, a Fable-style clothes closet is one in which new clothes are simply thrown in on top of the old. Nothing is thrown out. In contrast, in Martha Stewart fashion, a rearchitected closet is one in which the owner does a rolling "spring cleaning." New clothes are added, and the old are pruned. The owner also does not only shop during holiday season but constantly "rearchitects" sweaters, shoes, suits, and so on with new purchases that replace the old. Over time, the rearchitected closet is filled with a new and up-to-date wardrobe that is easy to access. This is like Midas' product line. In contrast, the layered closet becomes a junk pile. This is Fable's "House of Cards."

The second regeneration tactic, recombination, involves taking pieces of the past and recombining them in novel ways. Just as at Gap, Inc., where managers reassembled new combinations of existing store concepts like Gap-Kids and Old Navy to create Old Navy Kids, recombination is vital at Midas.

Recombination can be employed in different areas of the business. One example is the vast design library at Midas. The library is crammed with old circuit designs and software code that anyone in the corporation can use, so it is easy to assemble new designs using old ones. One team leader who frequently recombined old designs in new products claimed, "We found a way to use that single design in three different products." This is how the design library supports Midas' strategy to build a Ferrari from spare parts.

More striking from a strategic position is the way distinct technologies are recombined. A senior executive admitted, "The products could be imitated fairly easily. . . . The technology we provide isn't really anything new. There are many people out there with the skill sets to do it. But nobody has gone and put all the different technologies together." Another executive went on to describe how Midas was moving aggressively into multimedia using recombination. He described how "putting graphics and sound together is a new market. . . . The key is we are merging graphics and sound. We can either bring sound in, or we can put in graphics. . . . I'd like to think that Midas has more experience in integrating the two markets than any other computer company." So recombination is at the heart of the leading-edge strategy at Midas. Although outsiders are often awestruck by Midas technology, company managers more modestly claim that "our machines are just a union of things."

Modularity

Many managers are attracted to the short-term advantages of intertwining key aspects of their businesses tightly. But Midas managers forsake these often short-term gains for the long-term advantages of modularity. This compromise is striking when one considers that Midas is pushing the performance frontier. Firm managers are constantly tempted to achieve a performance boost by more tightly integrating their products, yet they are also aware of the dangers. A modular approach enables not only the rearchitecture and recombination described above but also adjustment to varying rates of change over time. Like the Naskapi, Midas managers value long-run adaptation over short-run efficiency.

A good illustration is how Midas "modularizes" its customers. Marketers separate customers according to types of performance that they demand. Some customers, like banks, want high reliability and security. Others, like engineering firms, want extensive graphics capabilities and sheer processing power. In response, Midas creates products with options that are responsive to these various performance demands. The result is that the company is able to adjust to different rates of change in its varied customer segments without having to adjust an entire product line. If the computing demands of engineering change more quickly than those of banks, Midas simply upgrades the relevant parts of its products but *not* the entire product. A visual analogy is the independent suspension of 4-wheel drive, in which the wheels adjust independently to changing terrain. This contrasts with passenger-car suspension, in which the wheels are much more linked and thus much less effective in off-road terrain.

Business Implications

At first glance, Midas' emphasis on the past is surprising. After all, the firm competes at the state of the art. When executing such a strategy, most executives, such as those at NewWave, worry about what is next. In contrast,

Modularity

Genetic algorithms and Darwinian evolutionary processes generally rely on modular components. Some of these components change through mutation or recombination from one generation to the next such that the system as a whole evolves. In living systems, these components are **genes**. In complexity simulations, they are **symbol strings**. In business, they are **competencies** such as brand image, logistics skill, product modules, and specific technical expertise. Modularity is central to the gradual change of businesses over time because it allows managers to fine-tune the combination of old and new, thereby allowing managers to "breed" high performance organizations.

Midas has learned that effectively capitalizing on the past makes it far simpler to attack the future. Relying on the past gives Midas the time and resources to excel at the truly new—the stunning technology that customers have come to expect. This past-conscious strategy is a primary reason why Midas has excelled as a futuristic company.

Nowhere are the advantages of the past more striking than in Midas products. Despite turning out increasingly complex and challenging products, Midas has actually cut product development time from about two years to nearly eighteen months. There are multiple reasons for this extraordinary performance, with the ability to gain cost and time advantages from the past being one of them. Accelerated product development has also helped the firm to widen the gap between itself and its also-ran competition in its traditional businesses.

Midas managers usually have been able to diversify successfully as well. Although the results of their Internet initiatives are unclear, the firm is certainly ahead of several competitors. Not every new venture is a success, of course, but the firm is moving out of its traditional stronghold into new areas of computing.

Finally, the links between old and new at Midas go in both directions: ideas have flowed back into the established and low-end businesses to extend the life of existing business models and pump up profitability. Managers at Midas use the new technology businesses to go back and refresh the low end in a strategy that they refer to as "drop in." In this way, the benefits of the past cycle back. Midas managers exploit the old, create the new, and refresh the old in a complex way that keeps Midas on the edge between the old and new.

Key Signals

The Midas case illustrates some critical features of effective regeneration:

1. *Blend the Old and the New.* Whether they are creating new products in existing businesses or diversifying into new ones, Midas managers always select the best of the old and something of the new. They always look to use their new activities to go back and refresh the old.

2. *Critical Mass of People.* Midas managers recognize that it takes a critical mass of people to carry the past forward. Without at least a few experienced people, nothing of the past will go forward and the business will, in effect, start from scratch.

3. *Speeding the Blend.* Midas managers look for ways to temper the old and the new through intermediate tactics that further blur the distinctions between old and new. Tactics such as rearchitecture and recombination not only accelerate adjustment to change, but they also temper risk.

4. *Modularity.* Modularity in strategy, customers, and products is critical to adjusting to change. Without modularity, it is impossible to rearchitect, recombine, or adjust to different rates of change. Midas managers pay attention to modularity.

Rules for Regeneration

In creating a new business, product line, or service always . . .

1. Pick the best of the past. At a minimum, carry forward some people.

2. Add something new.

3. When trying to diversify into more distant or unknown market spaces, shift the balance to the new.

4. Hasten change by recombining and rearchitecturing.

5. When the market is shifting very quickly or is very uncertain, add more that is new (especially random) and recombine more extensively from a wider variety of sources.

6. Remember to not only evolve from old to new, but also to reverse the process by refreshing the old with the new.

Table 4.2 • Regeneration at Midas

Business	Old	New	Not-So-New
High-end products	Developers with multiple generations of experience Product platform Customers Multimedia, ASIC, and channel expertise	Developers from outside Midas and other parts of Midas, especially R&D	Scheduled rearchitecture of product design Design library to recombine past designs Modularity of customer options
Low-end products	Same as high-end	Same as high-end	Transfer of high-end technology to regenerate low-end products
Internet venture	Developers Some product components	External GM and top managers Some developers and marketers Some customers Channel	Sound and graphics skills recombined

Regeneration resulted in leading-edge technology strategy that moderates cost and risk while focusing on the truly new and perennial market share leadership. As a competitor said, "Midas sets the standard."

Implementing Regeneration

Review the survey you took earlier in this chapter. You should have a good idea where your business falls. As an illustration, we have completed the survey for Fable (F), NewWave (N), and Midas (M).

To what extent do new businesses, products, or services reuse past concepts?

0 % •• 100%
    N   M   F

How old are your principal business, service, or product concepts?

Less than 1 year	1 to 3 years	3 to 5 years	More than 5 years
N	M		F

To what extent do your business, product, or service teams blend experienced and new members?

Extensively ••• Not at all
                         M   N, F

To what extent have your new businesses, products, or services refreshed your established ones?

Extensively ••• Not at all
   M   N, F

If your business is more like Fable, you need the managerial equivalent of caribou bones. Begin by looking for ways to get something new into what you do—new employees, new customers, new markets. Making new hires or simply transferring existing people is often the easiest way to get started. Also, ensure that something that you are doing has the potential to *surprise* you. Modularity takes a bit longer to achieve. But you should get started on thinking about how you can modularize what you are doing. Remember that modularity is the stepping stone to rearchitecture and recombination and so it has to come first. If this sounds complicated, think of your situation as getting out of debt. Develop a "newness and modularity" plan and then stick with it over time.

If your business is more like NewWave, your real problem is no continuity between yesterday and today. One way to create opportunity is to put some history in. Try putting experienced people in your new opportunities. Tactics like documentation or meetings are helpful, but they are no substitute for having at least a small cadre of experienced people who know the lessons of the past. In addition, consider teaming experienced people with new hires. At a minimum, build in incentives for experienced staff to help the new people, and for the new people to solicit and use their colleagues' help. Also, ensure that people use recombination and rearchitecture to look more creatively at the past. Here modularity is the necessary first step.

If your business is most like Midas, then you are regenerating well. It's important to be vigilant to maintain the edge of time between past and future. If you have a leading-edge strategy like Midas or are launching a new growth opportunity, the tendency is to underuse the past. The key is to guard against assigning all your best people to future projects and leaving no link with the past. Make it worth people's time to work on older products and to reuse past experience. Be wary of slipping schedule dates—they signal problems. If you are in highly competitive markets, pursuing a low-cost strategy, or competing where first-mover advantages and time-based competition are crucial, the tendency is to overuse the past. Here you should be sure to blend in new people or find a way to reinvigorate current staff. Watch out for creeping development times as well and passing by too many opportunities for doing something new. If you do not have a rearchitecture strategy, then develop one.

A Final Note on Winning Growth Opportunities

One of the most vexing challenges in contemporary business is diversification by established firms into new opportunities. Winning new, diversified growth opportunities is extraordinarily difficult for most big corporations. Quick movement to new opportunities is the fantasy, but inertia is the reality.

This chapter has two critical insights for managers of established firms facing this challenge. One is that diversification depends as much (maybe more) on using the past as it does on reaching into the future. Too often, managers are dazzled by what might be and so devalue the role of the past in winning those new opportunities. Our message is that the past is *the* advantage in diversification, especially for established firms. Wise leverage of the past improves the odds of success and frees managers from less critical details, leaving more time and resources to focus on winning the truly new.

The second critical insight is that diversification is as much about revitalizing mature businesses as it is about winning new opportunities. Frequently, managers fail to realize that new opportunities are not only about making the future happen but also about invigorating existing businesses. By transferring people and ideas from leading-edge businesses back to the mainstream of the corporation, managers increase the likelihood that the life and profitability of these established businesses can be increased and that the employees within them can be excited and recharged by glimpses of the future.

Time keeps on slippin',

slippin', slippin' . . .

into the future.

Fly Like an Eagle,

Steve Miller Band

winning tomorrow

THE "FRIENDLY SKIES"? For many air carriers, the skies have been distinctly unfriendly. United Airlines, for example, had a strategy much like that of many major U.S. carriers. One feature of that strategy was an extensive route structure that blanketed most of the United States. A second feature was a hub-and-spoke system that was built around a network of hubs in which a particular carrier dominated (often owning two-thirds of the flight slots). This system was the company's key revenue enabler, for it allowed the airline to charge premium fares in regions surrounding its hubs. A third feature was a byzantine rate structure that seemingly was always in flux.

Underlying this strategy was a vision of a particular future. This future was one in which there would be a small number of very large airlines, these airlines would profitably divide up the market along the boundaries of their fortresslike hubs, and the customer base would be primarily business travelers who flew frequently. These frequent travelers would be locked into a particular airline not only by proximity to the hubs but also by award programs that favored travel with that airline and so further limited price-based competition. Yet, strikingly, what was often missing from this vision were regional and international carriers, price-sensitive and infrequent flyers, and flyers who would pay for amenities.

Did this vision come true? No, or at least not in the way that many of these carriers and their shareholders would have liked. Despite the logic of fortress hubs and limited price competition, the reality of the high fixed-cost structure of the industry came into play. The high fixed costs were driven, in part, by extensive maintenance costs for large and varied aircraft fleets, and by organized labor. So despite the benefits of avoiding price wars for all, this high fixed-cost structure made it attractive to fill seats by reducing price. The temptation to cut price was intensified by chronic overcapacity in the industry. The resulting price wars drove the industry toward low margins.

But perhaps most significantly, not only did the anticipated vision not happen, but a new vision was closer to the mark. While the major domestic airlines battled for share in the business travel segment, managers at low-price airlines such as Southwest had an alternative vision. They saw a huge, price-sensitive market that was ignored by the majors. Their vision was a more egalitarian view of air travel—that is, a way of travel that *everyone* could afford. These low-price carriers usually created point-to-point service, rather than the hub-and-spoke systems of the major airlines. Rather than dominating hubs, the low-price carriers dominated routes. They offered standard fares, operated similar aircraft across all routes (thus lowering maintenance costs), used less expensive airport facilities such as Dallas' Love Field or Houston-Hobby, often eliminated the costs of travel agents and food, and employed a flexible, lower-wage, nonunion labor force. The results were lower prices and expanded markets.

Despite the increasing number of price-sensitive flyers and the success of some low-price carriers in generating higher profits in the industry, most of the majors stuck with their vision of the future. Early on, these carriers could have altered that vision to be more in line with the future that was really taking shape. And the low-price carriers would have been much more vulnerable at this point. But most managers at the major carriers did not make these adjustments. This was not the future that they were apparently planning.

Eventually, with their hubs under threat, the majors did react. For example, United started its own brand of low-price, point-to-point service, "Shuttle by United." But by the time United reacted, low-price carriers competed on more than a third of U.S. domestic routes and could no longer be eliminated by a simple focused effort. Moreover, United had to learn how to execute point-to-point service, whereas experienced competitors like Southwest already understood the formula. As it turned out, United's cost structure made profitable competition a difficult challenge. Ironically, Shuttle by United could have been started as a small experiment much earlier on. Rather than closing hubs in areas under attack from low-price carriers, United could have used the hubs as the foundation for building Shuttle by United point-to-point service. A relatively small investment by United in an alternative future scenario would have significantly improved their insight into how the future would actually evolve and how to compete when it arrived. Instead, it appears that company management, along with those at many other majors, assumed a different vision of how the future would evolve.

What has happened? Competition from low-price carriers has brought down profit margins. United and the other majors have been forced off routes by low-price carriers. Bolstered by strong performance, the low-price carriers attacked major airlines at their core—the fortress hubs. In Denver, Colorado, for example, United was forced by Western Pacific Airlines and Frontier Airlines to make steep cuts in its fares. In its San Jose hub, American has reduced the number of gates, even as Southwest has expanded. At the same time, the efforts by the majors to mimic low-price service have not prospered so far. Continental Lite has been discontinued. United's Shuttle reportedly lost money well into its second year of service, and the airline also gave up several routes

Vision of the Company, Not Industry	Southwest is in the business of freedom. Their mission is to open up the skies.
	It's not a job, it's a crusade. What Southwest has done is create a democracy in the airline business.
Probes, Not a Plan	Southwest prepares for the future by practicing the art of "What if ... ?" Future scenario generation gets the group thinking about all possible situations Southwest could face.
	Herb Kelleher says, "We have a plan. It's called doing things." He adds, "The meticulous nit-picking that goes on in most strategic planning processes creates a mental straitjacket that becomes disabling in an industry where things change radically from one day to the next."
Constant Attention	Good preparation can look like prophecy in retrospect. Southwest is a company of people who do their homework–thoroughly.
	Southwest is always scanning the horizon, trying to anticipate what the other airlines are doing, how they are altering their approaches, and what dominates their thinking.

Figure 5.1 • How Does Southwest Do It?

Source: Jackie and Kevin Freiberg, *Nuts!* (Austin, Texas: Bard Press, 1996).

where Southwest reigns. The majors are now creating a strategy for an unanticipated future.

The experience of these airlines illustrates that a viable strategy for the future is essential for effective competition. Mismanaging the future puts a firm in a position of constant catch-up. Such firms end up losing leading-edge customers while gaining an often undesirable image of being stodgy and out of touch. Frequently, these firms are blindsided by unexpected events. In contrast, firms that manage the future well end up adapting quickly and perhaps even creating the future in which other firms must compete. In the airline industry, Southwest and others created the future for their competitors in low-budget travel. Virgin Atlantic and British Airways have done the same in amenity-based, international business travel. In contrast, other airlines have been forced to compete in the future that their competitors have shaped.

Why is strategy for the future so challenging? On the one hand, the inherent uncertainty of the future means that planning is not an effective approach. It is difficult to know what will happen and even more difficult to forecast when. So flexibility is vital. On the other hand, intense competition and fast-paced change make reacting a poor strategy. Reacting means always playing catch-up, always competing in the future that others have defined. Thus, placing some bets on the future is critical. The dilemma is how to make a commitment to *a* future and provide flexibility for *the* future.

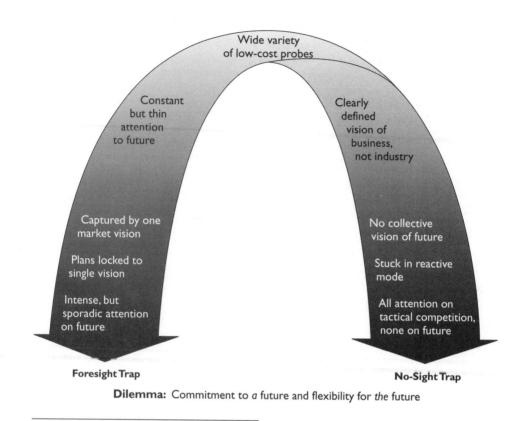

Foresight Trap   No-Sight Trap

Dilemma: Commitment to *a* future and flexibility for *the* future

Figure 5.2 • The Experimentation Edge

Survey Your Company

How does your management team think about the future? Take a few minutes to ask yourself the following:

The collective vision of our business is:
Clear ••• Ambiguous

Our future success depends on a particular industry scenario:
Yes •• No

Our approach to the future is to:
Plan •• React

Our attention to the future is:
Frequent •• Rare

We have several meaningful experimental products and future-oriented
strategic alliances:
Yes •• No

Our business is considered to be a:
Leader •• Follower

ABCs of Experimentation

The key to resolving the dilemma of making a commitment to a future and
providing flexibility for the future is another edge of time process, *experimentation*. If managers focus their attention too much on the present, they end up
chaotically reacting to the moves that others make. If their focus is too much
on the future, then they tend to lock into a particular future, lose flexibility,
and end up in the rigidity of a planned future. In contrast, experimentation
relies on small, fast, and cheap probes to create a more complex and dynamic
strategy for the future than either planning or reacting provides. Experimentation attempts to gain insight into the future that may unfold without losing
flexibility to react to the future that does unfold.

Exploring Space

Perhaps you remember the late 1960s, when Jean-Claude Killy skied his way
to a record-smashing three gold medals at the 1968 Winter Olympics. Lyndon
Johnson agonizingly stepped aside as the beleaguered president bogged down
in the war in Vietnam. The Rolling Stones and the Supremes, a very unlikely
pair, topped the global rock charts. And the moon was about to become a
travel destination.

Less than a decade after John Kennedy pledged to put men on the moon,
the U.S. space program was about to do just that. After several years of flirtation with earth's nearest neighbor, the United States launched a series of
Apollo missions to the moon. Beginning with Neil Armstrong's small but historic step for mankind onto the moon, five more manned Apollo missions followed. Of course, it was expensive to get to the moon and even harder to get
back . . . just ask the veterans of Apollo 13. But at the time, it seemed as

though a lunar colony was just around the corner, and then tourist flights. Could Club Med be far behind?

But this scenario never happened. Apollo 17 marked the last visit to the moon in the manned U.S. space program. U.S. voters lost interest in space exploration as Watergate, the oil crisis, and inflation captured their attention. The Russian space program also languished, and the Europeans and Asians did not take up the challenge. Space exploration was now equated with more earthly concerns, like the launch of globe-spinning satellites for telephone communication and television channels. Satellite broadcast of hit television shows like *Dallas* seemed more essential than space exploration.

But in the 1990s, the spectacular photos of Jupiter and Saturn taken by the Hubble mission and the first hints of life on Mars rekindled public interest. This excitement coincided with a renewed (and revamped) push into space from both the U.S. and Russian space programs. For Mars, the United States and Russia joined forces to launch a series of probes, a surface station, and a land rover. As an operations space official declared, "After a hiatus of 20 years, America returns to Mars."[1] For the moon, NASA rolled out a new probe, the Lunar Prospector. Some twenty-five years after the last Apollo mission, the Lunar mission manager, Scott Hubbard, claimed, "This is a key step in NASA's return to the moon."[2]

But this latest foray into space exploration looks nothing like the space programs of the late 1960s. Traditional space exploration involved big risk. Enormous Saturn rockets and complex manned space vehicles were the hallmarks of the "big science" approach of the 1960s. Thirty years later, NASA's big science approach was gone. The last straw was the 1993 debacle of the Mars Observer. This massive, almost billion-dollar mission to Mars mysteriously went off course and failed to function.

With probes such as the Lunar Prospector and Mars Sojourner, NASA is exploring the unknown in a whole new way that has been dubbed "smaller, faster, cheaper." The Sojourner, for example, a Martian rover that is the first vehicle to roam the surface of another planet, is the size of a child's riding toy. It weighs just twenty-three pounds and, at top speed, crawls along at just sixteen inches a minute. Its solar power cells are only 1.9 square feet in surface area. As backup, the rover packs D-cell batteries, nonrechargeable for the sake of simplicity and cost. The Sojourner's brain is an Intel 80C85 processor, selected for its low cost and ruggedness. But it lags behind many processors available on commercial systems in terms of speed and power.

The Lunar Prospector is equally striking. It has a simple design and was built from off-the-shelf components. The probe is small—4.5 feet by 4 feet. It has no backup capabilities. It is remarkably "dumb"—there is no computer on

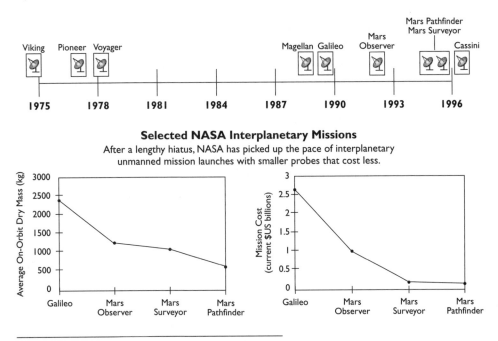

Figure 5.3 • NASA Interplanetary Exploration

Sources: JPL-NASA (http://www.jpl.nasa.gov); NSSDC-NASA (http://nssdc.gsfc.nasa.gov); and J. Flanigan, "JPL Think Small, Cheap," *Los Angeles Times*, September 4, 1996.

board, and all commands come from Earth. It has no tape system but rather radios directly back to Earth. Solar cells provide the power. Engineers designed the Lunar Prospector in only seventeen months. They built and launched it on a $60 million budget, as compared with $266 million for an Apollo launch. Yet it can scan the moon and accomplish in one very cheap (by space standards) mission more than *all* six Apollo landings combined. Even if the first Lunar Prospector fails, NASA would still have money for four more tries. NASA scientists have learned that experimentation through lots of small, cheap probes is the way to explore the unknown.

Lessons from Pharmaceuticals

The experience of the firms in the pharmaceuticals industry, where the future is very high stakes and enormously uncertain, shows the value of experimentation. Merck, a famously high-flying pharmaceutical firm, invests more than $1 billion each year in the future through its portfolio of research projects. Like space exploration, Merck's research projects have long timelines, about ten to twelve years for a new product. These projects are extraordinarily uncertain and extremely pricey—more than $200 million to develop a new product. Yet despite the challenges of managing leading-edge science, scientists and executives at Merck have astutely managed the future in a way that has played a major role in enabling Merck's long-standing leadership within the pharmaceutical industry.

Like NASA, Merck managers manage the unknown through small, fast, and cheap probes. Merck managers have become masters of scenario planning and Monte Carlo simulation, an analytic technique that simulates the interplay of variables like scientific viability, therapeutic impact, and exchange rates using probability distributions to yield a range of possible outcomes for a research portfolio, rather than simplistic, single-point estimates. These techniques allow Merck managers to probe the future quickly and without major expense.

Equally striking is Merck's reliance on a variety of thrusts into the future. Merck research projects target a variety of medical problem areas, from osteoporosis to schizophrenia. The portfolio is also balanced across an array of project time horizons. Some research is designed to probe into areas of fundamental science with distant payoffs. Other research is targeted more directly on short-term products and likely winners. The portfolio is varied in other ways as well. Some projects are in-house research efforts, and some are collaborations. Some of the collaborations are with universities; others are with small, biotechnology firms and large, established corporations, such as DuPont and Johnson & Johnson. Some are acquisitions like Medco, a firm that manages purchases of drugs for major health benefit plan buyers.

Finally, options are key to managing the future at Merck. Faced with long-term, major research projects, Merck managers and scientists break up research into a series of shorter-term "options" that can be exercised on a shorter time horizon. Major research projects that in other companies are managed as large and long-term bets are managed as smaller and shorter-term purchases of information about the future. Options do two things at Merck. They transform basic research into the small, fast, and cheap model that has become the style at NASA. They also transform the corporate perspective to one not of planning the future or reacting to it but rather of gaining insight about the future in a variety of ways. Options redefine success and failure. In the options mindset, a project may fail therapeutically or commercially but still be a success if it adds to the stock of insight about the future within the firm.

Space Exploration and Basic Science Meet Business

The space and pharmaceuticals examples suggest that successful strategy for the future centers on experimentation through a wide variety of low-cost probes that are designed to reveal the unexpected. The NASA example illustrates the power of "smaller, cheaper, faster" probes, whereas Merck's experience highlights the importance of variety, varying time lengths, and options. Taken together, these examples reveal how experimentation—the edge between reacting today and planning tomorrow—can help managers to gain insight into the future without committing to a future.

But the loss of control implied by experimentation is uncomfortable for many managers. It is easy to slip back into the comfort of planning, as many major airlines did, or into reacting, as others have done. How can managers avoid these traps?

Too Much Planning: The Foresight Trap

Many managers wisely approach the future by creating plans. Given the need to have an often-complex array of resources available for future moves, some planning is clearly desirable. Strategic planning can also serve a significant, symbolic role in pulling employees together around a set of common themes that energize the entire corporation. But especially in rapidly changing industries, managers can easily plan more than they know. Quickly shifting technologies, changing customer demands, and aggressive moves by competitors can all make substantial planning a significant waste of time. Even worse, some managers neglect to update their plans and so further trap their firms in visions of futures that never happen.

What is the impact of being caught in the foresight trap? Managers do, of course, occasionally guess right about the future or are at least not too far off from it. They are the lucky ones. More commonly, managers who extensively plan the future get the timing wrong. Sometimes they arrive to market too early and so must wait for the demand to catch up. Sometimes they are too late and so must accelerate to rejoin the future. Most often, managers bet on the wrong future. Competitors make unanticipated moves. New technologies are introduced. Customers prefer "green," not "blue," and so forth. These managers are left with a one-way ticket to the wrong future.

What type of firm is likely to slip into the foresight trap? In our experience, managers from slow-moving industries are at particular risk because they have often seen strategic planning applied successfully. Also at risk are large, established companies in which a planning bureaucracy has grown up over the years. In such firms, there is frequently a "planning religion." Surprisingly, managers of entrepreneurial firms often plan too much as well. In these firms, managers may be pressed into extensive planning in order to raise funds, or they may simply have the arrogance to believe that they are smart enough to plan what others cannot. But regardless of source, firms in the foresight trap tend to plan too much for a particular future.

A good illustration is Monsanto. In the mid-1980s, senior executives at this St. Louis-based firm created a strategic vision that included a major bet on genetically engineered agricultural products. These executives invested well over $1 billion in an orchestrated product development portfolio that ranged from seeds that grow without pesticides to genetically altered tomatoes. A favorite of Monsanto's then-president, the plan was a mammoth, ten-year wager on an emergent market. The first product was a costly and controversial hormone, BST, that increased the milk production of cows. But the product, once considered to be a $1 billion per year business by former CEO Richard Mahoney, took off slowly. Consumer acceptance of such products stalled because of concerns over health and safety. Further, farmers found the hormone too awkward and time consuming to use. In contrast, rivals such as DuPont took an experimentation approach to the future and created products that may have hit the future more squarely and, certainly, more cheaply. Though few doubt that Monsanto will be a major player in the industry and Mahoney's successor, Robert Shapiro, appears to have taken a more experimental approach, Monsanto's plan may have led managers to overspend, spend too soon, and spend in ill-advised ways. As one publication observed, "some are quietly wondering whether Monsanto will ever grab enough market share to justify its huge expenditures."[3]

Another example is Motorola. Wireless personal communication is a major piece of the strategy for this global electronics player. In this business, technology is in constant flux and the right technology bet is crucial. And no bet was more crucial than the one between the GSM (Global System for Mobile Communications) and CDMA (Code Division Multiple Access) standards in the U.S. digital cellular communications market. CDMA is considered by many to be technically superior, with far higher call-carrying capability, but GSM has already taken hold in other parts of the world, most notably in Europe. In the United States, most competitors hedged their bets on the future by allowing subscribers to choose between the two options. But not Motorola executives, who saw a CDMA future. At least in the short run, this was the wrong choice. Belatedly, Motorola managers reversed their position and offered choice. But most customers had by then committed to other suppliers. As one analyst noted, "It looks as if Motorola has all but guaranteed itself a trailing position."[4]

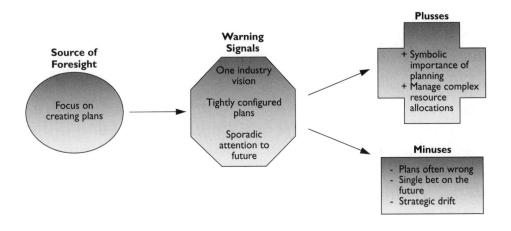

Figure 5.4 • The Foresight Trap

There are several signs that indicate a business is sliding into the foresight trap. First, its managers center their strategic thinking on one market vision. Despite the high uncertainty and fast change that often characterize their markets, these management teams tend to settle on a single view of when and how their markets are likely to evolve. This vision then becomes the lens through which the future is viewed.

Second, these managers often create tightly configured plans that fit their market vision. They lay out textbook strategic positioning for their firms in terms of cost, product or service differentiation, and technology. Using the logic of strategy-structure fit, these plans are then further locked into elaborate product or service development schedules, plans for manufacturing capacity, and hiring plans for individuals with related skills.

A third trait of businesses in this trap is that their managers pay sporadic attention to the future. Although these managers spend a significant amount of time studying their industries to formulate their view of the future and then elaborating that view into plans, they spend much less time reevaluating their efforts as the real future unfolds. They lock into a vision and a plan that they rarely revisit.

Perilous Planning at Pulsar

Another business in which managers were caught in the foresight trap was Pulsar (a pseudonym), a business unit within Galaxy, the leading-edge computing firm that we discussed in Chapter 3. As we described earlier, Galaxy attracts high-energy achievers who work intense hours to create some of the most exciting computing products in the world. Galaxy has a sugar-high, caffeine-powered work environment, and Pulsar is a part of Galaxy.

Pulsar competed in the interactive video segment of the industry. This segment was ill defined but potentially lucrative. Senior executives at Galaxy believed that playing in this market was essential for the corporation. Pulsar executives were charged with making this market happen.

One Market Vision

A striking feature of the Pulsar experience was the single vision of the market that its managers forged. These managers spent several months studying trends and developing their market vision. Although they recognized the tremendous uncertainty within the marketplace, they nonetheless ended up conceptualizing the future of the interactive video market in surprisingly specific terms. They envisioned a convergence of video games, consumer electronics, and consumer software in the home. As one executive said, the market will be "much more than games. . . . It will be the entire home." They also conjectured that this convergence would be realized in the form of an interactive product with a price point that "Joe Six-Pack" could afford and with features that he would want. The other part of the vision centered on the significance of computing technology in creating the market. Another senior executive described it to us this way: "It is technology that is really going to drive us to the future." He went on to claim that computing would be the centerpiece and that "the industry needs a new platform and the old technology isn't going to be around forever."

Surprisingly, Pulsar executives reached this vision without much in the way of product probing or reliance on outside futurists. They relied heavily on their own conjectures about the future. Yet their vision was not widely shared by managers at other firms. Whereas Pulsar executives saw the convergence in terms of the computer (Galaxy's expertise), other firms were making plans around the television and the telephone as the centerpiece of the family room of the future. Pulsar executives also saw the convergence as a technology play, but here too others differed, seeing it much more from a consumer products point of view in which branding, access to high-volume distribution channels, and low-cost manufacturing would be key. So Pulsar executives pressed ahead with one industry vision centered on computing and technology even as others foresaw a future based on television, the telephone, and consumer electronics marketing.

Tightly Configured Plans

Pulsar managers set their strategic course based on their industry vision. First and foremost, the group picked a leading-edge technology that was consistent both with their view that technology would drive the future and with Galaxy's competence in working with such technologies. According to one manager, "We are pushing the boundaries." Another said, "The strategy was to be pretty much out on the outer edge of technology. We wanted to push the technology pretty hard." Related to their leading-edge technology approach was a differentiation strategy that involved focusing on high-end consumers who could afford the premium technology that Pulsar would provide. Pulsar managers planned to begin in the U.S. market but then quickly move to Japan. They set the goal "to be first or second to markets with products that will give us 25 to 40 percent market share within the first year."

The differentiation/technology leadership strategy was then to be realized in product plans. This meant creating a feature set within the product line that would appeal to upscale consumers. As one manager recalled, "We picked products that we felt would have some appeal to people who would have $700 to spend on a cool piece of new technology." Another said, "We picked things where you could see a noticeable difference between us and the competition." The specific product rollout involved an initial portfolio of six products and then an additional ten more, for a total of sixteen, some of which would be jointly developed with partnering firms. As one executive explained, "Our strategy is to do the first six products internally. We will penetrate the market with these and then let knowledge trickle down. We plan to release three on this date, then one more soon after that, and then the final two. This rollout is based on largest potential sales." Why six initial products? Pulsar managers simply calculated that "one product will cost about $1,200,000 and 12 man-years and we divide our budget by that and get six projects."

Related to the product plans were staffing plans. Pulsar managers decided that they needed people skilled in the use of graphics and complex rendering software. They transferred some people back to other parts of Galaxy, canceled some projects that were already underway, and hired staff with more relevant skills.

Surprising to us was the absence of any experimental products, futurists, or forward-looking strategic alliances. Once the vision was in hand, there was no attempt to hedge bets or create options. Rather, Pulsar managers formulated an elaborate set of tightly configured plans for their strategy, product development, and human resource staffing that fit with their vision of where interactive video would evolve.

Sporadic Attention

This tight coordination between vision, strategy, and operating plans had the feel of "good organization." Pulsar managers believed that they were on top of their business—and perhaps they were . . . briefly. But Pulsar's managers dangerously did not revisit their plans. One admitted, "We have to follow what has been laid out." Yet their configuration of plans became dated. Another manager told us, "The overall strategy was put in place about eighteen months ago." Eighteen months! That is an eternity in the computer industry.

Instead of spending time to reassess their plans for the future, Pulsar managers put all their energy into the present. They did make some adjustments of resources among development projects, but they never wavered from their vision of the future. One manager said, "Our view is let's forget about the future and worry about it later in order to bring the products in." Another summarized, "It's a luxury to worry about the future." The result was punctuated attention on the future—that is, intense focus on the future followed by intense focus on the present.

Business Implications

The major problem with planning is that plans are virtually always wrong. Pulsar's plans were no different. A year into their plans, Pulsar executives recognized that they had seriously underestimated the technical challenge of their approach. One manager described, "It's a difficult situation because this technology platform is being invented as we go along. . . . We don't really have the time to do a lot of the infrastructure development." This fact complicated and slowed strategic execution. Pulsar managers also learned that their chosen technology was not as good as they had hoped. One manager noted ruefully, "The technology boost turned out to be different from what we expected it to be. It was not as powerful." This meant that product schedules had to be adjusted and that their carefully crafted staffing plans had actually mismatched people and jobs. A program manager complained that "a lot of these people's skills were pretty much wasted," whereas another said, "Our skill set just doesn't match."

Pulsar managers also learned that their timing estimates were off. Interactive video was much further away than anyone had projected. Ironically, Pulsar had abandoned an older technology that turned out to have longer-than-anticipated shelf-life. One manager lamented, "We thought that everything was going to the new technology and we responded too soon, really. There is a large customer base out there [for our older products]." Finally, a competitor introduced a better technology that leapfrogged Pulsar's position.

Left with the wrong strategic vision, the wrong technology, and the wrong people, Pulsar executives were in a quandary. Not only did their vision of the future not come true, but they lacked options, alternative visions, and contingency plans. An executive said, "Strategically, we don't know what in the world we are doing." Although Pulsar's managers went back to planning again, they had only a weak grasp of the future that did arrive. Pulsar fell behind and remains a mediocre performer in Galaxy's constellation of stars.

Warning Signals

There were several warning signals that indicated that Pulsar was slipping into the foresight trap.

1. *One Industry Vision.* Pulsar managers created a single view of how the industry would evolve despite numerous signs that this was unwise. The industry was just too new. Other sage observers had alternative views that were both plausible and different.

2. *Tightly Configured Plans.* Pulsar managers wrapped the firm into a neatly fitting configuration of vision, strategy, and structure. They did textbook industry analysis and strategy-structure fit. But the tight fit left Pulsar managers with little strategic flexibility when the real future arrived.

3. *Punctuated Attention.* Pulsar managers spent a lot of upfront time on their strategy for the future but then ignored it. They cycled back to their strategy for the future only when their plans soured.

Too Much Reacting: The No-Sight Trap

Although some managers, such as those at Pulsar, see more in the future than there is to see, other managers see less. In the no-sight trap, there is no strategy for the future, no experimenting with possible futures, and in fact, very little thought about the future. Managers simply respond to what happens around them. But in so doing, these managers have no anticipation of what might happen and no hope of shaping what could happen. Like ships in the fog, everything is a surprise for managers in the no-sight trap.

Managers tend to fall into the no-sight trap when they face intense competition. In frenetically competitive markets, it requires extraordinary discipline to spend time and resources on tomorrow's strategy when the needs of today's business are so all-consuming. Downsized and reengineered firms are also vulnerable. Excessive pruning can leave a work force that has no time to spend on strategy and that is focused on internal efficiencies rather than on external opportunities. Sometimes, managers slide into the no-sight trap because they believe that there is no point in thinking about the future. The marketplace is changing too quickly or unexpectedly to have a worthwhile strategy for the future. Although these managers may create a rough sense of the future and where they want to be, they never quite get around to thinking through the details. Regardless of how they are ensnared, managers in the no-sight trap end up stuck in today, reacting to various events—sometimes successfully, but more often not.

An example of a firm reacting to the future is the United Kingdom's Laura Ashley. Laura and Bernard Ashley began their retail business by producing printed scarves in their London flat. The prints reflected Laura's enjoyment of English romanticism and the floral designs of the Victorian idealists. Ashley and her designers became enormously successful in creating a distinctive fashion look with global appeal for the 1980s consumer who valued tradition. The Ashleys parlayed these designs into a vibrant garden of pastel clothing, accessories, and to a lesser extent, home furnishings, such as wallpaper, linens, and curtains. The result was that the Ashleys created one of the most successful fashion and retail empires of the decade. But after Laura Ashley's death in the mid-1980s, firm executives seemed to lose their vision of the future. By the early 1990s, the garden had become a weed patch of hundreds of shops in about forty countries. Managers in different regions built their own inventory systems, financial controls, and warehousing approaches in reaction to the particular demands of their regions and their own idiosyncrasies. Likewise, shops reacted to their particular customers' immediate shopping needs. But there was no central vision for the firm. The result was a chaotic, reactive, and sometimes contradictory approach to the marketplace. Laura Ashley's flowers wilted.

Another illustration is AT&T. The comfortable world in which the telecommunications giant called the shots on technologies and standards within the long-distance telephone industry in the United States ended. The Telecommunications Act of 1996 opened the door to hordes of competitors, including the powerful Baby Bells. As a result, AT&T was forced to offer local calling as a complement to its long-distance service and faced new competitors like electric utilities and cable TV operators. But it was not clear that AT&T managers had a new vision of their firm, postdivestiture and in the deregulated Internet future of telecommunications services. Initial forays into proprietary online services were unsuccessful. AT&T therefore had to play catch-up on Internet services with its rivals Sprint and MCI. Even in the core business of long-distance phoning, AT&T managers admitted to being blindsided by aggressive small competitors. Competition forced the firm to drop prices. As one industry executive noted, "Any observer has to conclude that their strategy over the last four or five years has been kind of ad hoc."[5] With no apparent vision of the AT&T of the future, AT&T executives became mired in a pattern of reacting to the moves of the competition.

How can managers spot when they are falling into the no-sight trap? We observed several characteristic traits. The first is that management teams in this trap have no vision about their business in the future. Although these managers may be exceptionally well informed about the latest tactical maneuvering by competitors, they have a surprising lack of knowledge about market trends. At best, these managers have individual points of view about the future, but they lack a collective vision of either their business or their market for the future.

A second trait is reaction to events. Managers in the no-sight trap characteristically respond to events. They do not try to plan the future. They do not try to learn about the future through probes such as experimental products or forward-focused strategic alliances. They just react.

A third trait that characterizes this trap is no attention to the future. Managers in this trap are so focused on executing current businesses that they have no time for the future. They are simply not paying much attention to it.

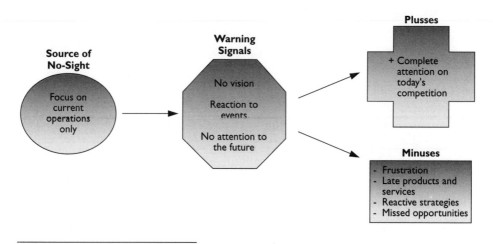

Figure 5.5 • The No-Sight Trap

Reacting to the Future at Nautilus

One business that is clearly caught in the no-sight trap is Nautilus, which we introduced in Chapter 2. This well-known global competitor was involved in intensely competitive market segments where it was crucial to balance the latest technology with low cost and the right features. When we studied Nautilus, managers had just finished an extensive reengineering of basic processes. As we mentioned earlier, they had developed very efficient, process-bound systems, with extensive use of decision gates and lockstep procedures. The result was disciplined efficiency that rendered the business unable to adapt effectively to change in current markets. In this chapter, we look at how these same managers tackled the future.

No Vision

The managers at Nautilus could easily describe their own market share, competitive position, and core competences as well as those of the competition. But when the subject turned to the future, they did not have much to say. They could not articulate a collective vision of the future: They had little ability to discuss trends within the industry; they did not know where their competitors were taking the competitive space; and they did not know how their customers were changing. They had little view of the future.

At best, Nautilus managers understood their business in terms of a dated perspective on the success drivers of the industry. One senior executive described the industry as a "horsepower race," meaning that the key to success was faster computing power. He claimed, "The market we are in is driven almost totally by a horsepower race. The one who wins is the one who has the biggest engine in his car." Yet, ironically, most competitors and customers had left this view long ago for a more complex one that included price, software availability, and reliability as success drivers. Overall, Nautilus managers had little perspective on the future and no sense of where they were going, beyond a few short-term profit goals. These managers were caught up in a very simple and tactical view of the future that one executive described as, "We're ahead, then someone else gets ahead, then we jump ahead again." But when pressed, most managers agreed that they were in "strategic drift." An executive remarked, "Well, I'm sure somebody does think strategically. . . . I hope somebody does it. . . . I'm actually not positive that they do."

Reaction to Events

At Nautilus, managers not only lacked a vision of the future, but they also had no way to gain insight about the future. There were, for example, no

everyone else focused on current business. When he spotted change, he signaled everyone else to react.

3. *No Attention.* Nautilus managers focused exclusively on the current operations, with almost no attention given to the future. They could not anticipate or even react very well.

Experimentation at the Edge of Time

Whether it is airlines, space exploration, or pharmaceuticals, the dilemma of
strategy in an uncertain, changing future involves balancing between the need
to commit to a future while retaining the strategic flexibility to adjust to the
future. The most effective managers achieve this balance by straddling
between the rigidity of planning for tomorrow and the chaos of reacting to
today. They understand that they cannot just take a wait-and-see approach,
because reacting is fundamentally a catch-up, not a winning, strategy. They
must make some commitments. But they also know that extensive planning is
naïve because it assumes an unchanging marketplace and their own omni-
science. So these managers navigate the edge between today's reacting and
tomorrow's planning by experimenting. Like NASA scientists, they engage in a
wide variety of simple, low-cost probes that provide insight about the future
while maintaining strategic flexibility. The result is quicker reaction to market
shifts, better anticipation of the future, and more opportunities for reinvention
and growth.

Charles Schwab, the pioneering discount broker, is a good example of a
firm that engages in experimentation. As rivals from Wall Street, along with
Internet trading companies like e-trade, and full-service brokerage houses like
Merrill Lynch, invaded Schwab's turf, Schwab managers fought back in several ways. Most prominent was the use of a variety of low-cost probes to
shape their next strategic moves. Managers used experimental products such
as simplified mutual funds selection and a futures trading program to test new
concepts in their traditional discount-brokerage business. In addition, they
probed the Internet with a broad range of transaction and information services such as Market Buzz. Surprisingly, they used probes to explore ways to
offer more service to their customers in the future, thus extending their business model into the competitive space of the full-service brokers. For example,
Schwab managers began talking with investment banks—notably Goldman
Sachs—about forming an exploratory alliance that would allow Schwab

clients to participate in initial public offering (IPO) underwritings. Of course, not all Schwab probes were successful: trials for mortgages and credit cards led to decisions not to introduce these products. But unsuccessful and successful probes are valuable. Rather than assuming that they can foresee the future, Schwab managers rely on a wide variety of probes that allow the firm to reinvent the brokerage establishment time and time again.

Another example is Sun Microsystems. This California-based computer firm pioneered the area of nonproprietary workstation products. Launched in the early 1980s, the firm proceeded to seize the lead in the hotly competitive workstation industry over much larger players, such as Hewlett-Packard, IBM, DEC, and Apollo. Sun accomplished this feat despite often lacking the best technologies. Key to the firm's success was experimentation through various low-cost tactics. Sun managers relied on the futurist insights of industry gurus (and Sun founders) Bill Joy in software and Andy Bechtolsheim in hardware. They also exploited strategic alliances that linked the firm to future customer opportunities with blue-chip firms like Kodak and AT&T. Later, managers aggressively pursued forward-looking alliances with complementary firms in software to create sales of Sun products. Sun managers have also funded a stable of experimental activities. The best recent example is Java, an object-oriented programming language that enables applications to run over the Internet. Locked away in a lab and focused on another application for set-top television controllers, Sun engineers stumbled upon what became Java. Sun senior executives wisely linked this R&D thrust with the Internet opportunity to give Sun a leadership position in the Internet future. Within the overarching theme of "the network is the computer," Sun management typically engages in a wide variety of futuristic probes that keep managers continuously reinventing this leading computer firm.

We identified several common traits among businesses that experiment effectively. One is that their managers have a simple and clearly defined vision of the business in the future. They do not try to predict any particular future of the industry, but rather they try to define their business' identity within whatever future comes. Nokia's "telecom, global, focus" identity is a good example, as is Sun's "the network is the computer." Then, as the future unfolds, these managers adjust their tactics in the context of their business vision.

Second, these managers rely on a wide variety of low-cost probes of the future. Like NASA scientists, they invest on an ongoing basis in probes such as strategic alliances, futurists, future-focused meetings, and experimental products and other probes that create insight into how their marketplace is evolving. These managers neither plan extensively nor react chaotically. Rather, they use their probes to incrementally shape strategic direction.

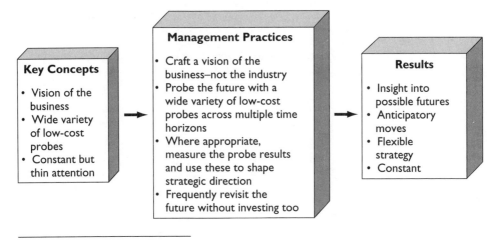

Key Concepts	Management Practices	Results
• Vision of the business • Wide variety of low-cost probes • Constant but thin attention	• Craft a vision of the business—not the industry • Probe the future with a wide variety of low-cost probes across multiple time horizons • Where appropriate, measure the probe results and use these to shape strategic direction • Frequently revisit the future without investing too	• Insight into possible futures • Anticipatory moves • Flexible strategy • Constant

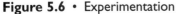

Figure 5.6 • Experimentation

Third, these managers give constant, but thin, attention to the future. They neither ignore the future like Nautilus managers nor do they swing between extremes like those at Pulsar. Rather, they constantly engage in forward-looking activities, but surprisingly, they do *not* spend a lot of time on the future. They know that the present is what matters most. Nonetheless, while the future is rarely on the front burner, it is always simmering on the back one.

Experimenting at Titan

Leave the airport and turn due east to head for Titan. Speed past scrub forest, an occasional strip mall, and farms. Pass a few traffic lights, and arrive at one of the most unlikely spots in the world for one of the premier firms in the business, Titan Computing (a pseudonym). The feel is one of precision, no nonsense, and nothing extra. Even the buildings at Titan look efficient. Concrete, steel, and glass give a supremely austere and controlled look. The image is of a well-oiled machine. Only the flowers in the landscaping soften the edge.

Titan creates systems solutions for both the mature mainframe computing market and newer markets based on client/server (C/S) technology. There is a constant juxtaposition of today's mainframe and tomorrow's C/S businesses.

The key to success within firms undergoing a major transition or paradigm shift is to maintain a careful balance between current and future businesses. At Titan, this means tending the mainframe business that is still an important source of current revenues, while simultaneously capitalizing on the high-growth C/S business that is the obvious future. Titan executives have managed the dual businesses extraordinarily well, at least in part because they are adept at managing the future. The firm's managers have an extraordinary sense of the future. They typically anticipate and sometimes even lead the industry. And even when they do not, they respond very quickly. In the process, they have reinvented their business.

Vision of the Business, Not the Future

Executives at Titan have a clear vision of their business. Since the company's founding, they have had a remarkably constant understanding of what they wish their business to be—"a provider of complete business solutions for global corporations." They have supported this vision over the past fifteen years, despite vast changes in the commercial computing landscape.

Yet even though Titan executives have maintained this constant vision of their business, they have not had a fixed view of their marketplace. Titan managers appreciate the inherent uncertainty of the future. They anticipate that markets and technologies will evolve. They know that competitors will come and go. They are aware that customer needs shift. And so they adjust their tactics but not what they envision as Titan's role in whatever future may come. A senior executive described this blend of company identity and strategic flexibility to us: "It is a mixture. We have a goal in mind. . . . It is clear we have a map and want to go in a certain direction. On the other hand, you have business opportunities. They are not in your map, but you feel good about them, they fit, and you add them."

Wide Variety of Low-Cost Probes

To the outside observer, executives at Titan have made a series of high-risk guesses about future market trends that happen to have been right. The reality, however, is far different. The management team at Titan relies on an explicit pattern of futuristic probes from which they have built their strategy. These probes are distinctively low cost, numerous, and highly varied.

One part of the pattern is *experimental products*. Titan managers routinely create experimental products to probe new markets. The criteria for choosing these products is explicitly different from those used to evaluate more traditional projects that are evaluated against an internal hurdle rate. The primary purpose of the experimental products is to provide insight into the future. Given this goal, failure is not only possible, it is both probable and sometimes even desirable. The consensus among Titan managers is that failures create more learning than do successes.

Experimental products are chosen according to two criteria. One is potential market size. Given Titan's scale, a business case—which customers will buy the product and why—must be made to demonstrate a sufficiently large

Understanding the Logic of Probes

Implementing experimentation requires an understanding of the logic of probes because probing is at the heart of experimentation. Probes are another form of mutation. They are valuable because they are an effective way to learn about the future. Direct, hands-on experience through such probes as experimental products and strategic alliances creates "learning by doing," which is a much more powerful way to learn than is reliance on vicarious or second-hand experience. "Small losses" from experimental products or the failed predictions of futurists are very effective for learning because they engage attention without raising the mind-numbing defenses that accompany "big losses." A mix of probes enhances learning because of interplay among several sources of knowledge. Insights from one approach, such as strategic alliances, can powerfully enhance insights from another source, such as the predictions of futurists. The cheaper and smaller the probes, the more probes can be afforded. Ultimately, the use of a wide variety of low-cost probes creates powerful and rapid learning, allowing managers to gain insight into the future.

Probes are also valuable because they can be used to create options for the future. In fast-moving and highly competitive industries, it is particularly difficult to predict the future. Given this uncertainty, options are especially useful because they give managers more possible responses. When the future does arrive, managers are more likely to have something ready to do and can adjust adroitly.

Probes are valuable for defensive reasons. They lower the probability of being blindsided by unanticipated futures. By probing the corners of the competitive landscape, managers are more likely to uncover threats, such as new competitors or technologies. Multiple probes are particularly valuable. Relying on only one type of probe or a few probes leaves managers vulnerable in other areas. For example, focusing only on the articulated needs of current customers can leave businesses vulnerable to new entrants with fresh technologies.

Finally, the best probes reveal the unexpected, the unanticipated, and the previously unknown. Probes insert an element of randomness that freshens thinking. After all, why investigate what is already known? When probes surprise, they stimulate creative thinking. From a competitive point of view, probes that surprise can reveal frame-breaking ways to compete that alter "the rules of the game." Probes take creative thinking beyond the limitations of an office-bound, brainstorming exercise to possibilities that managers simply cannot imagine on their own.[6]

market size. Small markets are really not worth exploring for a corporation the size of Titan. The second criterion is low cost. The experimental product has to be achievable with few resources. Without low costs, it is difficult to maintain a learning attitude toward a product. Big investments need big wins. Moreover, low costs mean that more experiments can be conducted. Whereas standard development projects involve between thirty and forty people, Titan's experimental products require about five to eight people.

An executive explained how Titan uses experimental products to probe new markets: "We drive spearheads into what we think are potential new markets and try to get feedback as quickly as possible. We go after a market area and find out if there are people who want to use our products in that area. We determine how big we think the market is and then decide if we want to tailor our products for it."

One experimental product was for global financial services. Many companies face legal requirements to use multiple currencies throughout their financial systems, which creates extensive, complex computing demands. For example, one of Titan's energy sector customers kept track of all internal transactions in Mexican pesos, U.S. dollars, and British pounds simultaneously. The potential market for a product that delivered the capability to use multiple currencies in an integrated, highly reliable fashion was considered substantial within the corporation. So Titan managers decided to create an experimental product that would permit the complete integration of up to three currencies for several financial applications. Limiting the scope to three currencies and to only financial applications made the project much less expensive and faster to finish. Yet the project was of sufficient scope to give Titan managers valuable insight into how the future market might develop.

Titan also explored down-market possibilities. In particular, Titan developers created an experimental product that was a stripped-down version of an existing product—sort of a "Titan Lite." Technically, the design was very much "quick and dirty." Essentially, the design stripped back capabilities from existing products. This was a "kludge approach" from a product development standpoint, but it accomplished the objective of a quick and low-cost look at the potential of down-market expansion. Consistent with the experimentation attitude, Titan's managers anticipated failure. As one manager predicted, "We are likely to make a lot of mistakes with this experiment because we don't know anything about lower end markets." But they expected to learn.

Titan managers also relied on *futurists*. In contrast to experimental products, which were used to probe deeply into targeted markets or technical opportunities, futurists thought more broadly and long term about future landscapes. At Titan, four managers served as the futurists for the business. Although they all had some operating responsibility, their primary jobs were to envision alternative future scenarios and how Titan would fare within those. These futurists had advanced degrees in relevant technical fields and maintained close ties to their respective research communities. They matched their cutting-edge, technical knowledge with deep insight into the markets that Titan served. Each of them spent time with, on average, ten existing or potential customers each week.

Another aspect of the pattern of probes at Titan was *strategic alliances*. Typically, Titan managers tried to ally with "best in class" partners who were providers of complementary products or services. The focus of these collaborations was exploration of new markets and products. In one alliance, Titan partnered with a leading PC software firm. Although Titan's C/S based products could operate in a PC environment, the next step was to interface directly with desktop PC software. This partnership created a seamless interface between Titan C/S products and its partner's popular desktop software. In the short run, the partnership gave Titan easy access to the low-end markets that managers wanted to penetrate. In the long run, Titan developers gained valuable lessons in user interface designs.

Further, Titan managers occasionally switched partners to ensure that the firm was collaborating in partnerships that were clearly focused on the future. For example, at one time, Titan managers had a close partnership with a leading disk drive manufacturer. But as disk drive technology became a well-known commodity, Titan replaced that relationship with a partnership with a leader in state-of-the-art networking technology. Titan managers realized that disk drive technology was no longer key to their future. In contrast, they saw networking as particularly vital for the future of Titan's Internet-friendly products.

Titan managers probed the future through explicit and regularly scheduled *future-focused meetings* to address the future. These monthly meetings provided a forum for synthetic thinking among futurists and operating managers about the shape of the future. The regular schedule ensured that the meetings were not pushed aside by pressing operating concerns. They also served as the place to blend the insights of futurists, the status of experimental products, and the information from the exploratory strategic alliances so that the group could continue to update its collective sense of the future and to make commitments for the future.

Constant But Thin Attention

Surprisingly, despite superior management of the future, the central focus of attention at Titan was today, not the future—today's products and today's revenues. Effective execution of *today* was the most crucial priority for most Titan

Table 5.1 • Experimentation at Titan

Type	Description	Time Frame	Metric
Experimental products	Foreign currency product and	6 months	Beta customer reaction
	downmarket product	6 months	Test market penetration
Futurists	Four operating managers with PhDs meet with 10 customers/ week	1 to 3 years	
Strategic alliances	PC software firm, networking firm, and systems integrator	1 year 1 to 4 years 1 to 2 years	Qualitative assessment of technology as leading edge
Future-focused meetings	Monthly meetings with business heads and two corporate executives	6 months to 5 years	

A wide variety of low-cost probes led to consistent change via anticipatory products, evolution into the new business paradigm of client/server computing, and a reinvented corporation at the top of its industry segment.

managers. In this way, Titan resembled Pulsar and Nautilus. But what distinguished Titan from these other players was that the future was not forgotten. Although Titan managers did not dwell on the future, they thought about it constantly. A senior executive at Nokia described that firm's goal for the future: "We've taken strategy away from the yearly cycle that it was in and we're trying to make it a daily part of a manager's activity."[7] Titan managers have already achieved it. Their key was "background processing" the future through a continuing flow of probes throughout all levels of the business. Even though the present was usually in the foreground, the future was always percolating away in the background of experimental products, exploratory strategic alliances, futurist musings, and future-focused strategy meetings.

Business Implications

The direct impact of Titan's experimentation with the future was better anticipation into how the future was likely to unfold. In particular, the strategy of many small, low-cost probes was an especially effective way to develop insight, because people learn most effectively when they gain information through multiple information sources, not just one or two. In addition, these probes acted as options on the future. As a result, managers at Titan were rarely surprised by the future. For example, Titan maintained an alliance with a global accounting firm that led executives to understand, long before it became "official," impending changes in international trade rules that would have a significant impact on a number of Titan's products. As a result, Titan was the only enterprise computing provider able to make the necessary product enhancements and ship the new products to customers before the trade rules changes actually came into effect.

The Titan product line was the envy of the industry. The firm's products were constantly at the leading edge of what customers wanted, and Titan was rarely outmaneuvered in the marketplace. Much more often, the firm not only beat the competition but also led the way in creating new visions for enterprise computing. A Titan competitor admitted, "Titan is giving us hell."

During the time that we spent with Titan executives, the firm was in the process of using its strong global position in mainframe computing as a springboard to international expansion into the client/server paradigm. Since then, Titan has become the worldwide leader in its industry segment. A major business publication noted, "Titan is on top." Wise management of the future is a big reason why. Using experimentation, Titan managers have changed from their legacy systems into the future of computing. The reward for their corporate reinvention has been one of the fastest-growing computer firms on the globe.

Key Signals

To summarize, the Titan example illustrates several essential features of experimenting with the future:

1. *Vision of the Business.* Titan managers crafted a clear and constant vision of the business as "a provider of complete business solutions for global corporations" but did not lock into any particular future vision of the industry. Titan managers also used their vision of the business as a rallying point for employees.

2. *Wide Variety of Low-Cost Probes.* Titan managers neither extensively planned nor chaotically reacted. They stayed in between with a variety of low-cost probes that helped shape their next strategic moves. These probes

Rules for Picking Probes

1. Develop many types of low-cost probes. Vary the time frames of probes. Create short-term and long-term probes and allow them to emerge from many parts of the business.

2. Be sure to choose some probes that have a chance of failure, especially small failures, because people learn more effectively from small failure than from successes.

3. Pick some probes that require implementation followed by a measurement of results. People learn more from hands-on activity and concrete feedback than from blue-sky thinking.

4. Use more probes when your marketplace is particularly volatile.

5. If you must use big probes, whenever possible break them into a series of smaller options, or opportunities to learn.

6. Place more probes into the most likely future.

7. Pick some random probes. Random probes are the most likely to reveal the unexpected, the unanticipated, and the previously unknown. They are the most likely to surprise you and as such, to be the most valuable—especially when the marketplace is uncertain.

8. Build on the results of your probes to shape the next strategic moves.

9. Do not probe endlessly in a particular area. At some point, commit to one course of action.

covered the future in the short run and the long run, and across many conceivable markets.

3. *Constant But Thin Attention.* Titan managers understood that the future in fast-changing markets requires frequent attention but not a lot of attention. Today is the prime focus of attention, although the future is never far away.

Implementing Experimentation

Return to the survey from the beginning of the chapter. Look at where *Pulsar* (foresight), *Nautilus* (no-sight), and *Titan* (insight) fall.

The collective vision of our business is:

Clear ┆•┆•••••••••┆┆••••••••••••••••••••••••••••••┆•┆ Ambiguous
     T   P   N

Our future success depends on a particular industry scenario:

Yes ┆•┆••┆••┆ No
    P   N,T

Our approach to the future is to:

Plan ┆┆••••••••••••••••••••••••┆┆••••••••••••••┆•┆ React
    P   T   N

Our attention to the future is:

Frequent ┆•┆•••••••••••••••••••••••••••••••••••••┆••┆ Rare
       T   P, N

We have several meaningful experimental products and future-oriented strategic alliances:

Yes ┆•┆•••••••••••••••••••••••••••••••••••••••┆••┆ No
    T   P, N

Our business is considered to be a:

Leader ┆┆•••••••••••••••••••••┆┆•••••••••••••••••┆•┆ Follower
     T   P   N

This pattern should give you some sense of how your business manages the future. If your business is more like Pulsar or Nautilus, then you need to make some changes. A good place to start is with the role of the business in the future. Begin by brainstorming throughout the business to come up with possibilities. This is a good way to energize and involve a wide swath of your people . . . and to surface great ideas. If your business is more like Nautilus, you will also want to cut back on your efforts to predict where your industry is headed. Some thinking along these lines is recommended, but remember that your best guess will probably be wrong. Don't spend too much time trying to predict what you can't. As you begin to shape a vision of your business, test it out under various industry scenarios. A robust vision survives a variety of possible futures.

The heart of experimentation is probing. The best probes surprise and reveal the unexpected. Begin by taking stock of your existing probes. Order them by their type and timeframe. Although an effective probing strategy targets the most likely futures, it is also diverse. Ensure that your probes stretch from a few months to a few years. For the longer ones, use Merck's strategy of breaking them into short-term options. If you have too many for one time-frame, do some pruning. Also ensure that you have different types of probes, because balance is key here. Ten strategic alliances with new customers and no experimental products is a poor probe pattern. You should mix different alliance partners and engage a variety of futurists, even people who are normally not futurists. Don't be afraid to create experimental products. You should also adopt a real options perspective that emphasizes learning from your probes. The success of your probes should be evaluated, at least partially, by how much their results surprise you, as well as by metrics.

Finally, take stock of the time that you and your colleagues spend on the future: Measure it. If you are like Pulsar, then you are probably spending enough (maybe more than enough) time on the future. But you need to spread that time out. If you are like Nautilus, then you are shortchanging the future. In either case, ensure that you spend some part of every week on the future and that you look for ways to engage the future even as you go about today's business.

Note on Strategic Planning

As a final note, we touch upon the controversial subject of strategic planning. The Pulsar example is a textbook illustration of strategic planning: study the industry, select a strategy, and build tactics around it. Such strategic planning has several strengths. It serves a useful, symbolic role. At Pulsar, it provided a rallying point for employees. It generated excitement and a relentless work ethic at the firm. At other companies, such planning can usefully signal discipline and sophistication to constituents like lenders and stockholders. So strategic planning can have important symbolic value. Strategic planning also serves a useful purpose in coordinating a complex set of efforts among many people. It is a way to organize tasks and lay out a resource roadmap for people to follow. Without any kind of planning, there is chaos. Clearly, at Pulsar strategic planning helped managers to coordinate a large group of people engaged in complex tasks. Strategic planning can even be effective as the primary strategy for managing the future in slow-moving industries.

But Pulsar's managers made an all-too-common mistake with their strategic planning. They believed that strategic planning is about the future. In reality, strategic planning gives managers almost no help in gaining insight about the future. It is a passive approach that does not actively engage the future. And it can even be detrimental to managing the future when the plans are too rigid, as they were at Pulsar. Pulsar's managers simply did not understand that in high-velocity markets, a strategic plan is an emotional rallying point and a resource roadmap. It is not anything more, and certainly it does not provide insight about the future.

What could Pulsar's managers have done differently? They could have treated their strategic plan as a rough roadmap, budgetary guideline, and rallying point, not as a straitjacket that limited managers from adapting to the real future that unfolded. More important, Pulsar managers should have complemented their strategic planning by actually engaging the future through experimentation and building strategy based on insights from these experiments.

It was all in the rhythm.
Have you ever seen
Michael Jordan play when
he's on a rhythm run? It
was exactly like that.

Robert Kuok,

Malaysian businessman

(net worth $1.7 billion),

commenting on his

own success.

setting the **pace**

SAN FRANCISCO IS famous for great seafood, spectacular bridges, stunning scenery, and some of the most successful corporations in the world. Within the global economy, none of these companies has been more influential than Intel Corporation. Nestled in the heart of Silicon Valley, just south of San Francisco in what only a few decades ago was fruit orchards, Intel has become the dominant semiconductor firm in the world and a perennial leader among U.S. technology companies. In the decade between 1987 and 1997, Intel Corporation generated an average annual return to investors of about 44 percent. Even more impressive, Intel's annual earnings equal those of the top 10 PC firms *combined*.[1]

What has made Intel such an extraordinary firm? It is well known that Intel has benefited from a cadre of outstanding senior executives. From founders Gordon Moore, the co-inventor of the microprocessor, and Bob Noyce, the strategist and external relations expert, to their junior partner, Andy Grove, and more recently the former Stanford professor Craig Barrett, Intel has had superb leaders who have built the company and crafted an intense, high-performance culture around "constructive confrontation," "two in a box" responsibilities, and the infamous slogan "only the paranoid survive."

It is also well known that Intel has experienced much good luck. In the early 1980s, the firm was in a battle with Motorola and National Semiconductor for its product to become the chip of choice in the new microprocessor-based computer industry. Intel's big break came with its IBM design win. Intel's chip was selected to power the IBM PC, the PC went on to become the standard industry architecture, and the rest is history. Intel joined the equally fortunate Microsoft to ride the tsunami of the PC industry, and the twosome became the powers behind the Wintel standard.

But part of the story of Intel's success is not so widely known—that Intel is an extraordinarily time-paced corporation. Time pacing involves changing because of the passage of time, not the influence of events. Every company is at least somewhat event-paced, because it is impossible to predict all that will happen in the future. But only a few companies are dominated by time pacing. Yet time pacing is a major reason why Intel and other stellar firms have consistently outrun their competitors, outmaneuvered them, and generated a relentless flow of advantages. Intel's time pacing is a fundamental and yet often overlooked factor in the firm's rise to prominence and its ability to sustain industry dominance.

Central to time pacing at Intel is the so-called Moore's Law. In 1975, founder Gordon Moore prophesied that the power of the microprocessor computer chip would double every eighteen months. No firm took this law more to heart than Moore's own Intel. Moore's Law, however, is not a law of physics. Rather, it is a law of business that Intel's engineers have made come true. Moore's Law sets the internally driven pulse rate of the firm. Producing to Moore's Law made Intel at its core time-paced, and the firm still pulsates to the rhythm some twenty-plus years after Moore's pronouncement.

Over time, Intel managers have elaborated on Moore's Law to create a flow of new product introductions that has left the competition scrambling to catch up. In the late 1980s, for example, Intel's battles with would-be competitors AMD and NEC made headlines. AMD was challenging Intel's withholding of 386 licensing for PCs. Intel was suing NEC for copyright infringement. But while Intel lawyers were fighting legal battles, Intel engineers were quietly winning the competitive war with product development. They accelerated their pace of innovation, added time-paced cycles of smaller innovation within the dictates of Moore's Law, and scheduled regular "mid-life kickers" for their products. The result was that Intel sprinted ahead of the competition. They repeated this feat again in the 1990s, when they picked up the pace against Motorola's PowerPC microprocessor and again widened the gap.

More recently, Intel managers have added another rhythm to the firm—the time pacing of fabrication facilities. Intel constructs a new manufacturing facility or "fab" about every nine months. Each fab costs an impressive $2 billion. Keeping these massively expensive facilities busy has created a new discipline of time pacing to go along with Moore's Law. Says CEO Grove, "We build factories two years in advance of needing them, before we have the products to run in them, and before we know the industry's going to grow."[2] This construction of fab capacity sets a second rhythm of change within Intel. Why manufacturing capacity? Fab capacity keeps rivals from gaining a toehold because Intel cannot meet demand.

Intel managers have increasingly turned their attention to being synchronized with the marketplace. After all, time pacing depends not only on Intel's ability to execute the rhythm but also on being synchronized with customers and complementers. If Intel pumps out too many chips or chips with too much technology, the firm falters. So to keep a consistent rhythm, Intel must, as Grove says, "create users and uses for our microprocessors." Intel executives now show up in Hollywood, strike deals with video game companies, and in fact are almost

Andy Grove's Philosophy . . .

- Timing is everything.
- Act early while the momentum still exists.
- As with runners, it is necessary to pass the baton at precisely the right moment.
- The greatest danger is standing still.

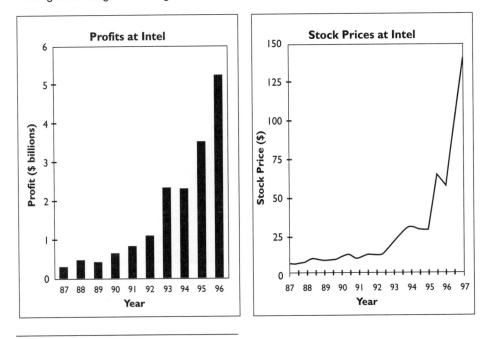

Figure 6.1 • And the Numbers at Intel

Sources: Andrew Grove, *Only the Paranoid Survive* (New York: Doubleday, 1996) and David Kirkpatrick, "Intel's Amazing Profit Machine," *Fortune*, 17 February 1997. Reprinted with permission. ©1998 Time Inc.

anywhere where computing power might be in demand. Staying synchronized with the market also means keeping complementers (such as software developers) in synch with the firm. After all, chips with no software will not sell. So key Intel complementers get early access to platforms to stay synchronized with the Intel rhythm and flow of new products.

Occasionally, Intel's microprocessors have sprinted ahead of the rest of the computing system and so threatened the rhythm. When this happens, Intel often builds up the platform with complementary products. This happened in 1991 with bus architecture (i.e., the input/output channel of a computer), and it happened more recently with network adapter cards (i.e., the circuit board that connects a PC to a network). In this latter case, slow and expensive access to networks was potentially slowing the sales of the high-performing microprocessors that are the heart of Intel. After all, why should customers buy

Company	Use of Time Pacing
British Airways	• "Five years is the maximum that you can go without refreshing the brand . . . We did it [relaunched Club Europe Service] because we wanted to stay ahead so that we could continue to win premium customers." –BA Chairman, Sir Colin Marshall
Emerson Electric	• "In each of the last three years we've introduced more than 100 major new products, which is about 70 percent above our pace of the early 1990s. We plan to maintain this rate and, overall, have targeted increasing new products to [equal] 35 percent of total sales."
Gillette	• Forty percent of Gillette's sales every five years must come from entirely new products. • Gillette raises prices at a pace set to match price increases in a basket of market goods (that includes items such as a newspaper, a candy bar, and a can of Coke). Gillette prices are never raised faster than the price of the market basket.
Netscape	• The inventor of the pace known as "Internet time." • "Netscape almost wrote the book on speed in product cycles." –Intuit Inc.'s CEO, Scott D. Cook • "Netscape forced the whole industry to move very fast." –VP for Technology, Corel Corporation, Eid E. Eid
3M	• Thirty percent of sales must come from products less than four years old.
Intel	• The inventor of Moore's Law–that the power of the computer chip would double every eighteen months. • Builds a new manufacturing facility ("fab") every nine months. • "We build factories two years in advance of needing them, before we have the products to run in them, and before we know the industry is going to grow." –Intel CEO, Andy Grove

Figure 6.2 • Time Pacing

Sources: Steven E. Prokesh, "Competing on Customer Service: An Interview with British Airways' Sir Colin Marshall," *Harvard Business Review* 73, no. 6 (1995): 101–116; Emerson Electric Annual Report, 1996, 4; Robert D. Hoff, "Netspeed at Netscape," *Business Week*, 10 February 1997, 79–86; and David Kirkpatrick, "Intel's Amazing Profit Machine," *Fortune*, 17 February 1997, 60–68.

exotic multimedia hardware if it takes too long to download the information from colleagues or from the Internet? Intel moved into the network adapter card market, owned almost exclusively by 3Com, in 1991. By the mid-nineties, Intel had taken about a third of the market. In 1997, Intel passed on low manufacturing costs to customers by slashing the prices of their network adapter cards by 40 percent and created demand for cheap, fast PC access to networks . . . and for Intel microprocessors.

Overall, Intel managers have succeeded in creating an extraordinarily time-paced corporation. The corporation pulsates to the beat of Moore's Law, elaborations to it, and the rhythm of expanding fab capacity. Intel managers have successfully orchestrated transitions, such as the ramp-up of manufacturing capacity, and they have helped complementers and customers to stay in synch by creating a predictable flow of new products. The result is an industry that is significantly led by the vision, and more important, the pace of Intel.

The experience of Intel illustrates the power of time pacing. Time pacing is the often unrecognized component of strategy behind the success of businesses that are able to create a continuous flow of competitive advantages. Although most businesses will never gain Intel's position, small companies and big businesses alike can be time paced and benefit from it. Time pacing is probably the most underrated and least known facet of strategy in rapidly and unpredictably changing markets.

Time pacing means creating new products, introducing new services, launching new businesses, and entering new markets according to the calendar. It means, for example, creating a new product every nine months, generating 20 percent of annual sales from new services, making major decisions within three months, or entering a new business every year. It is about running a business through routine and regular deadlines that become a rhythm. What time pacing does is set the rate of change within the business—the pace of how fast the business moves from past to present to future. Think of time pacing as an internal metronome.

In contrast, event pacing drives evolution according to occurrences such as moves by the competition, shifts in technology, or new customer demands. Event pacing is more erratic than time pacing, does not involve any kind of rhythm, and is typically reactive. Although managers are always somewhat event-paced because it is impossible to predict the future, time pacing is essential for creating a continuous flow of competitive advantages.

Time pacing is an effective strategy because it forces managers to look up from their businesses on a regular basis, survey the situation, adapt if necessary, and then get back to work. As a result, these managers can potentially react faster, anticipate better, and possibly lead the pace of change in their industry more effectively than managers who simply respond to events. Time pacing counteracts the tendency of most managers to wait too long, move too slowly, and lose momentum.

Time pacing involves two management concepts that many managers ignore. One is transitions. Time pacing relies on choreographed transitions to switch smoothly from engineering to manufacturing, from product to product, from one market to the next, from one business to the next. Without effective transitions, Intel managers, for example, cannot predictably ramp up new fabrication facilities or smoothly switch from one microprocessor design to the next. The creation of choreographed transitions is key and in fact, can help many managers to create advantage even if they do not time pace.

The second is rhythm. Time pacing relies on a rhythm that can actually be executed, is synchronized with the marketplace, and thwarts the competition. Rhythm creates the momentum of time pacing. Yet if the tempo of the rhythm

The Logic of Time Pacing

Time pacing is effective for many reasons. It counteracts managers' natural tendency to change too little and too late, while simultaneously forcing them to stop what they are doing, assess the effectiveness of their actions, and adjust their strategies before proceeding. This regular opportunity to assess position and make adjustments is particularly critical in uncertain and high-velocity markets where the need to change is difficult to predict and the temptation to keep working is strong. These periodic time-outs also become occasions to fix problems. Overall, they help ensure the early anticipation of future events.

Ironically, time pacing can also keep managers from changing **too often**. Although inertia is typically the greater problem, too much change occurs when managers try to adapt to every change in a fast-paced market. For example, they may pull out of new markets before these markets have had time to develop, rush through decisions with inadequate data, or drop a promising technology without a sufficient trial. Time pacing forces staying the course for a realistic period of time.

Additionally, time pacing reminds people to search for existing rhythms. Entraining to natural external rhythms can boost performance by allowing people to take advantage of the synergistic aspects of these rhythms.

Finally, time pacing creates a sense of relentless urgency. When this urgency is combined with predictable time intervals, managers can get into a rhythm or "flow" that allows them to focus, builds confidence, and can yield superior performance. In contrast, **event pacing** is reactive, often involves late responses to crises, and lacks momentum. Finally, although **choreography** is important, its specifics are often arbitrary. **Rhythm** is the more challenging aspect to manage in time pacing because it requires synchronization with the marketplace and with the internal capabilities of the business.[3]

is too fast, then managers may not be able to execute it or they may get too far ahead of the market. For example, products may be changed too frequently for customers to keep up. If it is too slow, companies will become laggards in the industry. Further, whereas choreography is often arbitrary, rhythm depends very much upon the marketplace, and so is more challenging to manage well.

Survey Your Company

Before going on in this chapter, take a few moments to answer the following questions about pacing:

New product or service concepts are introduced in your business at rhythmic intervals.   T or F

Your business has specific metrics, such as time to launch a global product, months to deliver a product, or percentage of annual revenue from new sources, that evaluate performance using time.   T or F

Your business has explicit procedures for transitions such as moving into new products or markets, integrating acquisitions, or ramping up to volume manufacturing.   T or F

Your business has a routine for leaving old business areas.   T or F

Your business is synchronized with the rhythms of key customers and suppliers.   T or F

Choreographed Transitions

Grabbing 4×100 Gold

Atlanta. August 3, 1996. On this languid southern evening straight out of a Tennessee Williams play, Olympic history was made. Canada's Donovan Bailey and his teammates wrote their own Olympic history as their 4×100 relay team bested the United States. It was the first time that the Americans had ever lost

---

Transition
• Create a choreography

Rhythm
• Establish a rhythm
• Stay in the discipline of the rhythm
• Fine-tune the rhythm

Figure 6.3 • Basics of Time Pacing

the Olympic event, except by disqualification. After intense speculation about whether Carl Lewis, the nine-time Olympic gold medal winner, would anchor the U.S. team, the Canadians ignored the hype and grabbed the gold. The United States had to be content with winning the three other track relays.

In the days leading up to the event, the Lewis story was front-page news in the United States. After sprinter Leroy Burrell went down with Achilles tendinitis, a debate raged in the media over Burrell's replacement on the 4×100 team. The primary choices were Tim Harden, a collegian from the University of Kentucky, and the old pro, Carl Lewis. Harden was probably the quicker man, but Lewis held the advantages of superior technical skills, such as baton passing, and vast international experience. It was leg speed vs. transition smarts. The choice was Harden, and the outcome was history. After waiting out the media blitz over whether Lewis should collect an historic tenth gold medal, the Canadians easily won the event by a .36-second margin, an eternity in international track. The victory margin could have been even larger if Donovan Bailey, the Canadian anchor man, had not celebrated the historic victory before he crossed the finish line.

What happened to the U.S. team? As any track aficionado knows, the key to winning relays is the exchange of the baton. In international track, a good exchange can make up between one-half to one second. It is both a matter of technique and of practiced judgment in assessing the speed of the incoming runner in the transition between runners. U.S. teams typically do not have enough time to practice these exchanges, and many track observers believe that this hurts their performance. In the past, U.S. teams have compensated with faster athletes. That strategy failed against the talented Canadian team. Would the transition skills of Lewis have changed the outcome?

Although the U.S. sprinter Jon Drummond hesitated at the start, he recovered to run a strong first leg against the Canadian lead-off man, Robert Esmie, who had celebrated his joining the 4×100 team by having his head shaved to read "relay." But possibly worried about poor American exchanges in recent competition and Harden's inexperience, Drummond became tentative, slowed down, and cautiously handed the baton to Tim Harden for the second U.S. leg. The cost of caution was time—the number one transition problem. Harden took the baton midway up the stick in the exchange with Drummond. As Harden realized, this grip would not give the third runner, Mike Marsh, enough room to grasp the baton in the next exchange. That was transition problem number two. So at top racing speed and in the middle of his leg, Harden adjusted the baton held in his left hand with his right. While successfully executing this difficult maneuver, Harden hitched his stride—transition problem number three. Canada's Glenroy Gilbert took advantage, won the second leg by beating

For long races, the incoming runner will probably experience fatigue and therefore the receiver must monitor for changes in speed. Thus, one should use a visual passing technique:

- Receiver watches the runner to gauge incoming speed.
- The receiver begins to run based on this speed.
- The receiver runs at the same speed as the incoming runner at the time of the baton pass.
- It is the responsibility of the receiver to take the baton from the outstretched hand of the passer.

For shorter races, the incoming runner should not be fatigued. In these situations, well coordinated teams can use a blind passing technique where the receiver begins to run when the incoming runner crosses a predetermined mark. After a few steps to gain speed, the receiver extends the hand back and grabs the baton from the outstretched hand of the runner.

Races can be lost if the team is too cautious by slowing down the transition to make it easier. Races can also be lost if the team is too reckless and the baton is dropped or the runner and receiver collide during the transition. Teams must frequently practice to determine the proper transition pace.

"Races are not won by increasing one's speed at the end, but rather by not slowing down."

Figure 6.4 • Rules for the Baton Pass

Source: Mel Rosen, *Sports Illustrated Track: Championship Running* (New York: Harper & Row, 1986).

Harden's sluggish time, and captured the lead. Marsh, the third U.S. runner, got off slowly in the passing zone, and Harden ran up on him. The pass was awkward, again costing the Americans valuable time. That was transition problem number four. Marsh then fell further behind on the turn against Canada's Bruny Surin, who, perhaps sensing the victory, set a torrid pace. By the time the U.S. anchorman, Dennis Mitchell, took the baton, Donovan Bailey (the world's fastest man by virtue of his 100-meter gold) had a two-step lead. He would not be caught, and the Canadians won the gold.

In looking back on the event, one can see that the United States left off their track team a more experienced transition man in Lewis, an athlete who had anchored six world record relays, and then made crucial errors in the transitions between their first three runners in the actual race. In contrast, the Canadians worked on their baton pass after a poor early round and transitioned flawlessly between athletes. Would Lewis have made a difference? The Canadians probably would have won even if the United States had been flawless. Although before the race the Americans had vowed to defeat the Canadians, the Canadians were confident that, as Gilbert said, "This was the opportunity to step it up one more notch and beat the Americans on their home turf."[4] No one will ever know what might have been, but the smooth Canadian baton passes, together with the slow and mistake-filled U.S. ones, certainly were part of the story.

Lessons from the Canadian Relay Gold

The Canadian 4×100 victory suggests several transition lessons. First, transitions are an essential aspect of winning. If transitions are ignored, teams lose position, stumble, and fall behind, as the U.S. team painfully learned. But if transitions are executed well, they can build a sense of drive and urgency within a team. Bruny Surin's surprisingly fast third leg for the Canadians suggests this phenomenon.

Second, transitions are rarely practiced and often forgotten. Among recreational athletes, neglect of transitions is especially common. In golf, for example, most players practice their long game (drives) and maybe their short game (putting), but few practice the all-important transition shots (chipping). Yet for many social golfers, the transition from fairway to green is where the strokes pile up. Similarly, in tennis, the tendency among club players is to practice the baseline game (i.e., groundstrokes and serves) and the net game (i.e., volleys and overheads). Often neglected is the critical transition between the two—the approach shot, which also happens to be one of the most difficult shots in the game. The same is true in sports with offense-to-defense transitions, such as special teams in American football. Transitions may not be where the glory is, but they are a basis for victory.

Third, transitions need to be choreographed. Transitions are often the most complicated aspect of a sport both in terms of what activities must be performed and the number of people involved. As a result, transitions are a time of high vulnerability because it is particularly easy to miscommunicate and have organizational breakdowns during the transition. Also, since in many sports transitions occur much less frequently than other plays, there are even fewer opportunities within the sport to gain experience with them.

Finally, although transitions need to be choreographed, the specifics of the choreography are often arbitrary. Any number of different steps in the transitions may work. For example, there are several alternative ways to execute the baton hand-off in track relays. The key is that each of the athletes knows the transition steps, understands them, and has practiced them with the group.

An example of a well-choreographed transition is the pit stop in Formula One (F-1) auto racing. Benetton's pit-stop crew set the F-1 pit-stop world record of 3.2 seconds at the 1993 Belgian Grand Prix. Steve Matchett, a member of the current Benetton crew, claims that the perfectly executed pit stop, in which every second counts, is equal to one, two, or maybe even three overtaking maneuvers on the track. Driver Jacques Villeneuve probably would not disagree, for a poor pit-stop call at the 1996 Belgian event cost him his shot at the overall Grand Prix title. How does the Benetton crew choreograph the pit stop? According to Matchett, on the Thursday before the Sunday race, the crew determine precisely where they will locate their equipment on race day. They meticulously mark the exact position of where the four tires should stop in the pit lane as well. Time is lost if the car stops even just two inches out of place, because even this slight error will require the mechanics to reposition themselves and their equipment. They also set the precise pit-stop routine for refueling and tire changes. They mark footprint locations and check the readiness of equipment, such as quick-release jacks and air guns. The crew practices the actual pit-stop transition approximately thirty-five times during the race weekend. Teamwork and repeated practice of a carefully choreographed transition routine are the keys to consistently fast pit stops. The result is lightning-fast pit stops and a clear advantage for Benetton drivers on the Grand Prix circuit.

4×100 Meets the X86 Intel Chip

What do transitions in track and other sports have to do with business? As in sports, businesses have critical transitions—from engineering to manufacturing, from one product to the next product, from one business to the next, from one market to the next. Yet, as in sports, these transitions are rarely managed or handled well despite their importance and high degree of complexity. The key to effective transitions in business, as in sports, is to choreograph them. Although the specifics of that choreography are often fairly arbitrary, choreographed transitions can make a difference in a firm's effectiveness in rapidly and unpredictably changing markets.

An example of a company that executes transitions well is the consumer-products superstar Gillette. With average earnings climbing at more than 15 percent annually through the 1990s, Boston-based Gillette had an exemplary financial track record and an equally famous skill for churning out a steady stream of products. Key to Gillette's success was the disciplined approach that firm managers took to transitions. Under the guidance of CEO Alfred Zeien, keeping the product pipeline full was central to Gillette's strategy. To this end, transitions between products were carefully scripted, with prototypes only getting the production go-ahead once a mockup for the next big project was ready for testing. Zeien modeled his approach to transitioning on pharmaceutical companies that "harvest products that are ten years old at the same time they are launching new ones. Meanwhile, future offerings are in the testing phase." As *Fortune* commented about Gillette's approach, "That formula may not sound complicated, but its execution requires extraordinary discipline."[5]

In contrast, the absence of well-choreographed transitions can be a disaster. For example, Blockbuster, a leading video rental company, stumbled badly in 1997, in part because of a mismanaged transition from one distribution system to the next. One analyst described the blunder as follows: "Blockbuster severed its relationship with East Texas Distribution, which used to distribute tapes to the Blockbuster stores. It went in-house because it could save money by cutting out a middleman. But its new central distribution facility was not yet in place."[6]

Another illustration of stumbling on the transition is America Online (AOL). Managers at this firm stayed with an approach of promotional blitzes to stimulate growth in their customer base long after its effectiveness had diminished and well after such competitors as AT&T and Netcom had switched from an hourly fee to flat-fee pricing as a more effective way to attract new customers. In response, AOL managers did make the switch, and that switch was consistent with AOL's long-term vision to become a broadcaster on the Internet. Yet the transition was disastrous. Far more customers than AOL anticipated signed up when the fee structure changed, and AOL did not have the infrastructure to support the demand. The capacity shortfall sabotaged, at least temporarily, AOL's attempt to boost revenues through advertising. So even though AOL managers focused on the issues of what their business model should look like today and where they wanted to go, they mishandled the transition between the two.

Choreographed Transitions at Zeus

Zeus (a pseudonym) is an excellent example of a business with well-managed transitions. Zeus is a major maker of software. Successful players in the packaged software game industry design strong products, get to the market quickly with them, and grab market share. In these winner-takes-all contests, the name of the strategy game is "hit" products, and Zeus has had a lot of hits.

Zeus has not so much an "idea" environment as it does a "product" one. Of course, everyone at Zeus loves "bells and whistles," but more than most technology-based companies, they prefer bells and whistles that are useful to their customers. The best design is one that delivers something newer, faster, and better that customers actually need. The best product is the one that gets to the marketplace at the right price and the right time. Zeus managers and engineers never forget that the heart of strategy in their business is getting the right products out of development and into the market again and again.

Paying Attention

Although it may seem very simple, one of the features that distinguishes Zeus managers from many others is that they believe in managing transitions. Initially, they focused on structuring transitions within product development . . . from one product to the next. As Zeus's product development portfolio grew, managers occasionally altered the transition process to handle the increasing number of products. Later, when we studied the business, managers were in the process of creating a formal transition process for entering new markets.

Choreography

As the 4×100 relay analogy illustrated, a critical aspect of effective transitions in track is their orchestration. Stellar teams have a clear routine for baton passes that they practice repeatedly. These athletes know whether an under-hand or overhand pass will be used and whether the transition will be visual or blind. They have planned the number of arm pumps for the outgoing runner and the timing for how long the incoming runner will hold the baton. Although the specifics of the baton pass vary from team to team, within any given team there is careful orchestration. The same is true of transitions at Zeus.

A good example of choreographed transitions is project-level transition. These procedures were carried out within a carefully choreographed cycle. Managers broke down the development of products into a three-month concept development phase and a nine-month execution phase. As development on a core product neared the end of its cycle, a small group of key designers and marketers (the "lead team") shifted their focus to concept development for the next-generation product. In the meantime, the rest of the development team finished the core project, with people being released from the project according to their technical specialty.

While the lead team engaged in building a concept for the next product, the rest of the team spread out into three-month assignments on experimental projects. These projects may have involved new technologies. Team members may also have been assigned to projects in a new market area or to "blue-sky" projects. Engineers were quickly matched to projects, with some attention given to their interests and skills but with some intended randomness as well. The assignment process was finished before the three-month window began, giving the teams a running start.

Activity was frenzied during this three-month period. Several managers commented that everyone worked at least as many hours during experimental product development as during core product development. The limited time-frame was one reason. Equally important, developers were excited about working on leading-edge technology. Moreover, the projects were small, and everyone had more responsibility than usual. There was a greater sense of teamwork. The projects also provided a welcome break from the grind of the nine-month core product development cycle. During this same three-month period, a small lead team of key technical and marketing experts created the overall product concept for the next-generation core product. At the end of the period, the engineers cycled back to the core product according to their technical specialty. The cycle then repeated.

Zeus managers also managed transitions into new markets. Although these transitions were not as highly orchestrated as those for new products, managers had a rough approach that centered on creating distinct new product categories. They assessed the technical and market results for the experimental options that they had included in their current products. They combined that information with insights from two or three selected customers and strategic alliance partners. That is, Zeus managers used the experimental probes described in Chapter 5 to come up with ideas for the new product categories. They also considered the recommendations of futurists. They picked promising new product categories based on criteria that included potential market size, likely competition, and technical feasibility. Their primary rule, however, was that the product category must be attractive to a significant number of current customers. The idea was to create new product categories from probes, to innovate on technology and functionality, but to use sales to existing customers as the beachhead into the market. Then they followed up with new customers.

Haphazard Transitions at Callisto

In contrast to Zeus, managers in many businesses neglect transitions. Although they may concentrate on current businesses or on the future like Callisto (a pseudonym), they seldom manage transitions actively.

Callisto was part of Jupiter's network of businesses. Callisto participated in a hotly contested oligopoly with three other strong players. So simply keeping up with the pace of business was challenging. There was constant pressure to innovate in the product line, in product after product. Yet surprisingly, Callisto's managers did not pay much attention to the transition between projects.

No Transition Awareness

Like many managers, those at Callisto simply were unaware that transitions can be managed. They were caught up in the demands of current markets and current product generations. Occasionally, they thought about the future. But they never thought about orchestrating the transition from one product generation to the next and, at the higher level, from one business opportunity to the next. They focused feverishly on current business and then scrambled to catch up between product generations. They spent even less time planning their strategic moves into new competitive spaces.

Haphazard Procedures

Because no one at Callisto was really aware of transition management, transitions to new products and new markets were haphazard. For example, Callisto's managers did not choreograph transition processes between successive product generations, even though the projects were highly organized. Indeed, the intensity of effort expended on projects was very high, but there was a lull between projects as managers figured out what to do next. In the interim, everyone else just waited around. When developers wrapped up their projects, they relaxed. They mingled with their colleagues to find out what they were doing. As one person described it to us, the experience is like "coffee time" where everyone is "sort of hanging out with anybody else who is in between projects, to see what's happening and to wait for something to be lined up."

Callisto managers also ignored the transitions into new markets. Callisto had an R&D group that was experimenting with new technologies. Callisto managers, however, had not developed a process for transitions between these forward-looking activities and actual new businesses. There were few personal connections between the people in R&D and those in the mainstream business. Rather, when managers attempted to build a new market opportunity, they scrambled to put something together. Sometimes these haphazard efforts worked, and sometimes they did not. Every transition was unique.

An example of a haphazard transition occurred with an experimental R&D product, Genesis (a pseudonym). Genesis could have formed the basis of a new business. Early market trials suggested that the project warranted movement from experimental status to being a part of Callisto's core business portfolio. Yet Callisto's managers put Genesis on hold because no one was available to manage the opportunity. Several months later, a competitor successfully created a new business around a product similar to Genesis. As we left Callisto, senior managers were rushing to respond. In the meantime, the people who had championed Genesis were upset and frustrated as they watched their business take off . . . with a competitor's product. One manager lamented that "a more structured approach would have forced us to staff-up Genesis; as it was, it could get continuously pushed off."

Setting a Rhythm

Choreographed transitions are one aspect of time pacing. Rhythm is the other. Rhythm emerges from the pulse of choreographed transitions that are repeated at regular time intervals. Rhythm gives time pacing its energy. It creates focus, confidence, and a relentless sense of urgency that drives change. Using a second sports example, we illustrate the power of rhythm.

Graf versus Sanchez-Vicario

Wimbledon is mandatory television viewing for tennis' many devotees. But how many times have you (or your tennis-watching friends) taken a quick break from the action, come back, and found that the match had changed completely? You were watching Boris Becker beat Pete Sampras, but now Pete has the upper hand. Or when you left, Monica Seles had taken the first set, but now Martina Hingis is on top. What happened? It is simple. While you were getting your strawberries and cream, control of the match switched. More precisely, one player imposed a rhythm on the other. Indeed, most of the top tennis players have a rhythm: They favor it, practice it, and use it to dominate their opponents and win. Rhythm arises from performing a specific set of behaviors, repeatedly, at regular time intervals. The advantage of rhythm is that it can often put players into the so-called zone of concentration and confidence in which performance is enhanced and domination becomes possible.

Take the match-up between Steffi Graf and Arantxa Sanchez-Vicario. With more than twenty Grand Slam titles, Steffi is one of the premier players of all time and Germany's greatest female tennis champion. Arantxa is the first Spaniard, male or female, ever to hold the number one world ranking in the Open era. These women are two great champions but with two decidedly different rhythms.

Steffi has a staccato rhythm. She likes a fast, no-nonsense, beeline-to-the-finish pace. Never running down her service clock, she moves quickly between points. She does not dwell on past points. Fast points and fast sets are her style. Steffi likes to get ahead, stay ahead, and quickly finish off the match. She is happy if she leaves the court without a sweat. Steffi's game reflects her preferred rhythm. She is at her best when playing serve and volley. Her powerful serve lets her finish her own service games quickly. Even when receiving serves, her strong return of service lets her attack quickly and decisively. Her strengths are powerful winning shots, especially her deadly forehand, that rapidly end points.

Arantxa prefers an altogether different rhythm. She savors the moment and enjoys the performance. A crowd pleaser, she takes the time to celebrate enthusiastically when she wins great points and talks to herself after unforced errors. Arantxa excels in long, arduous sets. She loves the battle. She gets into her rhythm when her fighting spirit is aroused. Arantxa's game also reflects her preferred rhythm. She is at her best in long, hard-fought points. Her piercing groundstrokes keep her opponents at bay. She uses long rallies to set up crafty winners. She is famous for her well-disguised drop shot. Her strength is her amazing retrieval ability. Arantxa covers the entire court, returns almost everything, and literally exhausts her opponents.

When these two players meet, it is a battle of opposing rhythms. Each tries to set the pace of play and to force the other to play her game. The one who succeeds in controlling the rhythm of the match for more points and more games ultimately wins the set. When the points are long and hard, Arantxa is more likely to get into her rhythm than Steffi. When the points are short and crisp, the rhythm is to Steffi's advantage.

In the classic battle between the two in the 1995 Wimbledon final, Arantxa won the first set, 6-4. After playing to Arantxa's rhythm in the first set, Steffi took control of the pace in the second set, winning it quickly in seven games. The third set was a seesaw battle. Arantxa took her time on the changeover between games and sets, then slowed the tempo by taking more time between points. During play, she redoubled her efforts to turn points into lengthy battles. Steffi countered by trying to finish points off quickly with service and forehand winners. In the third set, neither player could dominate. Steffi managed a 7-6 victory.

Top tennis players like Graf and Sanchez-Vicario stick with their rhythm, but they also alter their rhythms for different playing surfaces and opponents. Wimbledon, with its fast grass, and the French Open, with its slow clay, represent the two extremes in tennis court surfaces. When Steffi plays at the French Open, she alters her normal rhythm and prepares for a slower tempo of play. Similarly, when Arantxa plays at Wimbledon, she expects to tune her rhythm to a faster game. At times when she might normally serve and play a point out from the baseline, she will speed up her tempo and change her rhythm to play serve and volley more often. When she might normally tire an opponent out at the baseline, play a crafty drop shot, and finish with a deadly lob, on grass she will be more likely to attack the net and finish the point quickly with an angled drop volley.

Lessons from Wimbledon

The Graf vs. Sanchez-Vicario match-up illustrates several key lessons surrounding rhythm. First, it is critical to have a rhythm. Rhythm gets players into a "zone" that imparts confidence, focus, and a sense of control, all of which create the opportunity to dominate. Rhythm gets players into the style of play that suits them best and forces others to follow.

Second, staying in a rhythm requires discipline and concentration. Great champions stay in their rhythm and even intensify that rhythm as the match progresses. If an opponent begins to gain control, these champions redouble their efforts to stay in rhythm. In contrast, less successful players often lose their concentration, slip out of their rhythm, and end up losing the match.

Third, although top tennis players have a preferred rhythm, they strategically adjust that rhythm to different conditions. For example, the grass at Wimbledon might dictate one rhythm, whereas the heat at the Australian Open might dictate another. These players also sometimes change their rhythm or tempo to surprise their opponents. They recognize that rhythm is strategic—a weapon that can be adjusted depending upon circumstances.

Tennis Champions Meet Business

What does tennis playing have to do with managing? First, like tennis players, businesses can get into a rhythm. Performing activities like launching products or entering new markets at predictable intervals and with choreographed procedures creates rhythm. When the pattern of change in an organization is rhythmic, people adjust to the beat by pacing their activities and adjusting the intensity of their efforts. Although the tempo may be fast, rhythm creates a predictability that makes people feel in control, gives them greater focus and confidence, and often increases performance. Like top tennis players, skiers in a mogul field, or cross-country runners, they can get into a rhythmic "flow" (the so-called zone) that increases their sense of urgency and raises performance levels. Second, as in tennis, it takes discipline for managers to stay in rhythm. As managers become successful or the marketplace creates surprises, managers may lose their concentration and slip out of their rhythm. Momentum is lost that can be difficult to recapture. Finally, like great tennis players, managers sometimes consciously adjust their rhythm to changing conditions such as the shifting tempo of customer demand (*entrainment*), or they may strategically switch rhythms to gain advantage over the competition.

One company that uses rhythm effectively is 3M, which produces a wide variety of commercial and consumer products. Like Intel, 3M follows an internally generated rhythm. That rhythm is set by the corporate-wide dictum to deliver a fixed percentage of sales from new products. For a number of years, that percentage was 25 percent of sales from products introduced in the past

Entrainment

Entrainment is a biological concept that refers to the linking of related rhythmic processes. That is, related rhythmic processes tend to synchronize with one another over time. For example, human body rhythms tend to synchronize with night and day cycles. This is why some people manage jet lag when traveling by immediately adjusting their schedule to the day/night schedule of their destination. In business, it is possible to entrain internal processes to external rhythms, such as seasons, customer demand, or trade shows.

four years. In the mid-nineties, 3M managers picked up the pace by raising that percentage to 30 percent. The result is a relentless urgency to innovate and change.

In contrast, Motorola is a strong firm that found a rhythm but struggled to keep it. With average revenue growth of more than 25 percent in the early 1990s, this major high-technology company known primarily for semiconductors and mobile communications (e.g., cell phones, pagers, modems, and two-way radios) appeared to be in a strong rhythm. Then Motorola's growth engine stalled. The problem was in part that Motorola managers stumbled over rhythm. As one analyst put it, "The core businesses are eroding faster than expected and new products have not yet become significant."[7] In several critical businesses, such as cellular phones, the market became less attractive. Prices fell, and demand slowed more quickly than Motorola managers could respond. At the same time, intriguing new ventures, such as cable-modems, appeared to be a long way from being revenue-generating businesses. The result was lost momentum.

Setting Rhythm at Zeus

The Zeus example that we introduced earlier in the chapter provides a further elaboration of rhythm. As with transition procedures, products are the centerpiece of rhythm management at Zeus. Within each product line, a new generation of the core product is released every twelve months. Like clockwork, Zeus engineers produce product after product. They *never* miss that timing. As the engineering director told us, "We do a new product line every year and we never miss the beat." As the vice president of marketing described it, "My objective is a product life of four quarters and then a refresh." In an industry where there is always the "features for schedule" trade-off, Zeus managers may sometimes drop features, but they never miss schedule.

In addition to the twelve-month rhythm around major generations of established products, Zeus managers have also created a rhythm of predictable intervals around entry into significant new product categories. At this new business level, Zeus managers drive the organization to introduce one distinct new product category every year. They combine this rhythm with a choreographed transition procedure that involves trying options, picking a winner, and then establishing a beachhead with current customers. This combination of choreography and rhythmic timing allows Zeus managers to pump out a flow of new businesses.

Top athletes recognize that it takes discipline to stay within their rhythm. Yet for managers, it can be very tempting to slip out of the rhythm by adding "just one more product feature." Although Zeus managers recognized the need for this discipline in an abstract way, they learned its true value through experience.

A competitor introduced an unexpectedly strong product in the middle of Zeus's twelve-month core-product development cycle. Rather than making an improvisational shift to modify the product design that was currently underway, managers decided to introduce a stopgap product, Echo (a pseudonym). This decision added a new product into the development schedule and required Zeus managers to move some people from their main project to this stopgap one. The anticipated effect was a slight delay in the release of the next core product. The actual impact was significantly greater.

Adding the stopgap product to the development schedule did, of course, delay the release of the core product. But that was not all that was affected. First, the two products ended up with overlapping features that confused the sales force and customers. Sales of both products suffered, and ultimately neither fulfilled expectations. As one manager said, "In the end, customers never really understood the product. It was a bear to sell." Second, the delay in the release of the core product had a ripple effect on the experimental projects. Rather than delay the start of the next core-product development effort, managers shortened the time window for working on their experimental projects. This change affected Zeus's probing into the future, because they ended up missing a cycle of experimentation. Finally, the transition of engineers between projects was confused. Some were on the core product, while others were assigned to Echo or to both. There was a delay in the start-up of the next core project while some of the team waited for others to catch up and managers sorted out the mess. Zeus managers vowed never again to adjust their rhythm in an ad hoc fashion.

Although switching out of rhythm was a problem with the Echo project, it did not mean that Zeus's managers were never able to adapt. In fact, man-

Table 6.1 • Time Pacing at Zeus

Process	Rhythm	Choreographed Transitions
Core product development	9-month product cycle	Experts create specifications; others work on experimental projects and join at kickoff; developers roll off by specialty.
R&D experiments	3-month cycle between major products; prototypes timed to hit annual trade show	Almost random assignment of developers to projects while experts create core product specifications.
New market entry	1 new market each year	Target new market, assess probes, use existing customers as beachhead, then extend to new customers.

agers occasionally fine-tuned their rhythm and tempo as markets and competitors evolved and when they saw an opportunity to gain strategic advantage over the competition by changing their rhythm. A good example occurred a year before our research at Zeus. Executives dramatically changed the rhythm for introducing major generations of established products by slashing the release period from fifteen to twelve months. The reason was that these executives wanted to set a faster industry pace. They believed that they could provide a more rapid execution than the competition and that customers would respond favorably. They were right. So, much like Graf or Sanchez-Vicario, Zeus managers use rhythm to control the pace of the market.

Missing the Beat at Callisto

In contrast to Zeus, managers at Callisto did not rely on rhythm. They reactively managed their business in response to events, rather than the rhythmic pacing of predictable timing. For example, compare product development at Callisto and Zeus. At Callisto, there was no predictable timing for ending development projects. Projects were planned for varying time lengths, and those lengths were often adjusted, such as for adding new features. Sometimes projects ended earlier than expected. More often, projects stretched out much longer than anticipated. The lulls between projects, the so-called coffee time, added to the confusion and stifled opportunities to build momentum in the organization. Rather than pacing to time, Callisto managers changed with events. If a competitor introduced a new product, they reacted. If development completed a project, they introduced it to the market. If a new business opportunity appeared, Callisto managers responded if they could. Callisto never gained a rhythm and never found their "zone."

The only rhythmic process that we observed at Callisto was the annual corporate planning cycle. Once a year, managers at Callisto developed a business plan that was sent to corporate headquarters. The process involved the "roll-up" of functional plans (e.g., marketing, engineering, finance) into a business-level plan that also included a survey of the competitive landscape, major resource allocations, and commitments to specific bottom line results.

The rhythm of this annual planning cycle worked adequately well in Jupiter's slow-moving businesses like very high-performance computing. The rigidity of the annual planning process did make mid-course adjustments difficult. But market and technical change was usually slow enough to make a once a year transition workable. This process worked much less well for Callisto. The rhythm of annual planning was just too slow for the rate of change that was common in Callisto's segment of the industry. As a result, the process was not very valuable because plans were quickly outdated. Callisto managers ended up planning for a time horizon within which all they could do was guess, while having to take time away from running their real business.

Implications of Time Pacing

Time Pacing at Zeus

Time pacing, through a combination of choreography and rhythm, had several strategic implications at Zeus. First, it explicitly tied future strategy to current business. In many other firms, managers separate the two.

Second, choreography and rhythm efficiently orchestrated the very complicated and mistake-prone processes involving numerous people and resources that surround transitions. Just as a carefully routinized pit stop in F-1 car racing quickly brings competitors back into the race, so too did choreographed transition procedures get people at Zeus back into their business "race." The result was momentum and fast, smooth flow from today's to tomorrow's businesses. A telling visual image of this effect is Tarzan, an analogy suggested by one of the managers in our study. Think of a managerial "Tarzan" swinging from vine to vine (Zeus) versus another "Tarzan" dropping from one vine, landing on the ground, and then searching for the next vine (Callisto).

Time pacing also enabled people to pace the intensity of their work, synchronize with others, and sometimes get into a "zone" in which they were particularly focused, confident, and high performing. To capture the feeling at Zeus, think of walking into a stadium full of people doing the "wave." People are in synch, they have the beat, and they know what is coming next. There is a focused flow of attention and even an urgency that keeps people driven to maintain the wave.

More subtly, time pacing enhanced strategic options. As one Zeus manager astutely observed, "The structure from our cycle gives us the freedom we need to adjust." Zeus managers used the periodic transitions to survey the competitive landscape and reevaluate strategic direction before lowering their collective heads to get back to work. Zeus managers chose a rhythm (first fifteen months, then twelve months, then nine months) that they believed matched the demands of their markets. As a result, they created natural break points that were entrained with the rate of change in the industry. Moreover, when Zeus managers reevaluated pace, they did so strategically. Unlike most managers, they had an elaborate view of how to use pace as part of their strategic arsenal that went beyond simply being faster or preempting the market once or twice. Finally, Zeus's control of pacing made it a predictable partner for complementary business allies and for customers.

Overall, Zeus has a history of outstanding performance and has maintained leadership in its segment of the industry. Time pacing, built on choreographed transitions and setting a rhythm, has been a critical success factor. Through a relentless flow of new products and moves into new business opportunities, Zeus has outdistanced numerous competitors and set the pace of strategic change within its portion of the industry.

Event Pacing at Callisto

In contrast to the effective time pacing at Zeus, haphazard, unpredictable transitions at Callisto created an erratic flow of new products and transitions into new businesses. Unexpected beginnings and endings of projects often caught Callisto's managers with too few people. For example, one engineering manager described such a project that she had to staff: "I'm supposed to start this project immediately and I have no resources." This project was eventually late.

Sometimes managers had the wrong people and so had to wait or to staff projects with whomever was available. One Callisto manager described a typical experience. He recalled, "I wasn't the first choice by any stretch, but I was free and so this new project was offered to me." He told us that he actually did not know much about the new project but was trying to make do.

At other times, too many people were available, and so managers would take on make-work projects. Typically, these make-work projects were small in order to avoid tying up too many resources. Yet when there were several make-work projects at one time, they actually accounted for a substantial amount of resources. Moreover, they often had little to do with the central mission of the business. For example one manager said, "What many of my people are working on now is not really central to our business." Ironically, this manager eventually needed some of the people who were assigned to the make-work project for an important new one, but by then he had to wait for people to become available.

Overall, haphazard transitions and unpredictable timing created gaps between the present and the future at Callisto. These gaps were particularly apparent in the erratic flow of both new products and new businesses. Callisto has had success but has not been able to win consistently.

Getting into the Rhythm of Time Pacing

Below we have reprinted the time pacing survey from the beginning of the chapter.

New product or service concepts are introduced in your business at rhythmic intervals.   T or F

Your business has specific metrics, such as time to launch a global product, months to deliver a product, or percentage of annual revenue from new sources, that evaluate performance using time.   T or F

Your business has explicit procedures for transitions such as moving into new products or markets, integrating acquisitions, or ramping up to volume manufacturing.   T or F

Your business has a routine for leaving old business areas.   T or F

Your business is synchronized with the rhythms of key customers and suppliers.   T or F

If you answered "F" to many of the preceding questions, then your business resembles Callisto in that little attention is given to time pacing. A useful first step is to inventory your major transition processes, such as transitions between products, market entries, establishment of strategic alliances, or ramp-ups to volume production. Also consider processes like decision making where time limits might help people to pace their efforts. Figure out how long, on the average, each process takes to execute and whether the processes are choreographed. Also, inventory any rhythms that already exist in your business—like manufacturing cycle times or annual planning reviews. Then, choreograph some of the most critical transitions. The specifics of transition procedures are often arbitrary. What matters most is that they are specified and well-known. Remember that businesses can often benefit from choreographed transitions even if they never fully time pace.

The more challenging aspect of time pacing is setting the rhythm. List the important external rhythms of the business, such as seasonality, trade show dates, customer demand, and the rhythm of competitor product or service upgrades. Then match each internal rhythm with an important external one. For some processes, your internal pace may be too slow, requiring you to speed up these processes. Initially, you will probably underestimate your ability to time pace. Keep in mind that you probably can time pace more than you think you can.

If your business is like Zeus, then you answered "T" to many of the survey questions, and you are already practicing time pacing. It is important to recognize the significance of time pacing to your business success. Managers often underestimate the value of time pacing in what they do. Consequently, they either lose their time pacing discipline or miss opportunities to use time pacing as a strategic weapon. Be aware that your transition procedures and rhythm may need periodic adjustment to fit changing circumstances. For rhythm, this is particularly critical because the right rhythm often depends on forces outside your business—such as customers, complementers, and competitors. Be careful to manage the disruption that occurs when changing either transition procedures or rhythm. Finally, although time pacing is effective, every manager must also sometimes rely on event pacing as well.[8]

A Final Note on Time Pacing

One of the operative adjectives in thinking about time pacing is "relentless." When change is triggered by an internal rhythm that is entrained to a fast-moving marketplace, it creates an unremitting sense of urgency. At Zeus, some managers feel that they are pushing too hard and that their personal lives are suffering. Zeus is winning, but at what price?

There is no easy answer to this question. But it is important to contrast the stress created by pacing to that of working in a business that ignores time pacing. If a business is not driven by its own pace, it will be driven by the actions of other firms. The result is even greater uncertainty about the future and when the pace might change. Such event pacing also increases the likelihood of "death marches" to catch up with competitors who suddenly and unexpectedly jump ahead. Without time pacing, businesses are more likely to experience periods of poor performance. Overall, the result is often anxiety, managers who have not had time to re-energize themselves, and fatigued employees who leave the company after death marches. Although time pacing does inherently create a stressful environment, it is not necessarily more stressful than that created by the lack of time pacing.

There are a variety of options available to managers to alleviate the stress of time pacing. Zeus's creative approach, described earlier in this chapter, is one. Developers at Zeus are cycled onto experimental projects to give them relief from the grind of core-product development. Humor and a sense of fun also help. For longer term stress release, many Silicon Valley companies approach the problem by giving their employees sabbaticals—paid leaves of absence for several months—typically every five to seven years of service. Finally, simply realizing that time pacing is a stressful, but successful and efficient, competitive strategy can be very helpful.

A world of made is not a

world of born.

e. e. cummings

growing the strategy

$165 BILLION . . . That enormous accumulation of wealth is what *Business Week* claims is roughly the shareholder value created in the retail industry from the mid-80s to the mid-90s. Who were the big winners? Wal-Mart was responsible for $42 billion and Home Depot accounted for another $20 billion. All told, about twenty-five companies accounted for 85 percent of the value created. Who were the losers? America's largest retailer—arguably the icon of U.S. retailing—was one, creating a paltry $1 billion of value, at the most. Even as Wal-Mart moved aggressively to become the king of discount retailers and Home Depot shaped itself into a "category-killer," Sears, Roebuck & Co. took a beating. Sears was trapped in time, a dinosaur. Its market value was just one measure of how far the leading U.S. retailer had fallen.

Founded about a century ago, Sears had been a stunningly innovative firm, setting the pace for change in the retail industry. Its record shows a long string of successes. The firm pioneered the concept of catalog shopping. Then, in the years between the two world wars, Sears was the first to create the department store format. And in the post–World War II era, Sears was at the forefront of the parade again, this time in the march to the suburban shopping mall. By the 1960s, Sears seemed unassailable in its position as the dominant U.S. retailer . . . the retailer "where America shops."

Yet in the three decades since 1960, Sears has struggled. A succession of Sears senior executives (and certainly their employees) recognized that the firm was on a downward spiral to obscurity. Sears management eventually woke up to the fact that Kmart and Wal-Mart were their real competition and that these competitors had different and faster business models. So, realization of the need to revitalize Sears was not the issue. Rather, the issue was how to change . . . and not just once, but continually.

It's hard to pick a start date for when Sears executives began attempting to transform the firm.

- Maybe it was the early 1980s when Sears executives embarked on their financial services strategy by assembling, through acquisitions, a portfolio of businesses that included such firms as Dean Witter in brokerage, Coldwell Banker in real estate, and Allstate in insurance.

- Or maybe it was in 1988, when CEO Ed Brennan introduced the "everyday low pricing" strategy, calling it "the most important thing that we've done in 25 years."

- Or maybe it was when Sears launched the "Brand Central" strategy, which split the stores into boutiques organized around specific high-profile brands. As Brennan put it, "Our strategy is to position ourselves as a powerful specialty merchant in each of our individual businesses."

- Or maybe it was in the early 1990s, when senior executives restructured Sears by lopping off their financial services empire, the very successful Discover credit card, a stake in the Prodigy online computing service, and even the giant Sears Tower in downtown Chicago.

- Or maybe it was when Sears executives adopted a more conservative approach. Arthur Martinez, a senior executive at tony Saks Fifth Avenue, was brought on board in 1992, and he, in turn, closed more than 100 stores, laid off approximately 50,000 people, and even shuttered the venerable catalog business. Only the very core of the retail business was left. At the time, some observers questioned the moves. One noted, "Mr. Martinez' strategy is conservative, perhaps dangerously so."[1]

Until recently, the paths to revitalize Sears never seemed to lead anywhere. As one major news journal put it, "Can you really blame anyone for responding with an emphatic ho-hum to news of Sears, Roebuck & Co.'s latest turnaround effort? What is this, the third, fourth, or fifth strategy in so many years?"[2] Sears executives wanted to kickstart the company, launch it into new and growing markets, and transform the retailer into a truly world-class player again. They just could not seem to get there. The nadir was probably the 1992 automobile repair scandal, in which excessive financial pressure from corporate headquarters apparently led some personnel at Sears automotive centers to knowingly lead customers into buying unnecessary car repairs. California and other states responded with charges of massive consumer fraud.

Where did Sears executives go wrong? After all, they had visions for growing the company. They assembled competences that made sense in the context of those visions, and they knew how to pick promising markets, such as the booming financial services sector. Their disastrous everyday low pricing strategy, which flopped as a business approach and led to false advertising lawsuits, reportedly was the fruit of a relationship with a leading strategy consultant. Yet the company did not really transform into a business that could compete successfully in a highly competitive, rapidly changing industry.

The Sears story is not unique. The stagnation and even decline of established corporations around the globe, such as Japan's Nissan, Europe's Alcatel and Bull, and U.S. firms like Digital Equipment and most of Big Steel, is not news. It is obvious as well that companies pursuing more fast-paced, change-oriented business models like Nucor, Nokia, Home Depot, and Cisco Systems are prospering against these ponderous dinosaurs. As IBM's patriarch, Thomas J. Watson, Sr., once said, "It's harder to keep a business great than it is to build it."[3]

The challenge of transforming businesses into ones that can reinvent themselves is not just the province of big, bureaucratic dinosaurs. New firms often cannot change or ultimately grow beyond their first successes. The managers of Internet hotshots like Yahoo!, Amazon.com, and Netscape are clearly facing the challenge of discerning the formula for reinvention and growth in their own businesses.

A principal reason companies do not become businesses that can reinvent themselves is that their managers take a rational, even mechanistic approach to developing their businesses. These managers are often locked into the implicit assumption that a business is like a machine. They understand rational tasks like identifying markets, spotting competences, and creating visions, but they miss the insight that businesses are also living things. This distinction is absolutely fundamental. Living things grow. They adapt and evolve with shifting competition and varying climate. Change is what living things do. In contrast, machines run. They mostly don't change, or if they do, it is because they have been built, like neural nets, to mimic living things. Machines are built by assembling component pieces. Living things develop and evolve over time.

This chapter explores how a competing on the edge strategy is developed. A key distinction between businesses that are successful developers of the strategy and those that are not is the difference between machines versus living things, generally, and specifically, assembly versus growth. In the case of Sears, executives took a mechanistic approach. They tried to assemble their company from parts of businesses, flip a switch, and watch it run. They failed to realize that a company competing on the edge is not a machine. A constantly changing company is closer to an ecological community than a car. Whereas a car, a tank, or a toaster is assembled, an ecological community must be developed over time. Growing means that the starting point matters, order matters, and there are missing links in the process.

What has happened to Sears? In the 1990s, company executives have taken a strategic approach that is much closer to growing than to their assembly strategy of the past. When the new CEO, Arthur Martinez, took over in the early 1990s, his first step was to prune back the corporation and focus resources on regenerating the core retail business. After these steps, one observer commented, "Sears is—for the first time since 1931—just a retailer."[4] On this revived retailing base, Martinez began to branch out into new retail concepts like dealer stores (a collaborative arrangement with dealer-owners), stronger use of the powerful Sears brands, such as Craftsman, Kenmore, DieHard, and Weatherbeater, and stand-alone specialty outlets. As Martinez said at the time, "Only now have we earned the right to think about growth."[5] Sears appears to be finally moving on a path toward developing a competing on the edge strategy.

Creating a Prairie

Everyone who travels in the United States knows Chicago's O'Hare Airport. It's one of the busiest airports in the world. It's the airport to avoid in winter. It's the travel crossroads of the country, serving the third-largest U.S. city. It's even been a movie star—in *Airport*, of course. If you change planes there, O'Hare seems immense. If you need to get downtown, the Kennedy Expressway is usually impossibly jammed with cars and trucks. Throw in a Cubs game and you have an endless tie-up. But O'Hare wasn't always like this.

Imagine yourself at O'Hare at a far different time . . . not in 1998, but in 1898 or even in 1798, before the patchwork quilt of roads, fences, and farms had changed the midwestern landscape forever. Around you would be an abundance of plants, long grasses of various colors, a palette of flowers, some trees. You would see the original "amber waves of grain." If you waited a little while, you'd also see a variety of animals going about their daily ritual. You would be enjoying a living, breathing prairie that stretched a thousand miles to the Rocky Mountains. It is an ecological system that today is virtually extinct.

Suppose that you were given the task of re-creating that prairie as it was 200 years ago. Assume that you have no budget constraints. Also assume that you cannot buy the prairie but rather that you have to create your own. As you think about how you would approach the problem, jot down the key steps to your solution.

If you are like most people (or at least our friends), you probably came up with a list that is something like this:

Step 1: Buy a plot of land where a prairie likely thrived in the past, for example, on the outskirts of Chicago—O'Hare.

Step 2: Check the libraries. Look for old photos of the prairie. Obtain the most complete list available of all the plant and animal members of a prairie ecosystem.

Step 3: Collect samples of all the relevant species (e.g., seeds of plants and male/female pairs of animals).

Step 4: Clear the plot of land and plant your seeds, along with a few trees.

Step 5: Release the animals into the plot of land.

Step 6: Watch and wait.

Perhaps you added a few other steps with more intervention, like fertilization or watering, but overall you likely suggested some kind of approach that we will loosely call "assemble." That is, the steps you listed were to clear out your work space, get the component plants and animals, lay out the blueprint, follow the directions, and start assembling. You could then piece together the various components of the prairie . . . and hope that somehow a prairie emerges.

This approach is quite reasonable. It seems intuitively correct. If you were assembling a car, a house, or a toaster, it would probably work. All you would have to do would be to assemble the components of the desired system on a reasonably attractive plot of land, and eventually a prairie would emerge. It makes sense. Right?

Wrong. Assembly doesn't work, or at least not for a prairie. A prairie is something that grows. It has to start small. It has pieces that interact and build on each other. Once it is "up and running," the prairie works as a complex system that is dependent on the intricate interaction of all the components of the system. A prairie cannot be brought to life with one "abracadabra," one wave of the magic wand.

Ecologists have, in fact, experimented with trying to grow prairies. Early experimenters took the assemble approach, but they ran into complications. Urban weeds are one such complication. Relative to most prairie species, these noxious weeds are aggressive and fast growing. Given a chance, these tough weeds will "muscle out" the more timid prairie species and prohibit them from thriving. Knowing this, early ecologists began their work by clearing their fields of weeds and then planting prairie grass seeds. Then the prairie flourished. Right? Wrong—the prairie never emerged from these cleared plots.

What happened? The problem with this logic is that the first plants to sprout and grow in a freshly cleared field are the most aggressive, fastest-growing weeds. So even though the prairie seeds were planted first, the urban weeds took over the cleared soil, and the prairie never took hold. In contrast, an existing weed-filled field has a mixture of early aggressive weeds and slower growing, late-arrival weeds. This environment is much more hospitable to prairie seeds. In fact, some of the slower-growing, late-blooming weeds are actually members of the prairie family, and their presence facilitates the transition to a prairie. In contrast to earlier experiments, in later ones prairie seeds were added to weed-filled fields rather than cleared ones.

In later experiments, ecologists extended the grow—not assemble—approach. In particular, in one successful experiment in Illinois, ecologists grew a prairie savanna (i.e., a prairie with trees).[6] They began by planting a sample of choice prairie savanna seeds in wooded, weed-filled fields on the outskirts of Chicago. With careful management (e.g., clearing of underbrush), the fields filled with a myriad of rare wildflowers in only two years. Then, amid the bottlebrush grass and savanna blazing star, eastern bluebirds began to appear. These birds had not made an appearance in the area for decades. Next, species of plants that had not been seeded somehow emerged. The seeds for these endangered plants must have either been dormant, waiting for the right conditions, or were brought in by the growing bird population.

Butterflies that had not been in Illinois for decades found this emerging prairie savanna. Interestingly, the classic prairie savanna butterfly—an Edwards hairstreak—took its time to make an appearance. Not seeing it early on, entomologists questioned whether the Chicago experiment was really a prairie savanna. But by the fifth year of the experiment, the fields were filled with Edwards hairstreak butterflies. Slowly, the species came, and slowly the fields evolved from weeds toward becoming a true prairie savanna.

As the experiments continued, ecologists learned more lessons about re-creating prairies. They learned that order matters. Reversing the introduction of one species and another (e.g., reversing the order of entry of two predators) alters the ecosystem that emerges. Adding or subtracting a species also alters the system, affecting its final states and its resilience to change.

Perhaps the most subtle lesson to learn was that not all of the essential ingredients to growing a prairie savanna are visible at the end. Ecologists learned this lesson when they were stymied in their efforts. They were close to creating prairie, but something was not quite right. Half-breed prairies were being created—a mixture of prairie species and nonprairie species. The experiments didn't seem to be capable of evolving into that final step of a pure prairie. The ecologists searched for key components of a prairie that might be missing. But this was the whole problem: they were searching for something that they thought should be there, but wasn't. Instead, ecologists should have been looking for something that had been there, but did not stay. In other words, a fleeting member of the prairie system, a missing link.

Was there a missing link that was not present in the mature prairie but was essential to growing it? Yes—that missing link was fire. Initially, ecologists failed to introduce fire into their experimental prairie systems. Because its presence is not explicit in the final product, it was not an immediately obvious candidate to be deliberately added. Moreover, although ecologists were trying to mimic nature and minimally manage the fields of emerging prairie, the incidence of wildfires was far lower than it would have been in a true natural setting. Without fire, ecologists could not create the elusive pure-bred prairie. Fire triggers certain prairie seeds to sprout and eliminates many fire-intolerant urban plants. Without fire, there is no prairie.

Lessons from the Prairie

The prairie example illustrates the lessons of trying to create a living thing like an anthill, an ecosystem, or even a business . . . something that does not behave mechanically but rather something that can change and grow over time. There are several lessons here.

The first lesson is that living things are grown, not assembled. The various species of a prairie are too interdependent to be assembled in one single, massive act of change. It is not only difficult but also impossible to know beforehand how the myriad of components will interact to create the final system. Key to creating a prairie is realizing that it is not a highly controlled, single act of creation, but rather an evolution toward a desired end. With this in mind, ecologists approach the "re-create a prairie" problem we posed at the beginning of the chapter quite differently from most people. Rather than assemble all of the components at once, they create a small subsystem of their ultimate objective, a prairie. Then they nurture that subsystem, stabilize it, and use it as a foundation to grow more of the prairie. Their approach is to grow, not assemble.

The second lesson is that the starting point matters. In the prairie, for example, it is not effective to start with a cleared plot. Rather, you start with weeds and grow from there. A cleared plot will produce an ecosystem, but it will not be a prairie.

Third, the order matters. Build an ecosystem with one order and you get one result. Switch the order, and you get something else. Add a species, and you will get still another. Consider another example, the process of cooking a

---

- **Grow–do not assemble**
  Actually evolve into something different over time, not construct at one point in time

- **The starting point matters**
  Grow from current position

- **Order matters**
  A soufflé will only emerge, for example, if ingredients are added in the right order

- **Watch for missing links**
  Understand that what you temporarily have might not be part of the final system

---

Figure 7.1 • Basics of Growth

souffló—which is an art, not a science. The list of ingredients is simple—butter, egg yolks, egg whites, cheese, and milk. But despite the simple list, a beginning chef who is unaware that the egg whites must be added last will fail completely. In the right order, the simple ingredients grow into a splendid creation. In the wrong order, the result is nothing close to a soufflé.

Finally, it is important to understand that there may be missing links that are hidden from the final result but are nonetheless central to creating a living thing. They are temporary, but they are also essential. The appearance and disappearance of key components that are not part of the final system are often part of how living things grow.

Growing a Competing on the Edge Strategy

Although the prairie example reveals some of the basics of growth, it is rather distant from business. How do the lessons from creating a prairie actually play out in a business? A greenfields example, that of Hewlett-Packard's expansion move into Singapore, will help you gain some insight into how to grow a competing on the edge business.[7]

Creating HP-Singapore

In 1970 Hewlett-Packard (HP), a premier U.S. multinational, launched Computer Products Singapore (CPS). The objective was to establish a presence in Southeast Asia as part of an overall interest in globalization at HP. The goal was to create a design and development center in Asia with the potential for full-blown division status. Almost three decades later, the venture has become a vibrant global center for design, development, and manufacturing within HP. How did CPS get there?

Step 1: Start with a Current Business

At the outset, CPS was deliberately set up as a low-cost manufacturing operation. The focus was on the simplest kind of manufacturing, labor-intensive assembly of components, and simple products. The first components were core computer memories, and the first products were HP-35 calculators, transferred from factories in the United States. Although the manufacturing was very basic, HP planned to build the operation. So, from the beginning, HP managers included a quality improvement program that encouraged Singaporeans to develop their manufacturing skills.

People at CPS slowly built up their expertise in assembly manufacturing and thus enhanced their ability to deliver high-quality products at lower and lower cost. For the HP-35 calculator, for example, CPS reduced the manufacturing costs of the product substantially. With these successes and with continued enhancement of manufacturing capability, HP gradually transferred more products from the United States to Singapore. By the late 1970s, CPS was manufacturing not only calculators but keyboards, displays, and other computer components as well. This set the pattern at CPS of first developing a capability platform and then reproducing that capability across similar activities.

Step 2: Flesh Out the Current Business

In the early 1980s, CPS switched from a focus on assembling only to cost engineering as well. That is, they began to propose simple design changes to existing products in order to reduce the manufacturing costs even further. As always, HP took the time to build the capability within the Singaporean staff. A good example was the HP-41C, a sophisticated calculator. Managers at CPS set an ambitious goal of reducing costs by half, a goal that could only be achieved by redesigning the calculator at the level of the integrated circuit board. CPS sent about twenty Singaporean engineers and technicians to the United States for a year to learn about this kind of calculator design. When this group returned to Singapore, they brought with them sufficient expertise to enable CPS to reduce calculator manufacturing costs by 50 percent.

From their base in manufacturing and cost engineering, CPS extended into the redesign of more products and into higher-volume manufacturing. The group began with keyboards and then moved into more complicated products, such as printers. As CPS became more sophisticated in high-volume, low-cost manufacturing, the group continued to reduce production costs. A prime example was the ThinkJet printer, a strategically crucial product. The manufacturing of this product was given to CPS only four months after its introduction in the United States. Strikingly, CPS drove the manufacturing costs for the ThinkJet printer down by 30 percent in one year.

Eventually, CPS moved into product design for an established line of business. Under the guidance of a senior American manager, the Singapore engineering group built design and development skills. Again, CPS began with keyboards, and by 1986 the group had won sole responsibility for supplying HP with keyboards. At this point, CPS had complete responsibility for the keyboards business, including design and manufacturing.

Step 3: Regenerate from the Past, Experiment with the Future

With the current business in keyboards operating effectively, CPS management began to look to the future and how to continue reinventing the business. The CPS team decided that the logical move was to build their future around serving Asian markets. With this vision in mind, they began to discuss strategies for getting into the Asian printer market. This led to the development of Capricorn, their entry product into the Japanese printer market. This was the first printer product developed entirely at CPS. To enter the market quickly, the CPS team leveraged heavily off of existing DeskJet product designs and the experience they had gained from co-managing other printer projects. Yet the design challenge was still significant, because the new printer had to be substantially smaller than existing HP printers to meet the needs of the Asian market. Moreover, the CPS team recognized the importance of creating a brand image in Japan and the lasting impact their first product release would have. The CPS team knew that Capricorn was not the ideal product, but the compromises made were carefully thought through; the team also knew that they could only really start to learn about the Japanese market once they were playing in it. So Capricorn became a CPS experiment within the context of the vision of CPS as a center of Asian business.

Step 4: Time Pacing

As a final step, CPS created a series of linked moves to get in sync with the pace of Asian markets. CPS managers understood that they needed to have an organization that could continuously create new products if they were to be a viable stand-alone division over the long term. Through a series of adroit moves, the management team established a sense of rhythm at CPS that was tied to the demands of the Japanese market. The first move was the release of Capricorn. Capricorn was not a "home run," but it certainly accomplished its objective of establishing a toehold for HP in the Japanese printer market.

CPS managers followed Capricorn quickly with the release of a color printer (code named Scorpio). Again, this was leveraged from a U.S. design, which allowed CPS to rapidly release a new product to the Japanese market. Again, however, the product was not perfect. Even so, it did offer a unique feature—customized postcard creation—that was very attractive to the Japanese market. The CPS team decided that continued presence in the market was essential (Japanese customers were accustomed to very rapid new model introductions) and released Scorpio in Japan only nine months after the introduction of Capricorn.

Scorpio was suprisingly successful. With their toehold now a foothold, CPS could concentrate on a completely redesigned printer that would meet all the needs of the Japanese market. Working with Japanese vendors, CPS created a completely new product—a portable DeskJet. It was released in Japan only five months after the introduction of Scorpio. This was the first HP product ever released in Japan before being introduced in the United States and Europe. The product was very successful, and a U.S. release soon followed. Having established its presence in Asia, CPS subsequently received worldwide responsibility for all portable printer products. It was now an independent HP business unit.

Lessons from HP-Singapore

With the creation of HP-Singapore, HP established a vibrant, growing part of the corporation that has continued to flourish and change. This example indicates how some of the basic lessons about assemble versus growth, developed earlier in the prairie example, are achieved in a business. There are several lessons to be drawn from the experience of HP-Singapore.

First, like a prairie, HP-Singapore was grown over time, not assembled. Taking one step at a time, CPS evolved toward the business that everyone wanted them to be—an organization that could continue to reinvent itself. A simple pattern of growth emerged. The steps were to start with something simple (e.g., assembly manufacturing), build the capability to execute that simple thing very well (e.g., quality improvement programs, U.S. training), reproduce that capability in other contexts (e.g., new products, volume manufacturing), and add another capability (e.g., product design) on top of the existing platform of capabilities. Then the process would be repeated. It's

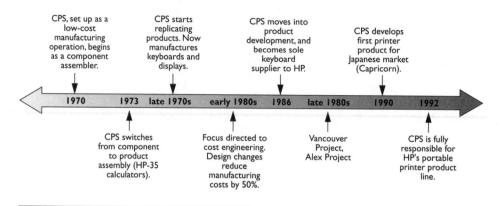

Figure 7.2 • Hewlett-Packard, Singapore

what we call the "inch-worm" approach to creating a competing on the edge business.

Second, the experience of HP-Singapore suggests that the smart starting point for growing a business is a simple, well-known aspect of a current business. In this case, the starting point was assembly manufacturing. HP managers did not begin by trying to launch something futuristic or to do something that went well beyond the existing expertise of the Singaporeans.

Third, the HP-Singapore example provides insight into the order that we see in the successful development of a competing on the edge strategy. CPS managers first created the foundation of a stable current business. Then they added growth opportunities built on that foundation and around a vision of the future business. As a final step, the CPS team developed a rhythm that was entrained to their target Asian markets.

What about missing links? As usual, missing links are subtle, but they are there. They show up in the history of HP-Singapore as failed opportunities that were turned into learning. This learning then had a later, more tangible impact. One example occurred just prior to the development of the Capricorn printer. Singaporean and U.S. engineers joined together to co-design a new, very low-cost printer, which was code-named ALEX. Although the experience was not particularly successful and the printer was never finished, the Singaporeans learned a tremendous amount about the product, project management, and strategy, more generally. Without this experience, the CPS team would have struggled to manage their first Japanese products. Yet a snapshot of HP-Singapore's successful portable printer division today would show no evidence of the influence of ALEX on the evolution of CPS. ALEX was a missing link.

Converting to a Competing on the Edge Strategy

The approach described so far applies to creating ecosystems like prairies and new ventures like HP-Singapore. But what about transforming established businesses? Do the same principles like starting position and order entry matter? Are there still missing links? And can the transformation process go faster than the twenty-plus years it took to launch HP-Singapore?

Two of the firms that we studied provide some answers to these questions. Both faced performance declines that led their managers to attempt to transform their respective firms. Our data from these experiences let us analyze how transformation really occurs. Moreover, since one firm was successful and one was not, the comparison allowed us also to draw some conclusions about how effective (and not so effective) transformation occurs. As it turned out, the more successful firm followed the lessons of the prairie and HP-Singapore in order to develop a competing on the edge strategy.

Tai-pan versus Royal

Tai-pan is the high-flying, diversified computing firm profiled in Chapter 3 in the discussion of cross-business synergies. Although Tai-pan is now an undisputed market leader in the industry, its fortunes were not always so rosy. The company underwent a major turnaround in the 1990s. The once-successful firm had slipped into bureaucratic gridlock. Its business pace had slowed, its competitors were sprinting by, and its products were becoming dated.

Royal also had once been a strong performer but was now struggling in the industry. We introduced Royal in Chapter 2, where we described its chaotic multimedia venture. Royal also had a long-time, core business of mainframes. This part of Royal had become entrenched in its traditional market and had not really figured out how to change.

Royal and Tai-pan faced some similar performance difficulties. They had both been strong players in the industry, but they were being overtaken by firms with faster business models. The question was how could both firms recover. Tai-pan was successful in transforming, but Royal was not. What was the difference between them?

The Starting Point

Both Tai-pan and Royal had many problems, ranging from poor product development processes to weak creation of new market opportunities and duplication of efforts across business units. At Tai-pan, products were overengineered and overpriced. At Royal, products were late to market and dated. In their core businesses, both firms were losing market share and were being successfully attacked by faster, leaner competitors with more efficient business models. In terms of the future, neither firm was effectively launching entries into the new markets of client/server computing, Internet applications, and multimedia. To use a basketball analogy, both Tai-pan and Royal were playing at half-speed in a full-court press game. There were many possible starting points to begin their transformations.

Royal: Starting with the Future

Royal's senior executive team started with the future. They reacted to their problems by spending six months in developing a new five-year strategic plan for the corporation. These executives had tried to kickstart Royal before, but this was the first time that they had extensively involved many of the key executives within the firm for an extensive period.

The detailed new plan required Royal to transform itself from a mainframe computing firm into a client/server based company, and to do so on a fast track. The reinvention strategy called for milking the current business as the cash cow. As one executive described it, "We want to exploit the relatively mature business, give it some mid-life kickers, and ramp it down." This meant a modest set of new products to keep extending the old business, coupled with layoffs, and ultimately shuttering the business.

Part two of the plan was to use this cash to fund an aggressive switch to client/server and other new computing markets. Client/server, in particular, was a natural extension of Royal's older business of mainframes because of the similarity in customers and their fundamental computing needs. As one manager said, "We want to keep the revenues up as long as possible on the legacy systems, try to draw the time out that we can squeeze revenue out of the cash cows, while we move into new business opportunities." The company's multimedia move described in Chapter 2 was part of this future-oriented focus as well.

Timing was an especially critical aspect of the plan. Royal managers figured that they would be able to have a viable client/server business soon, and so they concentrated on building up that business rapidly while gradually moving people out of the old Royal. A manager told us, "As with anything else, it's a mixture of providing products that the customer will actually buy today and having the vision to start to develop those products they want in the future."

Royal managers therefore directed their efforts toward developing a plan for the future—a strategy of phasing out the current business while ramping up the new. The strategy had both the overall approach and the specific product plans for what each business would roll out. But Royal managers forgot about actually executing these plans, especially in their current businesses. They stripped the best people from the existing businesses and jumped boldly into the future. They headed full steam into new computing markets and the development of next-generation computing products.

Tai-pan: Starting with the Present

In contrast to Royal's approach of starting the transformation process by focusing on the future, Tai-pan's management team began with current operations. They looked at the firm's underperformance in day-to-day competition in its core businesses. A quick analysis of current operations revealed high costs, declining market share, and a tendency to put the wrong features into products. In Tai-pan's core businesses, competitors had come in with lower costs and the features that people wanted. This is where Tai-pan's managers decided to put their emphasis. In some ways, this was a surprising choice. This business was maturing, cutthroat, and it had declining margins. Yet Tai-pan began by reviving its current businesses, not jumping to future ones.

The outside world saw a reengineering strategy. Tai-pan managers slashed product costs and cut technology investment. They also revamped the product line and shifted their emphasis to high-reliability computing at a low price. They brought manufacturing costs down through logistics improvements and global partnerships. From the inside, it was a more complete story. Tai-pan's managers accomplished these external moves by shifting the internal organization to what we would term the edge of chaos. Throughout the corporation, Tai-pan's managers revamped their way of managing the current businesses to more closely resemble the improvisational and coadaptive processes described in Chapters 2 and 3.

For example, in one business unit, managers determined (with some prodding from corporate headquarters) that they were partly understructured and partly overstructured. Analyses revealed that the setting of priorities and the assignment of responsibilities needed to be much more structured and deliberate. Moreover, communication was scattershot and less frequent than most managers perceived to be appropriate. Yet the business was also overstructured. For example, product innovation was very lockstep and linear. There were elaborate systems for creating new products, such as extensive specification procedures and progress checkpoints that constrained engineers from adapting to new technologies and customer shifts. It was almost impossible to improvise.

What Tai-pan managers did first was strip away much of the old structure that had channeled key operating processes like product innovation into a lockstep march. They ended up with a much more fluid approach to structuring the organization. Second, these managers established some new procedures for the key structure points (see Chapter 2), such as accountability for tangible goals (e.g., profitability), priorities, and communication. Key to this adjustment was to match the specifics of what was structured to the new market strategy that Tai-pan was pursuing. This strategy deemphasized technology leadership in favor of a more balanced approach. This meant that the marketing group was given much more responsibility than before (e.g., for profitability).

Finally, much like HP-Singapore, Tai-pan executives then relied on their newly honed skills in executing their businesses to flood the market with a wave of new products. In contrast to Royal, where the starting point was the future, Tai-pan managers focused on their current businesses. Surprisingly, these managers chose this starting point even though at least one and maybe several of their principal businesses were facing slowing growth. From the perspective of industry analysts, there were probably better opportunities elsewhere. Yet by concentrating on operational effectiveness, Tai-pan executives were able to move their organization to the edge of chaos. The result was lower costs, better products, leaner manufacturing, and a secure platform from which to move to the future. As one manager summarized at this point in the transformation, "Our primary competence is better implementation than anybody else."

The Right Order

In the prairie and HP-Singapore examples, the order of transformation mattered; for example, introducing a specific flower to the prairie before a particular butterfly affected both these species. But what about Tai-pan and Royal—did order matter?

Tai-pan: Edge of Chaos to Edge of Time

With quarterly results in their core businesses stabilized in the short term, the management team at Tai-pan shifted their attention to the edge of time. As one manager said, "We've been reactive, our history's reactive, and how we appear proactive is just because we react on a short schedule and can beat everybody to the market . . . but we've got to be able to start being able to tell what's going to happen and pick out those types of things that need to be part of the future. We're in the process of doing that so we're in a transition that says we don't want to be reacting, we want to be more proactive."

To the outside world, this next phase of Tai-pan's transformation looked like the company was moving toward a well-planned future. And that perception was partly correct. After all, Tai-pan managers did engage a major strategy consulting firm to help them with long-term thinking about their future businesses and potential growth opportunities. This visible aspect of the transformation at Tai-pan was helpful, but it was not the whole story. The inside view revealed more explicitly what had happened within the firm: although the outside rhetoric was planning, the inside reality was experimentation. What Tai-pan managers did was to execute a set of probes.

One probe involved *futurists*. Tai-pan managers moved several key people into futurist roles, where their jobs centered on thinking about new ways to use computers. As part of their jobs, these people joined the marketing group in setting up a new kind of focus group. Like many companies, Tai-pan already used focus groups extensively to evaluate aspects of products in the core businesses and to understand better the preferences of current product users. In contrast, the new future-oriented focus groups explicitly involved consumers who were nonusers of technology. Moreover, the focus was not on current businesses but rather more broadly on why these consumers did not use computer technology and what features might make them want to do so.

Tai-pan managers also revamped their approach to *strategic alliances*. They had some old alliances with firms in technologies such as disk drives, where the products had become commodities. Although they maintained manufacturing relationships with many of these firms, the joint product-innovation activities were scrapped. Instead, Tai-pan executives moved to relationships with companies with more leading-edge technology that might provide an advantage to the firm in future projects. The emphasis was much more on alliances that would provide a window of opportunity into the future.

Tai-pan managers also added more *experimental products* to their development portfolio. For example, they added some experimental projects that probed the future of mobile communicators for new applications and markets. They also made more use of experimental options on standard products as a way to understand better what consumer preferences for future products might be.

Moreover, Tai-pan managers instigated formal *future focused meetings*. Previously, future thinking had been primarily a corporate activity. With the transformation, executives moved this responsibility down to the heads of the various business units. In this way, Tai-pan lowered the location of the primary action on strategic decisions. Business-unit heads became central to the strategy process as the key integrators of corporate and business-level strategic thinking.

Although the past is often neglected by managers engaged in transformation, it was not at Tai-pan. Like the very best competitors, Tai-pan managers thought carefully about the edge between the past and the present. At the corporate level, senior executives made several well-publicized moves that leveraged the past. Imitating Intel's "Intel Inside" branding strategy, they focused on brand building—a smart decision given Tai-pan's excellent name recognition in this very competitive industry. They also made some choices about which aspects of manufacturing should be retained and leveraged, and which could be outsourced.

Inside Tai-pan, there were other moves, especially in product innovation. Traditionally, marketing and engineering teams had moved as a team from one generation of products to the next. To counteract the possibility of becoming mired in the past, Tai-pan managers reorganized their staffing of new teams so that only a critical mass of people would transfer from one generation to the next. On a rolling basis, individuals switched off of teams they had been involved with for several generations of products and moved into completely different product groups. This change added some freshness to the pursuit of new products while maintaining a core of experienced people.

Royal: Stalled in a Planned Future

Royal, however, was not faring as well. The firm was stalled in its leap into the future. One problem was that Royal managers completely divorced their current business from the future one. Although the strategy called for the profits from the old Royal to carry the firm, people in the old Royal became disillusioned. There was no "future" in their future. There was nothing new coming into their part of the company, and few of these people were being transferred to the new businesses. So there was no critical mass of experienced people moving from the older businesses into the new. As a result, little expertise was leveraged forward, and nothing from the new businesses refreshed the older ones.

The bigger issue, however, was that Royal managers never stabilized their current operations. As Chapter 2 showed, the new Royal was highly chaotic. In contrast, the old Royal was very rigid and bureaucratic. Ironically, although the two were culturally very different, neither could very effectively develop new products, which was the heart of the strategic plan for the future. As one manager related, "What exists already is a mixture of

The Science behind Order

There is a scientific basis for organizing the edge of chaos processes first, followed by the edge of time processes. Edge of time processes, such as experimentation and regeneration, are evolutionary. Evolutionary change requires systems to be structured, as with genes, and the range of possible change to be bounded by **complexity** and **error catastrophes**. Therefore, evolutionary change depends on previous **self-organization**, and the resulting change is gradual. In contrast, edge of chaos processes, such as improvisation and coadaptation, involve **dialectic** change through the competing tensions of structure and chaos. Dialectic change is faster and has more scale range. Therefore, edge of chaos processes can accommodate quick, major corrections to create structure, and so come first. Evolutionary processes require order and create gradual, finely tuned change. They come second. Finally, time pacing becomes relevant once the system is actually changing effectively.[8]

the old environment which was very procedure bound . . . and a new one which is not very organized yet, and we're sort of in between at the moment." From the perspective of the key structure points described in Chapter 2, both Royals had problems. Setting priorities was just one example. As a manager in the new Royal admitted, "I think some of those hard decisions about priorities just don't get closed down one way or another." A manager in the old Royal claimed, "We have found it extremely difficult to make the trade-offs between projects." Staff meetings were held every four to six weeks at both, and the assignment of responsibilities was poor. As a result, both Royals were functioning poorly, and neither could manage their current businesses well.

Finally, Royal's plan for the future was off the mark, as most plans usually are. Again, as is typical, timing was the problem. The new markets did not take off as fast as Royal senior executives had expected, whereas the old markets did not die as quickly as anticipated. Senior executives made major miscalculations of the pace of market change.

Final State

Like the managers at HP-Singapore, Tai-pan managers tackled time pacing as the final step in their transformation. In particular, they developed choreographed transitions and rhythms at two levels of the firm.

Tai-pan: Tying Timeframes, Getting into the Rhythm

At the business level, Tai-pan managers were just getting started with time-pacing changes when we left the firm. They had executed one particularly successful new business launch that they were trying to codify into a set of transition routines that they could use again and again. The objective was to enter a new business every eighteen months. Given Tai-pan's strong execution capabilities, the most promising markets were ones in which the dominant players relied on older, slower business models. Tai-pan managers were scanning for these opportunities first.

At the product level, Tai-pan managers had succeeded in choreographing a new set of sophisticated transition routines. Managers took a close look at how teams transitioned from one set of projects to the next. A much more structured approach to transitioning was created. For example, rather than follow the somewhat haphazard approach the organization had traditionally used, specific transition roles were assigned. Marketing managers became responsible for kickstarting teams. While engineering managers were still focused on finishing their current projects, marketing managers acted as catalysts to get new core teams (which usually included operations managers as well) set up for the next set of projects. The management team at Tai-pan also developed an explicit rhythm for project transitions. After some experimentation, the organization ultimately settled into an eight-quarter rhythm for the release of new products.

Royal: Disconnecting across Time

At Royal, transitions were not even in managers' consciousness. What's more, managers had actually severed their links between timeframes by ignoring their loyal mainframe customers. After about a year, a manager lamented, "We really annoyed our customers." This might have been acceptable if their new markets had taken off. But Royal managers misjudged the timing of the emergence of new markets and their own ability to have an impact in them. Royal was left with a damaged past and a late-arriving future.

Results

The story of Tai-pan is one in which the corporation has become a market leader in several significant businesses and a very good performer in the rest. Company executives have been widely praised for the turnaround. One major business journal termed it one of the fastest and most effective turnarounds ever. The outside view of the transformation trumpets the firm's cost cutting success, great new products, and well-planned future. But the inside story of how Tai-pan actually achieved the transformation of their businesses is much different. There the story was one of growing a competing on the edge strategy that ultimately enabled the bold and effective strategic moves reported in the press so widely.

In contrast, Royal had no stable base of performance from which to build. While managers at Royal focused on the new five-year plan, the firm's quarterly performance continued to stagnate. The pressure on the new client/server organization to generate revenues quickly was immense and ultimately it proved to be too much. Two years out, the business was struggling, and revenues were dropping on the older products. Royal managers started in the wrong place, never really got to the future, never organized the current businesses, and cut off their links to the past.

Lessons from Royal and Tai-pan

The comparison of Royal and Tai-pan takes the broad lessons from the prairie and HP-Singapore examples down to the specifics of developing a competing on the edge strategy. First, the key to developing a competing on the edge strategy is to think in terms of growth, not assembly. Competing on the edge is about change, so creating it should be much closer to growing a living thing than assembling a machine. At Tai-pan, managers did not try to execute all of the pieces of a competing-edge strategy at one time. Rather, they developed some aspects of the strategy, and once those parts were working, they moved to other pieces of the strategy. The development was quick (much quicker than at HP-Singapore), but it was not simultaneous.

Second, the starting place matters. Tai-pan managers began their transformation at the right location—their current business operations. They honed the basics of current strategy and operations, including logistics, manufacturing, and product development, before they moved on. Finding the edge of chaos was their first order of business in developing a competing on the edge strategy. In contrast, Royal managers started in the wrong place. Without moving to the edge of chaos, the firm's managers became bogged down in firefighting, and their lack of execution kept them from ever getting to the future.

Third, the order of implementation was important. Tai-pan managers started with the current timeframe and the corresponding edge of chaos processes. This stabilized their situation and provided the platform for reinvention. They then moved to the past and future, and to their corresponding edge of time processes. When we left Tai-pan, managerial attention was being

	Starting Position	Order	Final Steps	Results
Royal	**Future Vision** 5-year plan for corporation • Treat old business as cash cow while moving into new forms of computing • Assume fast transition to new businesses	**Stalled in the Future** Past: • No transfer from old Royal to new Current: • Constant firefighting Future: • Mis-timed both client/server emergence and mainframe demise	**Disconnected Time Frames** Past to present: • Severed connection between old mainframe business and new client/server	**Royal Stumbling**
Tai-pan	**Current Strategy** Strengthen core businesses by becoming improvisational • Drop lockstep procedures • Add semistructures Responsibilities: • Assign responsibility for profits, schedule, specifications Priorities: • Install monthly reassessment Metrics: • Prune measures; make real time Deadlines: • Add deadlines Real-time communication: • Add weekly cross-project meetings	**Edge of Chaos to Edge of Time** • Regenerate from past; assess capabilities for leverage potential; ensure some randomness • Add a pattern of probes for experimentation Futurists: • Move people to futurist role; establish futurist focus groups Strategic alliances: • Drop alliances on commodity products while adding ones with partners in leading-edge technology Experimental products: • Add products to development portfolio that relate to mobile communication and Internet; create experimental option features on standard products Future focused meetings: • Establish monthly meetings on future among business unit heads and at business level	**Time Pacing** Choreographed transitions: • Installed for product level; coming for business level Setting a rhythm: • Installed at 4 and 8 quarters at product level; in development at business level	**Tai-pan Soaring**

Figure 7.3 • Growing Competing on the Edge Strategy

focused on creating a rhythm. In a business that we studied extensively, Tai-pan managers had set a rhythm at the product level and were in the process of setting a pace at the business level.

Fourth, each step in the development of a competing on the edge strategy required Tai-pan managers to build new capabilities or skills. On the edge of chaos, the skills are improvisational and coadaptive. On the edge of time, regeneration and experimentation skills are critical.

Overall, the Royal versus Tai-pan comparison reveals two key points about development of a competing on the edge strategy. First, managers need to know *what* to develop. Here the core concepts of competing on the edge are relevant: edge of chaos, edge of time, and time pacing. Understanding that the related processes—improvisation, coadaptation, experimentation, regeneration, and time pacing—are fundamental in businesses that constantly change is essential. Tai-pan managers understood these core concepts. In contrast, Royal managers did not. They still believed in a planned future, not an experimental one. Their current businesses were not coadaptive and improvisational but rather chaotic and bureaucratic. They were unaware of time pacing.

The second key point is that knowing the core concepts is not enough. Managers must also understand *how* to develop competing on the edge. Like prairies and other systems that adapt and evolve, a competing on the edge strategy is grown, not assembled. This means that not everything can be done at once; it also means that the starting point and the order matter. Indeed, you can think of the key insights of this chapter as being the instructions for how to combine the core concepts of competing on the edge to create a business that can continuously reinvent itself.

Developing Competing on the Edge

Chapters 2 through 6 described the basics of each of the edge processes and how to implement them as stand-alone improvement opportunities. This chapter conveyed how to implement the entire competing on the edge strategy. At the beginning of the chapter, we asked how you would re-create a prairie. The obvious solution was to assemble it as you would construct a machine. The actual solution is to develop it as you would grow a living thing. Seeing competing on the edge as a strategy that must be grown is central to understanding its development.

From the Sears, prairie, HP-Singapore, and Royal versus Tai-pan examples, you probably have a good sense of how to proceed in developing a competing on the edge strategy. For clarification, here is a short checklist:

Begin with current operations . . .

1. Never forget that transforming the current businesses is the first priority. It is the base on which to grow. Like Tai-pan and Sears under Martinez, begin here even if there may be better opportunities for growth elsewhere. Focus on key operating issues, like manufacturing, selling, or product innovation. Prune back to your core, as Sears did, if you are too diverse.

2. Move to the edge of chaos. Test your organization to see where it is over-structured and where it is understructured. As at Tai-pan, there may be some of both.

3. Think small, if you can. Pick targeted areas to launch the transformation. Use them as exemplars or platforms to extend. This strategy, used by HP-Singapore, is the safest. But if your business situation is urgent, you can scale up more quickly, as Sears and especially Tai-pan did.

4. As you build your improvisational and coadaptive skills, reproduce in closely related strategic opportunities. For example, use your new product innovation skills to expand your product line. Use your logistics prowess to extend to new geographies or flow more products through your channels.

Once your current strategy is under control, you have, as Sears's Martinez says, "earned the right to think about growth" . . .

1. Move to the edge of time. Begin by making an inventory of your probes into the future. Ask yourself if your strategic alliances are giving you a window into the critical aspects of your future. If not, prune and find new ones. Create at least a few metrics to assess results.

2. Examine your product or service development portfolio. At least 15 percent of your efforts should be experimental, more if you have a leading-edge strategy or your market pace is extremely fast.

3. Add meetings focused on the future. Try some scenario planning. Employ futurists. Bring in a variety of people to open up your thinking about the future. Do it on a regular basis.

4. Don't forget your past. Often managers are so enthralled by the future that they forget that the past can be a source of regeneration. Specifically, take stock of your capabilities and see how to exploit them. Even "stuck in the past" businesses should keep some of what they do well.

5. Take your successes in new businesses and use them to regenerate your established businesses where you can.

Once your operations in each timeframe are effective . . .

1. Develop time pacing. There is tremendous opportunity to gain advantage here, but don't try to do it before you have stabilized your past and future. Most businesses are in their infancy in thinking about these issues. The keys are choreography and rhythm. It is easiest to start at low levels of the organization where transitions are more frequent and then move up as Tai-pan did.

2. Watch for missing links. Avoid the temptation to conceal failures. Instead, figure out what has gone wrong and why, and then use the insights, as managers at HP-Singapore did.

I cannot bring a world

quite round, Although I

patch it as I can.

Wallace Stevens,

The Man with the

Blue Guitar

leading the strategy

WHEN YOU THINK about coffee, what brand comes to mind? Folger's? Maxwell House? Nescafe? In the late 1990s, if you were like most people in North America, none of these names came readily to mind, even though they were the top-selling brands on grocery store shelves. Maybe ten years ago you would have thought of them . . . but by 1997, when it came to coffee, Starbucks was on the minds and in the mugs of America's coffee drinkers.

The Starbucks concept was the creation of Howard Schultz. In the early 1980s, Schultz was just another transplanted Brooklynite who worked for Starbucks, a small chain of coffee stores in Seattle. While vacationing in Europe, Schultz was struck by the excitement and style of Italy's outdoor cafés. He returned to Seattle and suggested that Starbucks launch the café concept. Exhortation failed, but dollars did not. In 1987, Schultz bought out his bosses' six Seattle stores for $3.8 million.

A decade later, Starbucks became the superstar of premium coffee in the United States. For example, in 1996, revenue was growing at an annual rate of 63 percent a year, with sales up from $285 million to $465 million. Earnings rose 156 percent to $26 million—ten times their 1991 level. From a base of about 900 stores, Starbucks managers hoped to grow the company to two thousand outlets by the end of the decade. To keep the profits flowing and the growth soaring, Starbucks managers found increasingly novel ways to keep their brand in front of consumers. They teamed with United Airlines for branded, in-flight coffee. They partnered with PepsiCo to put Frappuccino, a low fat blend of cold coffee and milk, on grocery-store shelves. They worked with Dreyer's to manufacture coffee ice cream and with Capitol Records for jazz compact discs to accompany coffee drinking. Starbucks even infiltrated the beer market by providing coffee extract for Redhook Brewery's Double Black Stout Beer. Continual reinvention and change was the strategy at Starbucks.

In contrast, Folger's, Nescafe, and Maxwell House were still on the store shelves engaging in their traditional battles. For these brands, coffee was still the low-priced commodity product that had a boring, bland image. These household names traded a few share points, engaged in the usual coupon wars, and even sometimes attempted to change. But they were rarely successful in their initiatives and were much less profitable than Starbucks.

Yet, even as Starbucks continued to change, prosper, and grow, concerns for the future emerged. Would Starbucks managers be able to sustain the performance? Could their business model be undone by poor weather in South America that would drive up coffee bean prices? Would anti-establishment competitors, like People's Coffee, be successful in attacking Starbucks' big-company image as the Wal-Mart of coffee? Did Starbucks managers dilute the brand with too much brand extension? Would most consumers decide that they were paying too much for a cup of coffee?

This brief history of Starbucks suggests some of the challenges of sustaining consistently superior performance, especially in unpredictable and fast-paced markets. Why is it so challenging? There are three primary reasons. One is that staying on top means remaining poised on the edges of chaos and time. Although these edges are places of adaptive behavior, they are also unstable (dissipative equilibria). This instability means that managers have to work at staying on the edge. It is all too easy to slip into the past, be lured too far into the future, or become trapped in either too much bureaucracy or too much chaos. The experience of being poised on the edge is like raising teenagers, when parents must constantly balance between giving their children enough freedom so that they become successful, independent adults, and enough structure so that they have sufficient guidance when their judgment is immature. For Starbucks, it is particularly easy to grow too fast or to move too precipitously into new opportunities, and so fly wildly out of control.

The second reason is that sustaining consistent performance requires keeping up with change. Consistent performance is a dynamic equilibrium, in the sense that the equilibrium point is constantly shifting. Starbucks' coffee prices may change, premium locations for Starbucks' shops may be taken, or their partnership with United Airlines might sour. The challenge for managers like those at Starbucks is to know when and how to move their equilibrium point, and so to keep pace with and even lead change.

The third reason is competition. Smart competitors often attempt to out-maneuver one another. For example, Starbucks faces threats from immediate competitors like People's Coffee, from traditional coffee producers like Procter & Gamble and General Foods, and from alternative beverages like iced tea and fruit drinks. The implication is that today's winner can easily become tomorrow's loser.

Another way to think about these challenges is to imagine a marble in a cup (a coffee cup, if you wish). In a static world, the marble remains at the bottom of the cup. Jiggle the cup and the marble will move, but it returns to the bottom of the cup. Now imagine turning that coffee cup over and putting the marble on the top. Jiggle the cup and the marble will fall off unless you pay attention and adjust the cup. That is dissipative equilibrium. Now, try to run holding the coffee cup upside-down with the marble on top. That is a dynamic equilibrium. Keeping the marble on the cup just became much more difficult. . . . Finally, suppose people are chasing you, trying to steal the marble. Now you have competition for the marble, and again you have made the task more difficult. Even worse, suppose that nobody wants your marble anymore. Now you have value-migration to the next business model. Sustaining superior performance in unpredictable, high velocity markets is like running with an upside-down cup, with a marble on the top, and with many fast and skilled competitors trying to steal your marble.

The imagery of the cup, however, is meant to be more than a clever play on Starbucks. It is a visual analogy of sustaining high performance in business, which emphasizes the simultaneity and dynamism of the managerial activities required. When the marble is on the cup, keeping it on top requires balancing the marble, watching where to run, looking out for the competition, and ensuring that your marble is still the marble that everybody wants. The managerial challenge is to effectively and simultaneously execute these enormously dynamic tasks.

Meeting this challenge requires rethinking—from the team room to the boardroom—what leaders actually do. In traditional management, there are two basic roles: strategist and implementer. Senior executives typically are the strategists and the business level managers are the implementers. In contrast, the dynamism and simultaneity of managing in rapidly changing, unpredictable markets suggests that leaders will have more, different, and shifted roles.

First, the role of *strategist* shifts to the business level, both in terms of setting business strategy and collectively shaping corporate strategy. Indeed, the heart of strategy is at the business level where the dual facets of strategy (i.e., "where do you want to go?" and "how do you want to get there?") meld together. The related tasks revolve around the processes of improvisation, coadaptation, regeneration, experimentation, and time pacing, which are at the core of this book. In terms of the coffee-cup analogy, this is the role of the runner who must balance the marble on top of the upside-down cup, watch where to run right now, and also help other runners on the same team to run well.

Second, a new leadership role emerges. This is the job of orchestrating multiple products, services, or businesses that emerges at the group or sector level (or at the corporate level in smaller firms). The primary task is to continually add, subtract, merge, and split businesses to match the relentlessly shifting mix of market opportunities. This is the critical role of *patcher* that rapid and unpredictable change creates. In coffee-cup terms, patching involves constantly matching and rematching the best marbles with the right runners in the face of changing competitive conditions.

Third, the role at the senior executive level changes from chief strategist to *synthesizer*. The key tasks involve channeling, synthesizing, and articulating the essence of the semicoherent strategic direction that characterizes the strategy that emerges as businesses reinvent themselves. In coffee-cup terms, this is the role of hiring the right runners and patchers, jogging alongside to cheer, and most important, articulating why everyone is engaged in the frenetic task of cup running that characterizes businesses in fast-moving, unpredictable markets. These three leadership roles are key to sustaining performance on the edge.

ABCs of Leading

Anyone from Boston knows the heartbreak of being a fan of the Red Sox, that perennial also-ran team in major league baseball's American League East. There has not been a World Series championship in Boston since . . . well, for years. The most agonizing aspect of the drought was the dominance of the New York Yankees. From the 1930s to the 1970s, every fall brought the World Series, and the Series seemed invariably to involve that New York nemesis, the Yankees, against the almost equally predictable Dodgers. From Babe Ruth and Joe DiMaggio, to Mickey Mantle and Whitey Ford, to Don Mattingly and the rest, the Yankees won the American League pennant almost 70 percent of the time in the forty years between 1930 and 1970. Regardless of whether the Red Sox fielded Ted Williams, Carl Yastrzemski, Jim Rice, or just some rookie in front of left field's "green monster," the outcome was almost always the same. The Yankees were in the Series, and the Red Sox were at home.

But by the mid-1970s, the Yankees were no longer the pinstriped pennant machine of the past. The reason may be summed up in two words: free agency. Journeyman players with a good year or two could now switch teams for big money and better deals. By the 1990s, major stars like Roger Clemens, Barry Bonds, or Ken Griffey, Jr. could cut their own deals. Baseball was now about pleasing prima donna players and about merchandising and massive television revenues. There were many more teams and divisional champions, and more interleague play. With all this change, no team could remain on top the way the old Yankees did. Back in the 1950s, a fan could count on the same Yankee lineup at the same positions, year after year: Skowron on first, Richardson at second, Mantle in center, and so on. With the advent of free agency, the lineups changed often. The Orioles, the Blue Jays, and the Indians were as likely to win the American League pennant as the Yankees. The structured and stable world that regularly produced professional sports dynasties like the Yankees, the great Boston Celtics basketball teams of the Bill Russell era, or the Montreal Canadiens hockey teams of the Richards era ended.

But a few teams have figured out how to win consistently in the era of free agency in professional sports. In the 1990s, the closest team to a dynasty in major league baseball was the Atlanta Braves. Between 1991 and 1996, Atlanta appeared in four of the five World Series as the National League pennant winner. (There was no Series in the 1994 strike year.) In 1997, they had the highest winning percentage. Once the doormat of their National League division, the Braves went from worst in 1990 to first in 1991 and continued to stay at or near the top. How did the Braves sustain their performance in the rapidly changing and uncertain world of free-agent baseball?

One part of the answer was manager Bobby Cox. The manager is the on-the-field leader in baseball. In the Atlanta organization, Cox focused on that leadership role. Together with his coaches, he set the defensive lineup, made the game-day moves, selected the starting pitcher, and specified the batting order. He motivated the prima donnas, kept track of the condition of the pitchers' arms, experimented with new defensive lineups, and strategized against the opponents. Put simply, his job (and that of the other managers in the Braves' farm system) was to go to the ballpark day after day during the season for 160-plus games, organize twenty-six players, focus, and win.

The second part of the answer was Braves owner Ted Turner. Whether the business was his global news station, CNN, or the Braves, or his other holdings, the Turner approach was often hands off. At CNN, for example, the legend is that he hired the people to set up the first broadcasts and then disappeared to pursue sailing's America's Cup. For the Braves, he made the major managerial hires and wrote the checks. But he was not in the dugout and he was not making the deals for players. Instead, he stayed in the stands cheerleading as the Braves' number one fan.

The third and probably most significant part of the answer was John Schuerholz. No, Schuerholz could not throw a 95-mile-per-hour fastball or hit for a .350 batting average. Rather, John Schuerholz was the general manager of the Braves. He joined the club from the Kansas City Royals after the 1990 season. His job was to troll constantly through the baseball world to get and keep the best players, at every position, for the Atlanta Braves. In the early 1990s, he made the key moves to keep starting pitchers John Smoltz, Tom Glavine, and Steve Avery and to snag starter Greg Maddux. They became the most-feared starting rotation in major league baseball. Maddux repeatedly

Leader	Leadership Role	
Bobby Cox, manager	Strategist	Cox has the rare ability to successfully mix young players with veterans on a championship team.
		Cox has an excellent understanding of the linkage between pitching and defense.
		Cox is adept at keeping just the right assortment of pinch hitters, pinch runners, and defensive replacements on the bench in specific roles.
John Schuerholz, general manager	Patcher	No other team wanted the not-so-glamorous free agents Terry Pendleton and Sid Bream as much as the Braves wanted them. Once they arrived in Atlanta, the team started winning championships.
		The Schuerholz deals are now legend: Fred McGriff, Otis Nixon, Marquis Grissom, and Greg Maddux, the biggest coup of all.
		The Neagle deal is just another in a series of master strokes by Schuerholz. Players like Terrell Wade and Jermaine Dye are part of the talent that just keeps coming.
Ted Turner, owner	Synthesizer	Though he makes an occasional clubhouse speech, Turner keeps his hands off the day-to-day operations.
		Turner says, "All I did was sit here and sign a few checks."

Performance

Between 1991 and 1997, the Atlanta Braves won six straight divisional championships (a National League record), appeared in four of the six World Series, and had the highest winning percentage in major league baseball . . . all after finishing in last place for four of the previous five years.

Figure 8.1 • Atlanta Braves' Dynasty of the 1990s

Source: Associated Press, Atlanta, 18 October 1996. Additional sources can be found in the bibliography.

won the Cy Young award as the National League's best pitcher during this stretch. Year after year, Schuerholz plucked the right players from the Atlanta farm system. Year after year, he did the midseason deals that brought the Braves key players during their stretch drives for the pennant. He signed Fred McGriff when the team needed a clutch power hitter. He signed Alejandro Pena when they needed a closing pitcher. He closed the offseason deals, like signing the lead-off man Kenny Lofton in 1997. He captured stars like Denny Neagle, who hurled his way to the best record on the Braves pitching staff in his first full season with the club. He signed less glamorous players like Terry Pendleton, who brought leadership, defense, and surprising home run hitting to the team. And, he let players go at opportune times. Managers at other teams *could have* made these moves. Schuerholz did make them. He surveyed the talent in the Braves organization, and kept track of the talent on the other ball clubs. He relentlessly patched and repatched the Braves to ensure that the Braves had the best team possible given the constantly changing pool of available baseball talent. Whereas the old Yankees fielded the same team, the new Braves fielded an ever-changing lineup. Creating this constantly shifting roster of players was Schuerholz's job—the job that the rapid and unpredictable change of free agent baseball made critical.

The Atlanta Braves baseball team's dominance during the 1990s suggests several key lessons for sustaining performance. First, when the marketplace is changing rapidly and unpredictably, the patching role of John Schuerholz is pivotal. In the case of Schuerholz, it was his ability to recognize the patterns, patch the quilt of Braves players together, and keep on patching the quilt that was at the core of reinventing the Braves as a pennant contender. Schuerholz had to do this season after season. This key managerial skill is recognizing patterns within and outside the organization and matching them to each other. For John Schuerholz, it was the ability to spot opportunities, commit quickly when a key player became available, plug the hole rapidly when a Brave went down with an injury, and build the team that Bobby Cox managed and Ted Turner cheered.

The second lesson is the significance of the on-the-field role of Bobby Cox. In baseball, the manager along with the batting, pitching, and other specialty coaches form a group that is parallel to the top management team of a business or product line. Prior to Schuerholz's arrival, Cox was both manager and general manager of the Braves, and the team was one of the worst in baseball. After Schuerholz came, Cox was able to focus on being the manager, and the Braves excelled. What changed? Cox could concentrate on managing the competing tensions in the clubhouse. Cox was able to focus on improvising on game day, balancing old veterans and new ballplayers, experimenting with different closing pitchers, and so forth. This key managerial skill is juggling the competing tensions that emerge in baseball's version of the edges of chaos and time. For Cox and the other team managers in the Braves organization, their ability to manage these tensions on the field . . . in game after game after game . . . was critical.

The third lesson is the concept of the senior executive as the synthesizer of a semicoherent direction. Ted Turner made the managerial hires, and occasionally committed extraordinary money to keep franchise players like the star pitcher Greg Maddux on the team. But unlike the equally rich and less successful Yankees' owner, George Steinbrenner, he mostly let others run the Braves organization.

Overall, the sustained superior performance of the Atlanta Braves is, in a significant way, a story of effectively dividing the leadership roles in a rapidly changing, highly competitive, and unpredictable business. The main components are to put strategy at the level of the business, ensure that patching is done well, and let the senior executive shape the essence of the business.

The Art of Patching

In 1960 Alfred Chandler, Harvard's eminent business historian, published a now-classic book about the strategy of the successful multibusiness corporation.[1] He chronicled the path that executives at DuPont, General Motors, Sears, and other firms followed, from the centralized, vertically integrated firm of the late 1800s to the modern, multidivisional (or M form) corporation. A message of that book was the necessity to align the firm around individual businesses that matched the particular markets that they served. Chandler described, for example, the transformation of DuPont in the 1920s from a functionally organized, vertically integrated corporation to a decentralized one organized around products like nylon, artificial leather, and paints. Yet, although the book is very insightful, some readers may have taken away an unintended "organization chart" mindset. This perspective suggests a neat and orderly, once-and-for-all matching between divisions and the markets that they serve, often captured by a chart showing the uniformly sized, equidistantly spaced rectangles of the traditional organization chart. The carefully drawn boxes in organization charts portray the businesses in an often unchanging match with the marketplace. The underlying perspective is that markets are reasonably fixed and hence the match between a business and a market is fixed as well.

Imagine a world in which the pace of markets is accelerated. Add new technologies (gene splicing, the Internet), blend in novel products and services (sport utility vehicles, depot stores, health maintenance organizations), and add a dash of new markets (the emerging Asian middle class, Hispanics in the United States, Eastern European entrepreneurs, yuppies). Put in an acquisition or two. Converge several markets (banking with stock brokerage, television with movies). What emerges is ubiquitous change. How does this kind of change affect a portfolio of businesses?

Sometimes new opportunities open up where there is no existing business (the emergence of cellular phones, digital photography, gourmet coffee cafes in the United States). In this case, it makes sense to add a business to the portfolio. Sometimes the flux produces converging opportunities, in which once-distinct businesses merge into each other (personal computers and televisions). In this case, it makes sense to consolidate the businesses or move activities from one to another. At other times, flux creates an explosion of opportunities (beer explodes into micro brews of all kinds, brew pubs, and brew mugs) that might be parceled out to new or existing businesses. Finally, sometimes opportunities fade. Then it may be time to shutter the related businesses.

The point is that when the marketplace is shifting rapidly and unpredictably, the match between businesses and opportunities is constantly falling out of alignment. As a result, today's clear-cut partitioning of businesses into neat, equidistant rectangles on an organization chart becomes tomorrow's out of date scramble as opportunities come and go, collide and separate, grow and shrink. In this landscape of constant flux, there is a frequent need to align businesses and new opportunities through patching.[2]

Modularity

Underlying the ability to patch is the idea of modularity, meaning that a company is composed of a set of distinct businesses that stand alone. For example, think of the analogy to a quilt. The patches on a quilt are distinct; most do not overlap. In other words, they are modular.

Modularity may seem arcane, but several companies that have historically been very modular are, not coincidentally, among the firms most noted for the ability to reinvent themselves and to sustain superior performance. Europe's ABB (much more modular than its organizational matrix suggests), Asia's Acer, and North America's Hewlett-Packard, 3M, Emerson Electric, and Johnson & Johnson are among the firms that routinely organize in modular fashion around small, strongly autonomous, entrepreneurial businesses that are constantly re-mapped onto evolving market opportunities. Acer managers, for example, patch their firm into very distinct geographic businesses to pursue their mission of joining consumer electronics and computing—then later revisit that patching. Similarly, Emerson Electric maps businesses into distinct product modules around specific market opportunities.

Managers at other businesses are just beginning to understand the power of modularity. They are creating more stand-alone, modular businesses by creating sharper business boundaries and are pushing decision making down to lower levels in the organization. For example, corporate executives at Gap shifted greater power to their retail divisions to more clearly delineate the modularity of these businesses. In 1996, Gap CEO Mickey Drexler moved authority for product development and marketing to each of the corporation's retail divisions, such as Old Navy, Gap, and Banana Republic. The division managers in turn began to make independent decisions, for example, about advertising agencies. The result is a more responsive firm.

Modularity is also practiced at Merck. One of CEO Ray Gilmartin's early moves was to create worldwide business strategy teams organized around key diseases. The teams brought together executives from diverse areas, including finance, manufacturing, and marketing, to assess everything from production costs to potential market size. An example was a thirteen-member osteoporosis team that oversaw doctor education programs and advertising to promote Fosamax, Merck's osteoporosis drug. The aim was to create a coordinated global strategy that would nonetheless be flexible.

Finally, modularity is not just the province of product-oriented businesses. For example, British Airways managers organized the firm's services into product-like modules, such as Executive Class service. Similarly, some health care and banking institutions have "productized" their service offerings to create modularity as well.

Patching

Patching refers to the dynamic mapping of modular businesses (or products or services) onto marketplace opportunities. It is about continuously realigning businesses with markets. Just as top general managers in major league baseball constantly troll the talent pool to make the best match between their needs on the field and the available players, so too do managers in firms that sustain superior performance constantly watch for the "white spaces" between existing businesses and then reposition their portfolio of activities to match them. Patching is therefore a fundamental motor of reinvention.

Patching involves two issues. One is size. Big patches position a company into a few very large businesses that are characterized by broad market scope or deep vertical integration. If these patches become too big, it is difficult to respond to changes occurring in subsections of the patch. Rigidity ensues. Businesses tend to be cumbersome and unresponsive to changing markets. In contrast, small patches organize a company into many fine-grained market niches. This type of patching can be enormously responsive to market change. Yet, if these patches are too small, businesses will be too closely related to each other and require too much coordination. The result is confusion and interference among them. These businesses might also lack critical mass to be successful. Patches that are too small create a quilt of businesses that is too chaotic to change effectively.

The second issue is content. Effective patching relies on correct mapping onto markets. If there is no patch on some particular market space, then there is a gap or white space in the product line of the firm. A new business is

Firms as Ecosystems of Patches

Complicated situations with many interacting components and constraints are usually best resolved by breaking the entire problem into
a set of non-overlapping (i.e., modular) smaller problems, or **patches**,
and then solving each patch independently. Despite little central control, solving small patches with high local autonomy is an effective
solution for two reasons. First, splitting a complicated problem into
many smaller problems typically produces the best overall solution.
Second, if the patches loosely communicate with one another as
described in Chapter 3, they will coevolve over time to an even better
solution to the problem. That is, autonomous patches that occasionally
communicate track changing landscapes most effectively.[3]

This reasoning suggests the counterintuitive observation that the
content of patches is less important than their **size**. When patches
are too small, the patches will interfere with one another as each tries
to optimize for its own purposes. In contrast, when patches are too
big, the ecosystem will become stable and rigid, with each patch unable
to coevolve out of a suboptimal situation. The middle ground is a patch
size that allows the ecosystem to stay on the edge of chaos, settled
into a mutually optimal and orderly pattern, from which it can evolve.

To draw an analogy to firms, assume that a firm consists of a set of
"patches" or businesses. When it is broken up into too many small
independent businesses, it becomes impossible for each business to
keep track of all the possible effects of the many interactions. The
result is chaos. In contrast, if the firm is patched into large businesses
with centrally controlled coordination, the outcome is likely to be
rigidity in the face of changing markets. Thus, finding the optimal patch
size is critical to the ability of firms to change.

needed. If there are overlapping patches, then the businesses may be confused
and cannibalize one another. In both cases, business boundaries need redraw-
ing. If patches do not match with markets, then there will be few sales.

An example of patching at the product level is Honda. In the early nineties,
Honda slumped when the Japanese economy sagged, a strong yen damaged
export sales, and the company missed the sports utility vehicle craze. In fact,
Honda's Japanese car sales fell in 1993 and 1994. Honda managers responded
with astute patching. They launched a deluge of new cars they termed "recreational vehicles" to attack the previously ignored sports utility market. In particular, Honda managers made two key patching moves. First, rather than
patch broadly by having just one product offering around sport utility vehi-

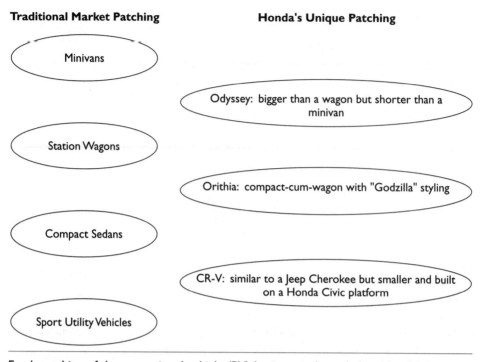

Traditional Market Patching

- Minivans
- Station Wagons
- Compact Sedans
- Sport Utility Vehicles

Honda's Unique Patching

- Odyssey: bigger than a wagon but shorter than a minivan
- Orithia: compact-cum-wagon with "Godzilla" styling
- CR-V: similar to a Jeep Cherokee but smaller and built on a Honda Civic platform

Fresh patching of the recreational vehicle (RV) business in Japan led to Honda's best-ever performance in that market. In Japan, the company manufactures four of the twelve top-selling cars, has RV sales that represent 60% of total sales, and has moved from number five to number three.

Figure 8.2 • Patching RV Products at Honda

Source: Alex Taylor III, "The Man Who Put Honda Back on Track," *Fortune*, 9 September 1996, 92–100.

cles, Honda engineers broke the market into more finely grained market niches. In other words, they created a smaller patch size. Second, rather than simply patching in the way that others had done, Honda managers chose some unique patches. Their Odyssey vehicle, for example, was patched across the traditional station wagon and minivan markets. It was larger than a station wagon but shorter than a minivan. Another patch product was the CR-V, which was positioned somewhat like a Jeep Cherokee but had a smaller size and lower cost. In other words, Honda managers varied from the way that the competition had organized the content of their patches. These patching moves proved to be enormously successful. By late 1996, 60 percent of Honda's new car sales in Japan came from these vehicles. And Honda had moved from number five to three in their domestic market. More significantly, Honda

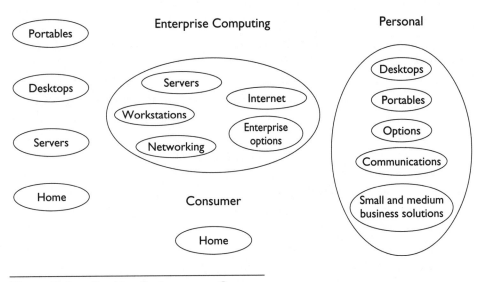

Figure 8.3 • Patching Businesses at Compaq

Source: "Compaq Announces Sweeping Organizational Changes Aimed at Supporting Growth, Expanding Global Leadership," Compaq Computer Corporation Press Release, 2 July 1996.

became the envy of the industry because their buyers were young Japanese who could become the base for future growth.

An illustration of patching at the business level is computing powerhouse, Compaq. In 1996, as the firm sprinted to the goal of $40 billion in annual sales by the year 2000, Compaq senior executives repatched their company into three groups and nine new business units, ranging from workstations to communications, Internet products, and options for personal computers. The size of the patches (relatively small) and their product content (favoring markets like networking and Internet) reflected how Compaq managers intended to approach the convergence of computing, telecommunications, and consumer electronics.

The Honda and Compaq examples illustrate how managers reinvent their products, businesses, and even companies through patching. Moreover, for firms like Hewlett-Packard and Emerson Electric, repatching is a routine event. The same is true at several of the firms that we studied.

Patching at Pioneer

Pioneer, a pseudonym, is a high growth venture that has emerged as one of the top new companies in the computing industry. What is unique about Pioneer is that its managers have cleverly married the concept of "engineer as king" with fiscal responsibility. Engineers are paid extremely well to play with exciting technol ogy and to produce industry-leading products that sell. It is "geek heaven"— but there's a catch. Pioneer's customers have to like the products that their developers create. It is this "exciting-technology-that-sells" approach that has kept Pioneer an industry pace-setter in both financial and technical terms.

Pioneer attracts technical talent. Engineers flock to Pioneer for three reasons. First, they get to work with the very latest technology. The work is difficult, challenging, and cutting-edge . . . exactly what engineers often want. Second, the compensation is outstanding and merit-based. Third and most important, engineers work on products that are actually released. Unlike many firms, an engineer's time at Pioneer is rarely spent on products that do not get shipped. And engineers love to see the products they designed used by people to do amazing things.

A critical part of Pioneer management is a modular approach to their businesses. Managers patch the company into multiple small divisions in which the business-level managers (and their management teams) dictate strategy. Consistent with the improvisation described in Chapter 2, these managers are accountable for a few specific measures related to profitability, innovation, and growth in market share. Otherwise, they are free to create their own business models.

A striking feature of Pioneer is that its managers rely on patching and regard it as pivotal to their success. In fact, patching is the primary task of one key corporate executive. This manager constantly scans market opportunities and adds businesses when they make sense, combines them, splits them apart when necessary, and closes them down. Patching means constantly realigning the match between businesses and market opportunities to create the patchwork quilt of businesses that is critical to how Pioneer managers constantly reinvent the firm. By making patching a focus of management attention, Pioneer sustains its position as a top computer firm. Below we describe how Pioneer managers patch.

Grafting a New Business

One patching situation that we encountered at Pioneer involved an acquisition. Pioneer's industry segment is so explosive that acquisitions are commonplace. In this case, Pioneer managers purchased Performance Computing (a pseudonym). Along with the primary business target, they acquired a product line in interactive video that had little to do with the rationale underlying the acquisition. This product line may be thought of as an orphan business or, to keep within our metaphor, as a piece of fabric without a place in Pioneer's quilt of businesses. The patching question that managers faced was where to put it.

There were several options. Option 1 was to put the interactive video business with an existing business at Pioneer that was in a related software technology. This would build critical mass and create technical synergies in interactive video. Option 2 was to add the business to a more established business where the sales channel was similar. This move would infuse new products into a division that had an excellent selling channel but too few new products flowing through it. Option 3 was to keep the acquired business as a stand-alone division. Option 4 was to sell the business. After all, Pioneer managers had not planned to be in this business, were very busy, and did not know much about it.

Like many patching situations, there were multiple viable options. In other words, there were a variety of ways to fit the interactive video product line into the quilt. As in most patching decisions, the key was to move quickly. The options in patching decisions are usually relatively clear and straightforward to analyze and so are not time consuming to assess. Two to three months is the usual timeframe at Pioneer for committing to a new patch. Slower patching decisions rarely yield new insights and instead exacerbate the tensions and confusion surrounding what will happen in the affected business areas. Moreover, at Pioneer, patching decisions are routine. They can be changed if a significantly better option emerges.

Pioneer managers chose to combine the two streams of technology (option 1) in about ten weeks. They believed that the combination of the related technologies would create a critical mass for pursuing a distinctive growth opportunity. Patch size was clearly critical in this choice. Together, these technologies would crosspollinate and so create a more robust entry into the interactive video market.

Colliding Businesses

Collisions among businesses are a particularly common patching situation. The general pattern is that managers in one business unit begin to pursue a new opportunity in the same market space as managers from another business. This is not surprising, because the pursuit of new products and growth opportunities is part of Pioneer's culture. Sometimes the managers of the colliding businesses are aware of each other, and sometimes they are not. Eventually, the managers and the relevant patching executive recognize the overlap and then repatch to keep each business modular and focused. We observed one of these collisions when we were studying Pioneer.

The collision of businesses involved the server and desktop units. Engineers in the desktop business had developed a "network computer" (i.e., a less intelligent or "dumbed-down" version of the PC) for use on the Internet. They had introduced the product to a few select customers and generated some initial interest. A few months later, managers in the server business recognized the same marketplace opportunity. They too began to develop a network computer. Eventually, both sets of managers and the patching executive noticed the overlap. The overlap continued for about two months to ensure that there really was an overlap and to gain some sense of the different technical directions (if any). When it became apparent that the opportunity was roughly the same, the managers decided to repatch.

As is typical of patching decisions, the options were clear. Option 1 was a stand-alone business that combined the operations from both desktops and servers; option 2 was to consolidate the business in desktops; and option 3 was to consolidate in servers. Option 1 was quickly rejected because the scale was insufficient to support a full division. Again, patch size was critical. That left a choice between the two existing divisions.

Like most patching decisions, the choice was not a simple one. The decision went beyond simply the business case for the better fit. The desktop division was further along in the product development cycle. It was the larger and more established business. Even though its managers were interested in the new product, it was a modest addition to their product portfolio. In contrast, the server business was smaller and newer. To combine the fledgling businesses in servers would give that business an opportunity to develop engineering skills from working on this particular type of product that would be useful for the future. In addition, the network computer would bolster employment in a geographic region where senior managers wanted to expand employment. Finally, the managers of the new products in both servers and desktops preferred a home with servers. The patching executive made the choice to consolidate the businesses within servers. Among the people in the desktop division there was some unhappiness with the choice, but they went along with the decision.

Modularity Miscue

Managers who patch routinely realize that modularity is essential for patching. Yet because patching options often are in conflict, managers are frequently tempted to compromise in a way that damages this modularity. Usually they resist, but we studied one situation at Pioneer in which they did not.

This situation involved an opportunity to create a software product to measure the performance of interconnected systems of computers. Managers in two businesses spotted the same opportunity. Again, it was a matter of businesses colliding. In this situation, each business made a very compelling argument for the opportunity to create the software. Given the strong case for both options, the group executive, together with the heads of the two businesses, decided to share the new opportunity. She gave the lead to develop the software to one business and the lead to market it and to be responsible for profitability to the other. Her reasoning was that this software project would develop critical skills in the first business but that the business opportunity fit better with the second.

Initially, everyone involved favored this compromise choice. Teamwork seemed assured. Reality set in about two months later, when it became apparent that no one felt responsible for the software products. Responsibility for the product line had been delegated to a lower-level manager in one of the divisions to oversee. But he lacked the power and the time to pursue the new business effectively. Pioneer was ultimately late to the market. Eventually, the software business was realigned and placed entirely in a single business unit.

Stuck at Jupiter

In contrast to the fluid mapping of businesses to market opportunities that we saw at Pioneer, the story was much different at Jupiter (see Chapter 3). Jupiter

---

Rules for Patching

1. Assign a senior manager whose responsibility it is to constantly scan for opportunities to add, merge, diverge, split, and realign businesses. Look for new markets. Look for novel ways to patch.

2. Pay attention to the critical variable of patch size.

3. Tie patching to experimentation so that the transition from probes to new products and businesses is executed well.

4. When an opportunity to patch appears:

   - Quickly formulate several options.

   - Avoid options that split opportunities across businesses.

   - Evaluate opportunity based on skills, geographic needs, and performance potential.

   - Decide rapidly, as speed matters more than precision.

5. As markets change faster, use smaller patches. Remember that big patches create rigidity, while many small ones create chaos.

was a generalist firm—the kind that Pioneer was fast becoming. But in contrast to Pioneer, Jupiter had no routine for patching and no executive for whom this was a major responsibility. As a result, Jupiter's managers ran their businesses without much thought about patching. In addition, there were historical fiefdoms at the company that made flexibility around business opportunities much more difficult to create. Enforced collaboration from the top further encouraged an attitude of protectiveness vis-à-vis turf issues within the businesses. Without a routine for patching and with turf barriers, managers at Jupiter often missed opportunities to readjust their patches. When these managers did see opportunities to realign businesses, they used extreme caution, because these decisions were seen as rare and largely irreversible choices. Ironically, this slow pace further increased the politicking around these kinds of divisive choices. As a result, Jupiter's managers missed this major driver of reinvention.

Lessons from Pioneer and Jupiter

Several lessons about patching may be drawn from the comparison between Pioneer and Jupiter. First, patching is a crucial activity in settings with rapid and unpredictable change. New markets arise, booming markets fragment, technologies appear, and markets collide. Patching is the process by which managers keep their businesses effectively aligned with a shifting marketplace.

Second, patching decisions typically involve several clear-cut options that have ramifications beyond the simple business case for where the opportunity will most likely prosper. There are often broader implications such as career development, employment, morale, and patch size that are important in patching decisions.

Third, although patching decisions present clear options, they are also often accompanied by high conflict. Patching decisions revolve around turf issues and so invariably pit managers against one another. As a result, most choices will make someone unhappy. The key to dealing with this conflict is to discuss the options broadly but make the patching decision quickly.

Finally, appropriate patch size and modularity are essential for effective patching. Pioneer managers violated their own precepts about modularity among businesses and regretted it.

Synthesizing Strategy

"Show me the money!" "It's the economy, stupid!" "Have lunch or be lunch." These and other sound bites are among the most maligned features of contemporary culture.[4] The term *sound bite* is itself a reference to the supposedly brief attention span of the MTV generation. But is there an advantage to the short, pointed exposition of a key thought? In science, for example, the revolutionary paper on DNA by Crick and Watson is less than two pages long. Einstein's theory of relativity may be summarized in less than a page. In rhetoric, memorable speeches are remembered by short phrases, not by their entirety. Douglas MacArthur's declaration, "I shall return," Martin Luther King's "I have a dream," and John Kennedy's ". . . ask what you can do for your country" are short and memorable. There is an elegance to simple rhetoric that captures the essence of complicated ideas and emotions. This is the sound bite at its best.

Sound bites are relevant here because the role of senior executives in high velocity and unpredictable markets involves the creation of what we might term sound bites. This role involves synthesizing an interpretation that captures the essence and excitement of a business or businesses in a way that only a short, elegantly crafted phrase can. In businesses whose people are faced with rapid and unpredictable change, a simple perspective that captures the heart of their activity can be critical to keeping the activity together.

At the Finnish telecommunications firm Nokia, for example, in 1992 CEO Jorma Ollila came out of a brainstorming session and jotted down the words "telecom-oriented, global, and focus" and then "value-added" on a piece of paper. These words became the cornerstone of the vision and direction of the company over the next several years.[5] On the one hand, these words convey a simple interpretation of the firm and not the future. They did not create a vision of what will happen within the telecommunications industry or a strategy about which market to enter first. Rather, they are a vision of being a global telecommunications company—whatever that might prove to be in the future. They also describe what Nokia is not.

On the other hand, the simplicity of these words captures reality. They named the semicoherent direction of numerous product lines, the actions of about 30,000 employees, and operations in about forty countries around the world. They described roughly what Nokia did and something of what Nokia managers would do in the future. They gave a name to the rapidly changing set of actions that characterized a firm that was branding cellular phones, creating high-end products like its $2,000 9000 Communicator, a phone/Internet device, and betting on new technologies like personal communications services (PCS). They captured the essence of what was fundamentally a semicoherent direction that was emerging from lower levels of the corporation. This simplicity built a sense of coherence and control in an otherwise complicated set of strategies.

Comparison of Three Leaders

Three senior executives from our cases provide a useful contrast in the synthesis and articulation of the strategy. At Titan, the dominant business that is moving from mainframe to client/server computing, the senior executive crafted a synthesis of the firm as a leader in "computing solutions for the global corporation." The synthesis is succinct, and yet captures the essence of Titan's business. At the same time, it permits variation from the central theme. As this executive told us, "We have a vision, but we deviate from it when we see a good opportunity." So not everything at Titan falls into line with this vision. Yet even though what the firm did or was likely to do did not exactly correspond with the vision, the vision is intimately related to the essence of the firm. In effect, this executive created a coherence that was partially true, but he also communicated more coherence than there really is.

Traditional Leadership versus Competing on the Edge

Traditional Leadership	Competing on the Edge
Group executives are span-breakers to ensure adequate control.	Group executives patch businesses to match changing markets.
Corporate leaders develop strategy.	Strategy emerges from businesses.
Strategy is developed by corporate leaders.	Corporate leaders distill the essence of the strategy from many businesses.
The best managers effectively analyze complex situations and develop strategic plans.	The best managers can see patterns in data and think across time frames.
To be competitive, detailed strategic plans must be executed.	Competition evolves in real time in surprising ways.
Success comes from sage planning followed by flawless execution.	Success comes from skilled, fast, and agile real-time moves at the business level, smart patching at the group level, and articulation of a simple vision at the senior level.

At a second firm, the senior executive is also quite visionary. He excels in looking ahead to the future of the industry and his firm's position within it. He also understands how his various businesses fit together. But this executive cannot simplify. He cannot convey coherence. He believes that the constellation of businesses is too complicated to simplify into a sound bite. For him, to simplify would be to mislead. His unwillingness (and perhaps inability) to articulate a focused, elegant interpretation of the firm frustrates other managers. They want a vision. As one implored, "We need to see someone out in front. It's so chaotic that we have to believe that someone is out there leading us and knowing what's going on. Other companies have their Scott [Sun], their Larry [Oracle], their Bill [Microsoft]. We need to have him."

At the third firm, the senior executive articulates an exciting interpretation of the firm. He is mesmerizing and charismatic when he expounds about the future. Yet the vision rings hollow. It is exciting . . . but it is not his company. Most of the people cannot see what the vision has to do with them or with the firm as a whole. The vision is too futuristic and too disjointed from the reality of the firm to be a compelling and rallying statement. This executive has framed a synthesis of the firm that is too disconnected from the truth.

Leading on the Edge

Earlier in this chapter we pointed out how tenuous maintaining superior performance was at Starbucks and is at any business, especially ones that compete in rapidly changing and unpredictable markets. It is very challenging to maintain such performance because it requires balancing on the edges of chaos and time, keeping up with the pace of change, and outwitting savvy competitors. The simultaneity and dynamism of these challenges suggest the rethinking of leadership roles. Below is a checklist that summarizes each of the roles.

At the business and functional levels . . .

1. The job is strategy. The bottom line is winning.

2. Create strategy by improvising, coadapting, experimenting, and regenerating. Next time pace.

3. Constantly test to ensure that you are still on the edge. Test the edges by adding or taking away some structure. Be vigilant for cues that you are slipping in one direction or another.

4. If the market speeds up, consider creating patches within your business.

5. Develop juggling skills to deal with competing tensions.

At the patching level of managing multiple businesses or product lines . . .

1. Keep businesses modular, focused on particular market opportunities, and accountable for a few key performance measures. Pay particular attention to business size.

2. Make patching decisions quickly, but with broad involvement, to limit politicking.

3. As markets become faster paced or more uncertain, make businesses smaller and more fine-grained. Loosen the connections between them.

4. Develop pattern recognition skills.

At the senior level . . .

1. Shape a simple synthesis of the firm—not the future—that captures the essence of the businesses without constraining, an interpretation that is not entirely faithful to reality but that is still grounded in reality.

2. Remember to articulate the synthesis, make the occasional big commitment, and cheerlead.

3. The firm will become less coherent as markets become faster paced or more uncertain, but the synthesis should not.

4. Watch for new market opportunities that even the patching-level managers may miss.

5. Develop pattern synthesis and articulation skills.

At every managerial level, managerial skills around time are essential. Timing and the ability to think across time frames that span from today to next month to next year and out several years—while still remaining focused on today—are essential to sustaining superior performance in fast-paced, competitive, and unpredictable markets.

The hallmark of great

companies is an ability to

recognize the game has

changed and to adapt.

Arthur Martinez,

Sears, Roebuck &

Company

rules of competing on the

THE PREMISE OF this book is that change is pervasive. The implication is that the key strategic challenge facing managers in many contemporary businesses is managing this change. The challenge is to react quickly, anticipate when possible, and lead change where appropriate. A manager's dilemma is how to do this, not just once or every now and then, but consistently. Our book has argued that competing on the edge is the unpredictable, often uncontrolled, and even inefficient strategy that nonetheless defines best practice when change is pervasive.

What are the "laws" of competing on the edge? The following summary distills the themes of this book into ten laws, or rules, that articulate the key assumptions and best practices about strategy, organization, and leadership that we have found to characterize firms that compete on the edge.

Strategy

Rule 1: Advantage Is Temporary

Treat any strategy as temporary. Managers who compete on the edge understand that competitive advantage is fleeting, and so they focus on continuously generating new sources of advantage. This casts change as an opportunity, not a threat. These managers ask "How can I turn change into new opportunities?" not just "How can I defend my position against these changes?" For example, executives at opportunity-oriented cable companies saw the uncertainty of the Internet not just as a threat to cable television, but as an opportunity to provide high-speed cable Internet access. These best practice managers act as though today's advantage will be gone tomorrow.

Rule 2: Strategy Is Diverse, Emergent, and Complicated

Rely on diverse strategic moves. Strategy is not a single, simple approach to the marketplace. It is a diverse collection of moves that are loosely linked together in a semicoherent strategic direction. Managers who compete on the edge let strategy emerge—as happened at Microsoft around the Internet—and then shape and articulate it. These managers make a variety of moves, observe what happens, and follow through with the ones that are successful. They play a broader range of strategic options and expect to shift strategy over time from, for example, driving differentiated brands, to pushing the technology envelope, to emphasizing cost leadership. Surprising strategies like discount broker Charles Schwab's unexpected moves toward full service brokerage defy prediction and keep competitors off-balance and guessing.

Rule 3: Reinvention Is the Goal

Managers who compete on the edge look for opportunities to reinvent their businesses and then let profits follow. They worry about finding new ways to create value, but not necessarily about being the most efficient firm. This emphasis on reinvention shows up in performance measures that track the sales of innovative products. One example is 3M's corporate edict that mandates 25 percent of sales come from products less than four years old. Emerson Electric's goal for new product sales making up 35 percent of total sales is another. This emphasis shows up in a focus on keeping pace with a changing marketplace, such as market share gain and sales growth relative to specific competitors. The emphasis on reinvention does not imply that profits are forgotten. Rather, these best practice managers recognize that profitable fortresses are rare, and that reinvention is the smarter path toward long-term profitability. So these managers ask, "What are next year's new sources of revenue?" as often as they ask, "What are the earnings in the core businesses today?"

Organization

Rule 4: Live in the Present

The present is the *most* important time frame. Today's product launch, today's manufacturing performance, and today's sales bookings matter most. The approach to managing today is to maximize minimum structure. Managers who compete on the edge structure their businesses as little as possible, paying attention to what is not structured as well. Necessary is structure found in priorities that everyone can recite and responsibilities that everyone knows. A few strict rules and a few slavishly monitored operating variables like cycle time, bookings, and metrics on order fulfillment indicate necessary—but minimal—structure. As described earlier, the result is service that is consistent yet personal like British Airways, and products that are innovative and efficiently distributed like Nike. These managers use just enough structure to keep things from flying apart, keep businesses poised for change, and keep managers aware of new opportunities. Across businesses, these managers look to capture some, but not all, synergies.

Rule 5: Stretch Out the Past

Although the present is the most important time frame, managers who compete on the edge nonetheless learn more from the past than their counterparts who don't compete on the edge. They keep their product and service platforms in the market longer than others, exploit derivative products more effectively, and extend their offerings into new geographies and customer segments more frequently. They often selectively use the past to jump-start new opportunities. Best practice managers realize that the past is often *the* competitive advantage when chasing new opportunities. Wise use of the past diminishes risk and frees resources to focus on new ideas. For example, managers at the Gap looked to their past to support the launch of Old Navy. The new venture combined existing world-class sourcing and logistics with fresh merchandise, new store locations, and a distinct retail format to appeal to a new customer segment. Gap executives took some risks, but not every decision was a risk. The most sophisticated of managers who compete on the edge reverse time by refreshing existing businesses with learnings from new ventures—as IBM managers did with their Lotus Notes acquisition that helped revitalize sales of their mainframe computers. But while using experience, these managers guard against becoming locked into dated competitive models. Best practice managers stretch the past, but stay on the edge.

Rule 6: Reach into the Future

Managers who compete on the edge reach further into the future. Simply put, they manage in a longer time horizon than most others. Driven by a belief that the future is unpredictable, they launch more experimental products and services, create more strategic alliances with a focus on nascent markets and technologies, and employ more futurists than other firms. Driven by a paranoia that the future is constantly changing, they revisit the future often. For example, they might evaluate the service mix of an experiment in grocery store banking daily, meet monthly with futurists, and monitor equity investments in fledgling ventures quarterly. Yet despite frequent reviews of the possible future, these managers do not spend a lot of time on the future, nor do they invest much in planning. Instead, they strike a balance. They avoid underinvesting in the future and constantly play. At the same time, they are not entranced by the future at the expense of the more important present.

Rule 7: Time Pace Change

Managers who compete on the edge pace change in their businesses with the passage of time as well as by the occurrence of events. They understand that pace—as distinct from speed—is a critical strategic weapon. So they set a rhythm and tempo around the number of new products or services launched per year (such as Emerson Electric's 35 percent target for new product sales), the number of store openings per quarter (such as Starbucks' and Canada's Chapters Bookstores' growth plans), rhythmic refreshment of brands (such as British Airways' refreshing of travel service brands on a regular basis), or the building of manufacturing capacity (such as Intel's plans for building a new manufacturing facility every nine months). Like a tennis player making an approach shot, a golfer chipping, or a football player returning a kick-off, these managers manage the transitions that rhythm creates. For example, they usually choreograph the switch from one product development project to the next. They may choreograph the assimilation of acquisitions as Banc One does, or new market entries as Gillette does. When they launch products, they orchestrate their logistics and coordinate with complementers. If they cannot set the pace, they try to match their tempo of change with the demands of the market and the rhythm of other firms. Managers who compete on the edge understand the power of rhythm to get their businesses into a groove and keep them there.

Leadership

Rule 8: Grow the Strategy

Managers who compete on the edge grow their businesses like prairies, rather than assemble them like toasters. This means that they do not build the pieces of strategy at once. To rejuvenate strategy, they begin by pruning back branches as Arthur Martinez did at Sears. They revamp current businesses and strategies by correcting the clearest cases of over- and under-structuring. They set priorities, major responsibilities, and operating measures if they do not exist, and dismantle mega-structure that does exist. They pay attention to the order in which strategy is grown—beginning with current businesses, then working to incorporate the past and linking future opportunities, and concluding with time pacing. These managers never start with the future when regrowing a business—they start with the basics of today.

Rule 9: Drive Strategy from the Business Level

The mindset is business-level driven strategy and accountability. Business managers control both parts of strategy: "where do you want to go?" and "how are you going to get there?" Managers in best practice companies realize that, in high-velocity markets, strategy cannot be driven top down. Too much changes too fast to wait for strategy to trickle down through a hierarchy. Success comes from skilled, fast, and agile moves at the business level.

Rule 10: Repatch Businesses to Markets and Articulate the Whole

The role of the senior managers also shifts. In a slowly changing world, a wise corporate architect could cleanly map businesses onto market opportunities once and for all. In a rapidly changing world, this is not feasible. Any neat match of businesses with markets is all too fleeting in a world where opportunities come and go, collide and divide, and merge and morph. This constant flux creates the challenge of continually re-examining the make-up of individual businesses and their matches with markets, as exemplified by Honda's realignment of its recreational vehicles for the Japanese market, and Compaq's remapping of businesses onto the converging opportunity space of the Internet, telecommunications, and consumer electronics. Continuously re-aligning businesses with emerging opportunities and articulating and occasionally shaping emergent strategy are the principal responsibilities for best practice senior managers. Pattern recognition and the articulation of the essence of patterns are the skills that can be found at the heart of the senior manager's job.

The ten rules of competing on the edge make sense in rapidly changing and uncertain industries where the two parts of strategy come together. Rooted in the logics of complexity thinking, the nature of speed, and time-paced evolution, they result in a semicoherent direction that is somewhat unpredictable, uncontrolled, maybe even inefficient, but also one that is robust and effective. Competing on the edge is complicated and demanding, but it is also an approach to strategy that works . . . when the name of the game is change.

APPENDIX: METHODS

The ideas behind competing on the edge emerged from our in-depth field research on firms in Asia, Europe, and North America. We focused our research on the computer industry because it is the prototypical illustration of a high-velocity industry for which managing change is the key strategic challenge. Each of the twelve businesses we studied competes in industry segments that are extremely competitive and have high rates of technological change. These businesses are thus ideal for studying strategy and organization in situations where the ability to change is central to superior performance.

Research Design

The research design is a multiple-case study that permits a "replication" logic in which the cases are treated as a series of independent experiments that confirm or disconfirm emerging conceptual insights. We usually gathered information on the perspectives of three levels of the management hierarchy. We incorporated into the analysis the impact of parent company and industry factors that might influence strategy-making. In addition, we included both real-time observations and retrospective data.

The research sample consisted of six pairs of businesses. Nine were headquartered in North America, two in Europe, and one in Asia. One member of each pair was considered a *dominant* player within its segment of the industry, using profitability, growth, market share, and general industry reputation to determine this measurement. This dominant business was matched with a *very good* business using the same measurements, but one that was not a segment leader. The dominant businesses had an average revenue growth of more than 20 percent per year during the 1990s. The very good businesses had an average revenue growth of approximately 5 percent per year over the same period. Although all of the businesses competed within the broadly-defined computer industry, each of these pairs faced unique strategic issues. The rationale for this variety was to ensure that these findings are general enough to apply across many strategic contexts.

The primary data for the book were drawn from our initial research in nine businesses. We chose the business-unit level of analysis because of its strategic centrality for firms that compete in rapidly changing markets. We then added data from three additional businesses, one of which balanced the sample to create a set of five pairs of businesses facing similar strategic issues. The other two additions were diversified, multidivisional firms with global reach that were the parent corporations of two businesses in the original sample.

Selection of Case Studies

Two of the businesses were *leading-edge technologists.* That is, they were competing at the frontier of the very latest technology. This let us capture the competitive dynamics of the extraordinarily fine line between the leading versus "bleeding" edge of technology.

Two businesses were *component integrators* competing in hotly contested, high growth industry segments. For the managers of these businesses, the critical strategic choices involved constantly making trade-offs regarding product features and new technologies in the context of an enormously competitive and cost-sensitive market segment.

Two businesses were making the major *corporate transformation* from mainframe to client/server markets. The critical strategic issues for these businesses centered on how and when to make that switch. Timing was the critical unknown. When and how would mainframes die? Moreover, the dramatic switch in computing regimes was as much cultural and organizational as it was technical and market driven. Businesses in the mainframe segment of the industry tended to be more bureaucratic and their pace of business was slower than the high-velocity and hotly aggressive client/server world.

Another two businesses, major purveyors of shrink-wrapped application software, were enmeshed in *standards battles.* Here the critical strategic issues revolved around managing in a segment of the industry where control of standards was the central competitive issue. Choosing the right hardware and software platforms, rapidly building an installed base, and building a network with the right set of collaborators were keys to ultimately dominating these winner-take-all markets.

Two businesses were *high-growth* ventures. The central strategic issue for these businesses was managing the torrid pace of growth. The critical challenge for managers was to keep running fast enough to stay on the growth treadmill without self-destructing in the process. The task was made that much more difficult by more established competitors constantly nipping at their heels.

Table A-1 • Case Studies by Chapter

Chapter	Case	Strategic Position
2	Royal	Corporate transformation
	Nautilus	Component integrator
	Cruising	Component integrator
3	Jupiter	Diversified multinational
	Galaxy	Leading-edge technologist
	Tai-pan	Diversified multinational
4	Fable	Standards battles
	NewWave	High-growth venture
	Midas	Leading-edge technologist
5	Pulsar (part of Galaxy)	Leading-edge technologist
	Nautilus	Component integrator
	Titan	Corporate transformation
6	Zeus	Standards battles
	Callisto (part of Jupiter)	Division of diversified multinational
7	Tai-pan	Diversified multinational
	Royal	Corporate transformation
8	Pioneer	High-growth venture
	Jupiter	Diversified multinational
	Titan	Corporate transformation

The final two businesses were *diversified, multinational corporations*. The key strategic issue for these large, complex, multidivisional organizations was orchestrating synergy among business units while keeping the corporation continuously aligned with constantly evolving market opportunities. Particularly challenging was balancing the unique demands of a single business with the advantages of capturing cross-business synergies.

We deliberately disguised the cases in the book in order to protect the identity of the firms and their managers. We promised anonymity to the executives we interviewed in order to obtain much greater candor and depth than would otherwise be possible. Details such as specific products and corporate location have therefore been disguised. In a few examples, we created composite cases where data drawn from several businesses has been attributed to only one. We did this in order to illustrate points in a way that would ensure anonymity.

Data Collection

For the initial nine cases, we collected data through interviews, questionnaires, observations, and secondary sources. The primary source of this data was semistructured interviews with more than eighty individual managers at several levels within the management hierarchy. These managers included lower level executives who were responsible in some capacity for individual projects or small portfolios of activities, and higher level managers such as general managers, vice presidents, and corporate executives. There was a mix of functional areas represented at both higher and lower levels, including engineering and marketing respondents.

We conducted these interviews during visits to the companies that spanned several days. Interviews typically lasted ninety minutes, although some ran as long as three hours. During site visits, we kept a daily record of impressions and recorded our informal observations during lunches, coffee breaks, and product demonstrations. Whenever possible, we audited meetings. These observations served to provide real-time data.

We began our interviews with questions that would uncover a manager's background as well as the competitive dynamics of the market segment in which the business competed. We covered the key strategic issues facing the business and particular product lines within the business. Depending on the identity of the interviewee, we also asked questions about relationships within and across different groups within the business, and with other parts of the corporation. We paid particular attention to the innovation process and the related product development portfolios that are the lifeblood of firms in rapidly changing markets.

In addition to qualitative data, we asked the managers to provide quantitative data. The survey they were asked to complete included questions on communication patterns, collaboration, organizational structure, role clarity, priorities, project and business performance, competitors, leveraging, and transition processes. We collected data on the financial performance of the business from the chief financial officer. In addition, we gathered extensive secondary data from the business press in order to build our understanding of the market and parent company forces that affected each business.

After the primary data collection, we added three additional cases and followed up with managers at many of the original businesses studied. This latter data collection was less structured than the first one, and occurred during visits to each site. It included open-ended interviews as well as real-time observations of executive meetings.

Data Analysis

As is typical of inductive research, we analyzed the data by first building extensive individual case studies and then comparing across cases to construct a conceptual framework. As a first step, we entered all transcribed interview responses into a database indexed by case, interview number, interview type, and question number. Next, we gathered responses to the same question to form a single response.

Using these synthesized responses and secondary sources, we wrote a case study for each site. This iterative process required frequently revisiting the data as important features of strategy and organization emerged within each case. Although we noted similarities and differences among the cases, we delayed further analysis until all case write-ups were completed to maintain the independence of the replication logic. A second researcher read through the original interviews and formed an independent view of each case. We then used this independent view to cross-check each emerging case study. The initial case-writing process took about six months to complete.

Once the individual case studies were completed, we used cross-case analysis to develop conceptual insights. We had no a priori hypotheses. Initially, we compared the cases to identify common dilemmas and refine the unique aspects of each particular case. We created tables and graphs to facilitate further comparisons and compared successive pairs of cases for similarities and differences to develop the emerging constructs and theoretical logic. With each iteration we used new permutations of case pairs to refine the conceptual insights. We took several breaks during the analysis process to refresh our thinking. As the analysis evolved, we raised the level of abstraction. We went back to our original cases to confirm and adjust our ideas as needed. We also went back to the original interviews to ensure our ideas continued to be consistent with the data.

Later we added three additional cases and brought our number of interviewed managers to over one hundred. We used these new data to confirm and elaborate the hypotheses and conceptual framework that we had developed and to give us a fresh pool of data to help refine our thinking. The two multidivisional company cases were particularly helpful in sharpening our understanding of capturing cross-business synergies.

We gathered secondary information, including books, teaching cases, and articles from the business press on additional firms from a wider set of industries in order to refine our thinking about the applicability of these ideas across a variety of industries and strategic positions. We honed our ideas by using them in the classroom as teaching material. We also explored the relationship between the insights that we developed from our twelve cases and those from our research on complexity and evolutionary theories, the nature of speed, and time-pacing, as well as from the more general research on strategy and organizations. The result of these efforts was the competing on the edge framework.

NOTES

Chapter I

1. This definition of strategy is taken from "Making Strategy," *Economist*, 1 March 1997.

2. David Kirkpatrick, "Intel's Amazing Profit Machine," *Fortune*, 17 February 1997.

3. Michael E. Porter, "What is Strategy?" *Harvard Business Review* 74, no. 6 (1996): 61.

4. Our thinking builds on the work on emergent strategy of a number of colleagues, including Joseph Bower, Robert Burgelman, Henry Mintzberg, James Brian Quinn, and Karl Weick.

5. Denise Caruso, "Microsoft Morphs into a Media Company," *Wired*, June 1996.

6. Ibid.

7. Stuart Kauffman, *At Home in the Universe* (New York: Oxford University Press, 1995).

8. Some debate surrounds the meaning of complexity and edge of chaos in the scientific community (see Horgan and Johnson in the complexity area of the subject bibliography). In light of this debate, we have used conceptualizations that are grounded in our data, and as such are relevant in the context of real corporations.

9. This insert relies on our and others' works cited in the *Subject Bibliography*, particularly in the areas of complexity and evolutionary theories and time-paced evolution.

10. All 3M quotations are from Thomas A. Stewart, "3M Fights Back," *Fortune*, 5 February 1996.

11. Kauffman.

12. This example is taken from chapter 7 of W. Mitchell Waldrop, *Complexity: The Emerging Science at the Edge of Order and Chaos* (New York: Touchstone, 1992).

Chapter 2

1. Anne Miner and Christine Moorman initially triggered our interest in improvisation. Jo Hatch, Deb Meyerson, Beth Bechky, and Karl Weick gave us invaluable insight into the workings of improvisation.

2. Ben & Jerry's makes social values an important goal that often supersedes traditional measures of financial performance.

3. Geoffrey Smith and Jeffrey M. Laderman, "Fixing Fidelity," *Business Week*, 6 May 1996.

4. Linda Grant, "Stirring It Up at Campbell," *Fortune*, 13 May 1996.

5. Both Campbell Soup and Mercedes-Benz have staged comebacks by becoming more improvisational.

6. Rajiv Rao, "Zen and the Art of Teamwork," *Fortune*, 25 December 1995.

Chapter 3

1. The Time Life illustration relies extensively on the case by David Garvin and Jonathan West, "Time Life Inc. (A)," Case 9-395-012 (Boston: Harvard Business School, 1995).

2. The work of D. Charles Galunic, Morten Hansen, and Gabriel Szulanski on cross-business coadaptation was helpful to us in writing this chapter. We also benefited from conversations with Robert Axelrod and Michael Cohen.

3. Greg Burns, "What Price the Snapple Debacle?" *Business Week*, 14 April 1997.

4. All Time Warner quotations are from "Ted Turner's Management Consultant," *Economist*, 22 March 1997.

5. This vignette appears in Arie de Geus' *The Living Company* (Boston: Harvard Business School Press, 1996), 134–135.

6. Hugo Uyterhoeven and Myra Hart, "Banc One–1993," Case 9-394-043 (Boston: Harvard Business School, 1993).

7. This communication is described in Stuart Kauffman's *At Home in the Universe* (New York: Oxford University Press, 1995), 267–271.

Chapter 4

1. The insights of Erhard Bruderer, Andrew Hargadon, Daniel Levinthal, James March, and Jitendra Singh were particularly helpful in our thinking about genetic algorithms and recombination. John Holand is our source for the explore versus exploit dichotomy.

2. Paul Colford, "New Cosmo Editor Won't Alter Magazine's Sassy Spirit," *San Jose Mercury News*, 20 February 1997.

3. Edith Updike, "Toyota: The Lion Awakens," *Business Week*, 11 November 1996.

4. Bill Saporito, "Fallen Arches," *Time*, 9 June 1997.

5. Kathy Rebello, "Spindler's Apple," *Business Week*, 3 October 1994.

6. "General Motors' Saturn: Success at a Price," *Economist*, 27 June 1992.

7. George Mannes, "Will Mario Find Love at 64?" *New York Daily News*, 29 September 1996.

8. Linda Himelstein, "The World According to GAP," *Business Week*, 27 January 1997.

Chapter 5

1. Jeffrey Kluger, "Next Stop: Mars," *Time*, 11 November 1996.

2. Frank Sweeney, "Another Small Step," *San Jose Mercury News*, 13 March 1997.

3. Ron Stodghill II, "So Shall Monsanto Reap?" *Business Week*, 1 April 1996.

4. Peter Elstrom, "Did Motorola Make the Wrong Call?" *Business Week*, 29 July 1996.

5. Catherine Arnst, "AT&T: Will the Bad News Ever End?" *Business Week*, 7 October 1996.

6. The research of Sim Sitkin, Paul Lave, and Etienne Wenger on learning was particularly helpful in our thinking.

7. John Byrne, "Strategic Planning," *Business Week*, 26 August 1996.

Chapter 6

1. David Kirkpatrick, "Intel's Amazing Profit Machine," *Fortune*, 17 February 1997.

2. Ibid.

3. We particularly appreciate the critical insights of Connie Gersick on time pacing.

4. "Canada Wins Gold in Relay," *Canadian Press Newswire*, 3 August 1996.

5. All Gillette quotations are from Linda Grant, "Gillette Knows Shaving—and How to Turn Out Hot New Products," *Fortune*, 14 October 1996.

6. Geraldine Fabrikant, "Blockbuster's Profit Is Now Seen Plunging," *New York Times*, 2 July 1997.

7. Lawrence A. Armour, "Can We Talk?" *Fortune*, 9 June 1997, 189–196.

8. For further information on implementing time pacing, refer to Kathleen M. Eisenhardt and Shona L. Brown, "Time Pacing: Competing in Markets That Don't Stand Still," *Harvard Business Review* (forthcoming).

Chapter 7

1. "American Retailing: Back to the Future," *Economist*, 9 October 1993.

2. Kevin Kelly, "The Big Store May Be on a Big Roll," *Business Week*, 30 August 1993.

3. Carol J. Loomis, "Dinosaurs?" *Fortune*, 3 May 1993.

4. Patricia Sellers, "Sears: In with the New . . . Out with the Old," *Fortune*, 16 October 1995.

5. Patricia Sellers, "Sears: The Turnaround Is Ending, the Revolution Has Begun," *Fortune*, 28 April 1997.

6. This experiment is described in Kevin Kelly's book *Out of Control* (Reading, MA: Addison-Wesley, 1994), 57–68. Our ideas on growing ecosystems build on the example discussed by Kevin Kelly as well as on work by J. A. Drake and Stuart Pimm.

7. We relied heavily on several cases prepared by Dorothy Leonard-Barton and George Thill, "Hewlett-Packard: Singapore (A), (B), (C)," Cases 9-694-035, -036, and -037 (Boston: Harvard Business School, 1993).

8. We relied on our academic research and the work of Stuart Kauffman for this insert.

Chapter 8

1. Alfred D. Chandler, *Strategy and Structure* (Cambridge: MIT Press, 1962).

2. The work of D. Charles Galunic was particularly helpful throughout this chapter.

3. Stuart Kauffman's *At Home in the Universe* was particularly helpful in our thinking about the importance of patch size.

4. Charles Krauthammer, "Make It Snappy," *Time*, 21 July 1997, was the source for some of the ideas about sound bites.

5. Rahul Jacob, "Nokia Fumbles, But Don't Count It Out," *Fortune*, 19 February 1996.

BIBLIOGRAPHY

Subject Listing

4×100 Relay

"Best in the World: Sprinters Set the Pace in a Record Medal Haul." *Maclean's* (Toronto edition), 12 August 1996.

Blockus, Gary R. "Thomas Runs Away from Field for Another State Title." *Morning Call*, 29 May 1994.

"Canada Wins Gold in Relay." *Canadian Press Newswire*, 3 August 1996.

Cox, Jennai. "GB Relay Team Pass on Their Experience." *Times*, 28 October 1996.

Davidson, Neil. "Canadian Quintet Easy Team Choice." *Charlottetown Guardian*, 2 January 1997.

Longman, Jere. "Canada Shocks US (Minus Lewis) in Relay." *New York Times*, 4 August 1996.

Rosen, Mel, and Karen Rosen. *Track Championship Running*. New York: Sports Illustrated, 1988.

"Smooth Baton Passing Key Factor in Relays." *Washington Post*, 8 August 1992.

Woods, David. "US Shocked in 4×100 Relay." *Indianapolis Star*, 4 August 1996.

Airline Industry

Associated Press. "Southwest Air Chief Flies an Unconventional Route." *San Jose Mercury News*, 29 November 1996.

"Bandits at Nine O'Clock." *Economist*, 17 February 1996, 57.

Boisseau, Charles. "Southwest's Pilot." *Houston Chronicle*, 10 March 1996.

Freiberg, Jackie, and Kevin Freiberg. "Is This Company Completely Nuts?" *Executive Excellence*, September 1996, 20.

Freiberg, Kevin. *Nuts!* Austin, Tex.: Bard Books, 1996.

Godsey, Kristin D. "Flying Lessons: Ten Southwest Strategies to Apply to Your Business." *Success*, October 1996, 23.

James, George W. "Big U.S. Airlines: Under Siege." *Journal of Commerce*, 1 February 1996.

Larson, Mark. "Southwest Is Declared Winner against United." *Business Journal—Sacramento*, 4 March 1996, 4.

Lowry-Miller, Karen. "Flying Cheap in Europe." *Business Week*, 31 March 1997, 50.

Murphy, Ian P. "Southwest Emphasizes Brand as Others Follow the Low-Fare Leader." *Marketing News*, 4 November 1996.

Atlanta Braves

Associated Press. "Series Brings Together Flamboyant Owners Turner, Steinbrenner." 18 October 1996.

Benson, John. "Building a Winner." http://www.johnbenson.com/building, October 1997.

"Bobby Cox." Major League Baseball Properties, Inc., http://www.majorleaguebaseball.com/bios, 1997.

Edes, Gordon. "It's Getting Old for the Rest of the NL, but the World Seems to Belong to the Braves." *Fort Lauderdale Sun-Sentinel,* 15 October 1996.

Hersch, Hank. "End of the Slide." *Sports Illustrated,* 19 August 1991.

Complexity Theory

Gell-Mann, Murray. *The Quark and the Jaguar: Adventures in the Simple and the Complex*. New York: W. H. Freeman, 1994.

Hatch, Mary Jo, and Haridimos Tsoukas. "Complex Thinking about Organizational Complexity," working paper, Warwick Business School, January 1997.

Holland, John. *Adaptation in Natural and Artificial Systems*. Ann Arbor: University of Michigan Press, 1975.

Horgan, John. "From Complexity to Perplexity." *Scientific American*, June 1995, 104–109.

Johnson, George. *Fire in the Mind*. New York: Vintage, 1995.

Kauffman, Stuart. *At Home in the Universe*. New York: Oxford University Press, 1995.

———. "Escaping the Red Queen Effect." *McKinsey Quarterly* 1 (Spring 1995), 119–129.

Waldrop, W. Mitchell. *Complexity: The Emerging Science at the Edge of Order and Chaos*. New York: Touchstone, 1992.

Core Competence

Barney, Jay B. *Gaining and Sustaining Competitive Advantage*. Reading, Mass.: Addison-Wesley, 1997.

Peteraf, Margaret. "The Cornerstones of Competitive Advantage: A Resource-Based View." *Strategic Management Journal* (March 1993), 179.

Prahalad, C. K., and Gary Hamel. *Competing for the Future*. Boston: Harvard Business School Press, 1994.

———. "The Core Competence of the Corporation." *Harvard Business Review* (May-June 1990), 79.

Stalk, George, Philip Evans, and Lawrence E. Shulman. "Competing on Capabilities: The New Rules of Corporate Strategy." *Harvard Business Review* (March-April 1992), 57.

Cross-Business Coadaptation

Galunic, D. Charles, and Kathleen M. Eisenhardt. "The Evolution of Intracorporate Domains: Divisional Charter Losses in High-Technology, Multidivisional Corporations." *Organization Science* 7, no. 3 (1996): 255–282.

Hansen, Morten. "The Search-Transfer Problem: The Role of Weak Ties in Sharing Knowledge Across Subunits," working paper, Harvard University, 1997.

Hargadon, Andrew and Robert I. Sutton. "Technology Brokering and Innovation in a Product Development Firm." *Administrative Science Quarterly* 42, no. 4 (1997): 716–749.

Szulanski, Gabriel. "Appropriability and the Challenge of Scope: Banc One Routinizes Replication," working paper, University of Pennsylvania, 1997.

Emergent Strategy

Bower, Joseph L. *Managing the Resource Allocation Process.* Boston: Harvard Business School Press, 1970.

Burgelman, Robert A. "A Process Model of Internal Corporate Venturing in the Major Diversified Firm." *Administrative Science Quarterly* 38 (1993): 223–224.

———. "Intraorganizational Ecology of Strategy Making and Organizational Adaptation: Theory and Field Research." *Organization Science* 2 (1991): 239–262.

Mintzberg, Henry, and Alexandra McHugh. "Strategy Formation in an Adhocracy." *Administrative Science Quarterly* 30 (1985): 160–197.

Quinn, J. Brian. *Strategies for Change.* Homewood, IL: R. D. Irwin, 1980.

Evolutionary Theory

Bruderer, Erhard, and Jitendra V. Singh. "Organizational Evolution, Learning, and Selection: A Genetic-Algorithm-Based Model." *Academy of Management Journal* 39, no. 5 (1996): 1322–1349.

Baum, Joel A. C., and Jitendra V. Singh, eds. *Evolutionary Dynamics of Organizations.* New York: Oxford University Press, 1994, 3–20.

Hargadon, Andrew and Robert I. Sutton. "Technology Brokering and Innovation in a Product Development Firm." *Administrative Science Quarterly* 42, no. 4 (1997): 716–749.

Kogut, Bruce, and Udo Zander. "Knowledge of the Firm, Combative Capabilities, and the Replication of Technology." *Organization Science* 3 (1992): 383–397.

Levinthal, Daniel A. "Organizational Adaptation and Environmental Selection—Interrelated Processes of Change." *Organization Science* 2 (1991): 140–145.

March, James G. "Exploration and Exploitation in Organizational Learning." *Organization Science* 2 (1991): 71–87.

Van de Ven, Andrew H., and Scott M. Poole. "Explaining Development and Change in Organizations." *Academy of Management Review* 20, no. 3 (1995): 510–540.

Five Forces

Porter, Michael E. *Competitive Strategy*. New York: The Free Press, 1980.

———. "What Is Strategy?" *Harvard Business Review* (November-December 1996), 61.

Formula One Pit Stops

Beattie, Leal. "Winston Point Leader Not Overconfident." *Dayton Daily News*, 20 October 1995.

O'Keeffe, Chris. "9-4 Hill for Italy Glory." *Sporting Life*, 7 September 1996.

Matchett, Steve. "When Every Second Seems an Eternity." *London Sunday Times*, 31 March 1996.

———. "The Perfect Formula." *London Sunday Times*, 24 December 1995.

Game Theory

Brandenburger, Adam M., and Barry J. Nalebuff. *Co-opetition*. New York: Doubleday, 1996.

D'Aveni, Richard A. *Hypercompetition: Managing the Dynamics of Strategic Maneuvering*. New York: Free Press, 1994.

Nalebuff, Barry J., and Adam M. Brandenburger. "The Right Game: Use Game Theory to Shape Strategy." *Harvard Business Review* (July-August 1995), 57.

Improvisation

Barrett, Frank J., and Mary Jo Hatch. "Organizational Innovation and Jazz Improvisation: Exploring a Postmodern Metaphor." Paper presented at the Academy of Management conference, Vancouver, Canada, August 1996.

Bastien, David T., and Todd J. Hostager. "Cooperation as Communicative Accomplishment: A Symbolic Interaction Analysis of an Improvised Jazz Concert." *Communication Studies* 43 (1992): 92–104.

———. "Jazz as a Process of Organizational Innovation." *Communication Studies* 15, no. 5 (1988): 582–602.

Berliner, Paul F. *Thinking in Jazz: The Infinite Art of Improvisation*. Chicago: University of Chicago Press, 1994.

Borko, Hilda, and Carol Livingston. "Cognition and Improvisation: Differences in Mathematics Instruction by Expert and Novice Teachers." *American Educational Research Journal* 26, no. 4 (1989): 473–498.

Hatch, Mary Jo. "Jazz as a Metaphor for Organizing in the 21st Century," working paper, Cranfield School of Management, 1996.

Moorman, Christine, and Anne S. Miner, "Organizational Improvisation and Organizational Memory," working paper, University of Wisconsin, 1997.

Rao, Rajiv M. "Zen and the Art of Teamwork." *Fortune*, 25 December 1995, 218.

Weick, Karl E. "The Aesthetic of Imperfection in Orchestras and Organizations," working paper, University of Michigan, 1997.

Learning Options

Lave, Jean and Etienne Wenger. *Situated Learning*. Cambridge: Cambridge University Press, 1991.

McGrath, Rita and Ian MacMillan. "The Effect of Uncertainty on Technology Investment Strategies in High Velocity Environments: A Real Options View," working paper, Columbia University, 1997.

Sitkin, Sim. "Learning Through Failure: the Strategy of Small Losses." *Research in Organizational Behavior* 14 (1992): 231–266.

Movie Industry

Grover, Ronald. "Lights, Camera, Less Action." *Business Week*, July 1996, 50.

"Hollywood's Fading Charms." *Economist*, 22 March 1997.

Parks, Christopher. "Screened for Viability." *Financial Times Limited*, 22 June 1996.

Naskapi

Moore, Omar Khayyam. "Divination—A New Perspective." *American Anthropologist* 59, no. 1 (1957): 69.

Vollweiller, Lothar Georg, and Alison B. Sanchez. "Divination—'Adaptive' From Whose Perspective?" *Ethnology* 202, no. 3 (1983): 193.

Weick, Karl E. *The Social Psychology of Organizing*, 2nd ed. Reading, Mass.: Addison-Wesley, 1975.

Prairie

Drake, J. A. "Community Assembly Mechanics and the Structure of an Experimental Species Ensemble." *American Naturalist* 137 (1991): 1.

———. "The Mechanics of Community Assembly and Succession." *Journal of Theoretical Biology* (147), 213.

Kelly, Kevin. *Out of Control*. Reading, Mass.: Addison-Wesley, 1994.

Pimm, Stuart L. *The Balance of Nature*. Chicago: University of Chicago Press, 1991.

Punctuated Equilibrium

Abernathy, William J., and James M. Utterback. "Patterns of Industrial Innovation." *Technology Review* (June-July 1978), 40–47.

Gersick, Connie J. G. "Revolutionary Change Theories: A Multilevel Exploration of the Punctuated Equilibrium Paradigm." *Academy of Management Review* 16, no. 1 (1991): 274.

Romanelli, Elaine, and Michael L. Tushman. "Organizational Transformation as Punctuated Equilibrium: An Empirical Test." *Academy of Management Journal* 37, no. 5 (1994): 1141.

Tushman, Michael L., and Philip Anderson. "Technological Discontinuities and Organizational Environments." *Administrative Science Quarterly* 31 (1986): 439.

Speed

Eisenhardt, Kathleen M. "Making Fast Strategic Decisions in High-Velocity Environments." *Academy of Management Journal* 32, no. 3 (1989): 543.

Eisenhardt, Kathleen M., and Behnam N. Tabrizi. "Accelerating Adaptive Processes: Product Innovation in the Global Computer Industry." *Administrative Science Quarterly* 40, no. 1 (March 1995): 84–110.

Strategic Planning

Byrne, John A. "Strategic Planning." *Business Week*, 26 August 1996, 46.

Mintzberg, Henry. "The Fall and Rise of Strategic Planning." *Harvard Business Review* 72, no. 1 (1994): 107.

Time-Paced Evolution

Ancona, Deborah G., and C. L. Chong. "Entrainment: Pace, Cycle and Rhythm in Organizational Behavior." *Research in Organizational Behavior* 18, (1996): 251–284.

Brown, Shona L., and Kathleen M. Eisenhardt. "The Art of Continuous Change: Tying Complexity Theory and Time-Paced Evolution to Relentlessly Shifting Organizations." *Administrative Science Quarterly* 42, no. 1 (1997): 1–34.

Gersick, Connie J. G. "Marking Time: Predictable Transitions in Task Groups." *Academy of Management Journal* 32, no. 2 (1989): 274.

———. "Time and Transition in Work Teams: Towards a New Model of Group Development." *Academy of Management Journal* 31, no. 1 (1988): 9.

————. "Pacing Strategic Change: The Case of a New Venture." *Academy of Management Journal* 37, no. 1 (1994): 9.

Tyre, Marcie, Leslie Perlow, Nancy Staudenmayer, and Christina Wasson. "Time as a Trigger for Organizational Change," working paper, MIT, 1996.

U.S. Space Program

Flanigan, James. "Solving a Space Problem: JPL Thinks Small, Cheap to Stay Aloft." *Los Angeles Times*, 4 September 1996.

Kluger, Jeffrey. "Next Stop: Mars." *Time*, 11 November 1996, 73.

Salisbury, David F. "Engineers Explore Ways to Replace Mechanical Devices with Tiny Machines." *Stanford Report*, 2 April 1997, 1.

————. "Stay Tuned: Weather Reports from Mars." *Stanford Report*, 6 November 1996, 1.

"Space Exploration: Small, Fast, Cheap and Erotic." *Economist*, 24 February 1996, 88.

Sweeney, Frank. "Another Small Step." *San Jose Mercury News*, 13 March 1997.

Company Listing

3M

Bartlett, Christopher A., and Afroze Mohammed. *3M Optical Systems: Managing Corporate Entrepreneurship*. Case 9-395-017. Boston: Harvard Business School, 1994.

———. *3M: Profile of an Innovating Company*. Case 9-395-016. Boston: Harvard Business School, 1995.

DeYoung, Garret. "Listen, Then Design." *Industry Week*, 17 February 1997, 76.

Kanter, Rosabeth Moss. "Don't Wait to Innovate." *Sales & Marketing Management* 149, no. 2 (1997): 22.

Peterson, Susan E. "How to Build a Board." *Star Tribune*, 5 January 1997.

Stevens, Tim. "Balancing Act." *Industry Week*, 17 March 1997, 40.

Stewart, Thomas A. "3M Fights Back." *Fortune*, 5 February 1996, 94.

Acer

Engardio, Pete. "For Acer, Breaking Up Is Smart to Do." *Business Week*, 4 July 1994, 82.

Engardio, Pete, and Peter Burrows. "Acer: A Global Powerhouse." *Business Week*, 1 July 1996, 94–96.

Kraar, Louis. "Acer's Edge: PCs to Go." *Fortune*, 30 October 1995, 187–204.

Air France

Balmer, Crispian. "Europe's Lame Duck Airlines Struggle to Take Off." *Reuters European Business Report*, 10 November 1995.

Edmondson, Gail. "The Fighter Piloting Air France." *Business Week International Editions*, 7 April 1997, 16.

"Final State Aid Installments for Air France and Tap Approved." *European Report*, no. 2217, 19 April 1997.

Follain, John. "Strike-Hit French Airline Limps into Open Skies." *Reuters Financial Services*, 1 April 1997.

McCormick, Jay. "Air France's Restructuring Taking Off." *USA Today*, 2 January 1997, 6B.

"News and Views." *Journal of Commerce*, 30 October 1995, 3.

Owen, David. "Europe on a Tight Schedule." *Financial Times*, 9 May 1996.

Ridding, John. "More Fuel Needed for Recovery." *Financial Times*, 18 September 1995, 16.

Toy, Stewart. "Can Air France Make Its Connection?" *Business Week*, 17 June 1996, 126.

Tran, Pierre. "Interview: Air France Flies into Turbulent Change." *Reuters European Business Report*, 28 March 1997.

Amazon.com

Krantz, Michael. "Amazonian Challenge." *Time*, 14 April 1997, 71.

Martin, Michael H. "The Next Big Thing: A Bookstore?" *Fortune*, 9 December 1996, 169–170.

Rebello, Kathy, Larry Armstrong, and Amy Cortese. "Making Money on the Net." *Business Week*, 23 September 1996, 104–118.

America Online

"America Online Posts $10.3 Million Loss But Says Revenue Rose by 250% in Quarter." *Washington Post*, 8 November 1995.

Barrett, Amy. "At AOL, More Holes by the Minute." *Business Week*, 24 February 1997, 37.

———. "Honey, What's on AOL Tonight?" *Business Week*, 2 June 1997, 131–132.

Barrett, Amy, and Paul Eng. "AOL Downloads a New Growth Plan." *Business Week*, 14 October 1996.

———. "Can Bob Pittman Upgrade AOL?" *Business Week*, 11 November 1996, 44.

Barrett, Amy, Paul Eng, and Kathy Rebello. "For $19.95 a Month, Unlimited Headaches for AOL." *Business Week*, 27 January 1997, 35.

Koprowski, Gene. "AOL CEO." *Forbes ASAP*, 7 October 1996.

Lohr, Steven. "On-Line Stars Hear Siren Calls to Free Agency." *New York Times*, 25 November 1995.

Oakes, Brian C. "America Online: The Most Powerful Online Media Franchise." *Lehman Brothers*, 11 October 1996.

Parekh, Michael, and Vik Mehta. "On-line/Internet Software and Services Highlights." *Goldman Sachs US Research*, 4 October 1996.

Ramo, Joshua Cooper. "How AOL Lost the Battles but Won the War." *Time*, 22 September 1997, 46–62.

Apple Computer

"Apple's Clouded Vision: MacWorld Expo." *Multimedia Monitor*, 1 February 1997.

Burgess, John. "Apple Bets on Newton, New Direction." *Washington Post*, 30 July 1993.

DeBare, Ilana. "The Future's in Hand." *Sacramento Bee*, 9 February 1993.

Fisher, Lawrence M. "Apple and IBM End Multimedia Joint Venture." *New York Times*, 18 November 1995.

Ford, Ric. "Developers Wish Apple Success, But Faith Slipping." *MacWeek*, 14 April 1997, 29.

Kalman, Edmund. "Tokyo Unveiling Proves Apple's Point." *Nikkei Weekly*, 15 February 1993, 9.

Haber, Lynn. "The Bruised Apple." *InfoWorld*, 8 January 1996.

"IBM, Apple to Dismantle Kalieda Venture." *Reuters Financial Service*, 17 November 1995.

"IBM to Adapt Taligent Programming Interfaces, Plans Modifications to Make Them Work with OpenDoc." *Computergram International*, 8 January 1996.

Mello, Adrian. "Beyond the Power Macs." *MacWorld* (August 1994): 19.

Miller, Michael J. "Unmet Promises." *PC Magazine*, 24 September 1996.

Nash, Jim. "Newton Gets Lukewarm Reception from Resellers." *Business Journal-San Jose*, 16 August 1993, 1.

Norr, Henry. "Passing Observations on a Corporation in Crisis." *MacWeek*, 5 February 1996.

O'Connor, Rory J. "Apple Goes Out on Limb for Newton." *Dallas Morning News*, 7 August 1993.

Potts, Mark. "Apple Gets to the Core of a Consumer Vision." *Washington Post*, 17 January 1993.

Rebello, Kathy, and Peter Burrows. "Apple's Uncertain Harvest." *Business Week*, 9 August 1993, 70.

Rebello, Kathy, Ira Sager, and Richard Brandt. "Spindler's Apple." *Business Week*, 3 October 1994, 88–96.

Schlack, Mark. "Apple's Opening Move." *Byte* (March 1997): 14.

Schneidawind, John. "Newton's Big Bang." *USA Today*, 29 May 1992.

"Taligent to Become IBM Subsidiary." *Business Wire*, 19 December 1995.

Thompson, Tom. "The MessagePad Makeover." *Byte* (March 1997): 44.

AT&T

Arnst, Catherine. "AT&T: Will the Bad News Ever End?" *Business Week*, 7 October 1996, 122.

———. "Ready, Set, Devour?" *Business Week*, 8 July 1996.

Byrne, John A., and Arnst, Catherine. "Can Walter Fix AT&T?" *Business Week*, 10 March 1997, 26.

Elstrom, Peter. "Dialing for Direction." *Business Week*, 14 July 1997, 25–26.

Kupfer, Andrew. "What, Me Worry?" *Fortune*, 30 September 1996, 121–124.

———. "For Long Distance Companies, Going Local Is a Grind." *Fortune*, 3 March 1997, 136.

———. "Is Lucent Really as Good as It Seems?" *Fortune*, 26 May 1997, 107–110.

———. "Why Allen's Latest Plan Won't Work." *Fortune*, 7 July 1997, 30–32.

Loomis, Carol J. "AT&T Has No Clothes." *Fortune*, 5 February 1996.

"The Passion of the Newly Converted." *Economist*, 8 June 1996, 74.

Banc One

"Adams Named Banc One's Chief Technology Officer." *PR Newswire*, 20 March 1997.

Albertson, Robert B. "Banc One Corporation: The Right Bank at the Right Time and the Right New Product." Goldman Sachs, *Investment Research*, 7 December 1992.

"Baldwin to Become National Business Banking Chief at Banc One Corporation." *PR Newswire*, 16 November 1995.

Bryant, Adam. "The Post of President Is Filled at Banc One." *New York Times*, 22 April 1992.

Fickenscher, Lisa. "Banc One Shifts Execs, Seeks More Coordination." *American Banker*, 16 December 1993.

"Strategize . . . Survive . . . Succeed." *Magazine of Bank Management*, July-August 1994.

Teitelman, Robert. "The Magnificent McCoys: Running America's Best Bank." *Institutional Investor*, July 1991.

Uyterhoeven, Hugo and Myra Hart. "Banc One–1993." Case 9-394-043. Boston: Harvard Business School, 1995.

Zack, Jeffrey. "Will the Super Community Concept Remain Viable?" *American Banker*, 9 October 1995.

Ben & Jerry's

Barna, Ed. "Ben & Jerry's Copes with a Changing Marketplace." *Vermont Business Magazine*, May 1995, 16.

Canedy, Dana. "Chief Leaving Ben & Jerry's as Its Sales Are Lagging." *New York Times*, 28 September 1996.

Judge, Paul C. "Is It Rainforest Crunch Time?" *Business Week*, 15 July 1996, 70.

Kadlec, Daniel. "A New Flavor at Ben & Jerry's." *Time*, 14 October 1996, 72.

Mackinnon, Malcolm. "The Ice Dream Team." *Hemp Times*, July-August 1997, 42–48.

Redman, Russel. "The Just Dessert." *Supermarket News*, 7 August 1995.

Taylor, Alex III. "Yo, Ben! Yo, Jerry! It's Just Ice Cream!" *Fortune*, 28 April 1997, 374.

Blockbuster Video

Fabrikant, Geraldine. "Blockbuster's Profit Is Now Seen Plunging." *New York Times*, 2 July 1997.

Forest, Stephanie Anderson, Gail DeGeorge, and Kathleen Morris. "The Script Doctor Is in at Blockbuster—Again." *Business Week*, 28 July 1997, 101.

Sellers, Patricia. "Wal-Mart's Big Man Puts Blockbuster on Fast-Forward." *Fortune*, 25 November 1996, 111–113.

British Airways

Colling, Trevor. "Experiencing Turbulence: Competition, Strategic Choice and the Management of Human Resources in British Airways." *Human Resource Management Journal* (Autumn 1995): 18.

Prokesch, Steven E. "Competing on Customer Service: An Interview with British Airways' Sir Colin Marshall." *Harvard Business Review* (November-December 1995): 101.

Reed, Stanley. "British Airways Sure Isn't Coasting." *Business Week*, 13 September 1996, 52.

British Petroleum

Lubin, Joann S. "BP Negotiating to Sell Minerals Business." *Wall Street Journal*, 15 December 1988.

"Swedish Ban Lifted to Allow BP Mine Venture." *Wall Street Journal*, 4 March 1983.

"US Minerals Exploration." *Wall Street Journal*, 20 July 1982.

Campbell Soup

Apt, Jay. "Gerber's Johnson Named by Campbell." *Focus*, 10 January 1990, 11.

Berman, Phyllis, and Alexandra Alger. "Reclaiming the Patrimony." *Forbes*, 14 March 1994, 50.

Donlon, J. P. "Top Spoon Stirs It Up; Interview with Campbell Soup CEO David Johnson." *Chief Executive* (November 1996): 44.

Mastrull, Diane. "Campbell and Pace Recipe: A Mixing of Disparate Cultures." *Philadelphia Business Journal*, 17 February 1995, 1.

Grant, Linda. "Stirring It Up at Campbell." *Fortune 500*, 13 May 1996, 80.

Weber, Joseph. "Now, Campbell's Makes House Calls." *Business Week*, 16 June 1997, 144–146.

Compaq

Brethour, Patrick. "How Compaq Runs its Virtual Network." *Globe and Mail*, 25 September 1996, B12.

Burrows, Peter. "Where Compaq's Kingdom Is Weak." *Business Week*, 8 May 1995, 98–102.

———. "Why Bother Making Home PCs?" *Business Week*, 30 September 1996, 72–74.

"Compaq Announces Sweeping Organization Changes Aimed at Supporting Growth, Expanding Global Leadership." Compaq Press Release, 2 July 1996.

"Compaq Launches New Workstation Division." Compaq Press Release, 5 August 1996.

Kirkpatrick, David. "Fast Times at Compaq." *Fortune*, 1 April 1996, 120–128.

———. "Houston, We Have Some Problems." *Fortune*, 23 June 1997, 102–103.

McCartney, Scott. "Compaq Says It Is Revamping into Three Divisions." *Wall Street Journal*, 3 July 1996, B4.

McWilliams, Gary. "At Compaq, A Desktop Crystal Ball." *Business Week*, 20 March 1995, 96–97.

———. "Compaq: All Things to All Networks?" *Business Week*, 31 July 1995, 79–80.

———. "Compaq at the 'Crossroads.'" *Business Week*, 22 July 1996, 70.

———. "Compaq's Unhappy Headhunting Ground." *Business Week*, 11 November 1996, 42.

———. "Compaq: There's No End to Its Drive." *Business Week*, 17 February 1997, 72.

———. "Battle Stations! Battle Stations!" *Business Week*, 11 August 1997, 34–35.

McWilliams, Gary, and Ira Sager. "Compaq Starts a PC Brawl." *Business Week*, 18 March 1996, 40.

Venetis, Tom. "Compaq Restructures Product Divisions." *Computing Canada* 12, no. 15, 25 July 1996, B4.

Wildstrom, Stephen H. "Compaq's Brave New Network." *Business Week*, 27 March 1995, 22.

———. "Compaq's $1000 Bargain." *Business Week*, 10 March 1997, 18.

Cosmopolitan

Brown, Helen Gurley. "Management Wisdom from the Ultimate Cosmo Girl." *Fortune*, 28 October 1996, 181–184.

Colford, Paul D. "New Cosmo Editor Won't Alter Magazine's Sassy Spirit." *San Jose Mercury News*, 20 February 1997.

Daimler-Benz

Nakanishi, Nao. "Mercedes Seen Depressing Daimler Earnings in 1992." *Reuters Financial Service*, 28 October 1992.

———. "Mercedes Seen Depressing Daimler Earnings this Year." *Reuter Asia-Pacific Business Report*, 28 October 1992.

Simonian, Haig. "Car Trip into the Unknown." *Financial Times*, 9 August 1996.

Taylor, Alex III. "Speed! Power! Status!" *Fortune 500*, 10 June 1996, 47.

Templeman, John. "A Mercedes for Every Driveway." *Business Week*, 26 August 1996, 38.

Vlasic, Bill. "In Alabama, the Soul of a New Mercedes?" *Business Week*, 31 March 1997, 70.

Woodruff, David. "Dustup Daimler." *Business Week*, 3 February 1997, 52–53.

———. "The Bulldozer at Daimler-Benz." *Business Week*, 10 February 1997, 52.

D. E. Shaw

Aley, James. "Wall Street's King Quant." *Fortune*, 5 February 1996, 108.

"B of A Teams Up with D. E. Shaw, A High-Tech Investment Boutique." *The American Banker*, 14 March 1997.

Bass, Thomas A. "The Phynancier." *Wired*, January 1997, 152–211.

"D. E. Shaw & Co., L. P.'s FarSight Subsidiary Enables Financial Institutions to Provide Integrated Financial Services Online." *Business Wire*, 11 February 1997.

"How Quants like Shaw Make their Money." *Fortune*, 5 February 1996.

Lux, Hal. "Reprogramming D. E. Shaw." *Investment Dealers' Digest*, 4 September 1995, 16.

———. "D. E. Shaw Chairman Predicts Major Impact from Internet." *Investment Dealers' Digest*, 8 July 1996, 11.

Peltz, Michael. "'Computational Finance' with David Shaw." *Institutional Investor* (March 1994): 88.

Segal, Julie. "D. E. Shaw Delivers Net Front End for Third-Market Trading." *Financial Net News* 2, no. 11 (1997): 1.

"Strategic Alliance between Bank of America and D.E. Shaw & Co. Creates New Force in Global Financial Markets." *Business Wire*, 13 March 1997.

Weisul, Kimberly. "D. E. Shaw Subsidiary Makes First Move into Retail." *Investment Dealers' Digest*, 17 February 1997, 11.

———. "First Web-based Trade Takes Place in Third Market." *Investment Dealers' Digest*, 24 March 1997, 13.

Wirth, Gregg. "Bank of America Forms Alliance with D. E. Shaw." *Investment Dealers' Digest*, 17 March 1997, 3.

Dell

Narayandas, Das. *Dell Computer Corporation*. Case 9-596-058. Boston: Harvard Business School, 1996.

Emerson Electric

Emerson Electric Annual Report, 1996.

Fidelity Investments

Collins, James. "The Money Machine." *Time*, 30 September 1996, 42.

Fromson, Brett D. "SEC Probing Personal Trading at Fidelity." *Washington Post*, 13 January 1994.

Smith, Geoffrey. "Fidelity Struggles to Soar Again." *Business Week*, 9 December 1996, 166.

Smith, Geoffrey, and Jeffrey M. Laderman. "Fixing Fidelity." *Business Week*, 6 May 1996, 100.

Whitford, David. "Is Fidelity Losing It?" *Fortune*, 13 January 1997, 20–21.

Whitford, David, and Joseph Nocera. "Has Fidelity Lost It?" *Fortune*, 9 June 1997, 58–70.

Wyatt, Edward. "Fidelity Limits Fund Managers' Comments on Stocks." *New York Times*, 10 January 1996.

———. "Who's Out to Topple Jeff Vinik?" *New York Times*, 5 May 1996.

GAP, Inc.

Brown, Ed. "Will Old Navy Fill the Gap?" *Fortune*, 18 March 1996, 59.

Emert, Carol. "Old Navy Chain Is Trying Out Separate Shops for Kids' Toys." *San Francisco Chronicle*, 17 May 1997.

"Gap Forms New Division: To Open 40 Stores." *Reuter Business Report*, 10 March 1994.

"Gap Plans to Open 185–200 Stores in 1994." *Reuters Financial Service*, 3 March 1994.

George, Melissa. "Gap Addresses Frugal Shoppers with New Unit." *Reuters Financial Service*, 10 March 1994.

Himelstein, Linda. "The World According to GAP." *Business Week*, 27 January 1997, 72.

Joyce, Tom. "Old Navy: New Aim at Clothes." *Burlington County Times*, 14 May 1995.

Pellet, Jennifer. "The Manhattan Stories." *Discount Merchandiser* (October 1995): 20.

Popiel, Leslie Albrecht. "'Old Navy' Store Is Gap's Answer to Penny-Pinching Shopper." *Christian Science Monitor*, 31 October 1994, 8.

Saccomano, Ann. "Few Gaps at Gap Inc." *Journal of Commerce*, 18 November 1996, 45.

Strom, Stephanie. "How Gap Inc. Spells Revenge." *New York Times*, 24 April 1994.

Wallace, David J. "Abercrombie & Fitch Stores Being Opened by the Limited." *Philadelphia Business Journal*, 20 May 1994.

General Motors

"GM's Saturn: Success at a Price." *Economist*, 27 June 1992, 80.

Hitchner, Earle. "A Bold Experiment: Saturn Corp." *National Productivity Review* 13, no. 2, 22 March 1994, 297.

Kerwin, Kathleen. "GM Warms Up the Branding Iron." *Business Week*, 23 September 1996, 153–154.

McWhirter, William A. "GM Gets Set to Hit the Road." *Time*, 14 April 1997, 62.

"Service Strategy Key to Car Sales." *Marketing Week*, 15 November 1996.

Teresko, John. "Engineering: Where Competitive Success Begins." *Industry Week*, 19 November 1990, 30.

Valigra, Lori. "Saturn's NT Effect." *Client/Server Company* 3, no. 6, June 1996, 40.

"Would Mid-Size Saturn Be Made the Old Way?" *Los Angeles Times*, 6 July 1996.

Gillette

Bulkeley, William M. "Duracell Pact Gives Gillette an Added Source of Power." *Wall Street Journal*, 13 September 1996.

———. "Gillette Gets $7.3 Billion Power Source." *Wall Street Journal*, 13 September 1996, A3.

Donlon, J. P. "An Iconoclast in a Cutthroat World." *Chief Executive*, no. 111 (1996): 34–38.

"Gillette-Duracell: A Great Marriage." *Reuters Financial Service*, 13 September 1996.

"Gillette Moving Quickly to Acquire Parker Pen." *New York Times*, 7 May 1993, D3.

"Gillette Reports Record Results for Fourth Quarter." *Business Wire*, 31 January 1997.

Grant, Linda. "Gillette Knows Shaving—And How to Turn Out Hot New Products." *Fortune*, 14 October 1996.

Lowenstein, Roger. "Blades, Batteries, and a Fifth of Gillette." *Wall Street Journal*, 19 September 1996, C1.

Maremont, Mark. "How Gillette Wowed Wall Street." *Business Week*, 30 September 1996, 36–37.

Morris, Betsy. "The Brand's the Thing." *Fortune*, 4 March 1996, 72–86.

Ramirez, Anthony. "Gillette to Buy Stake in Wilkinson Sword." *New York Times*, 21 December 1989.

"This Pregnant Guppy Bears Correction Fluid." *Wall Street Journal*, 14 August 1991.

Grateful Dead

Johnson, Greg. "A Dead Head for Business." *Los Angeles Times*, 18 August 1996.

Rifkin, Glenn. "How to Truck the Brand: Lessons from the Grateful Dead." *Strategy & Business*, no. 6, 1997, 51.

Swenson, John. "Grateful Dead Hit It Big 'In the Dark.'" United Press International, 4 September 1987.

Hewlett-Packard

Dickinson, Mike. "Is New HP Product Reason for Xerox to Mope?" *Rochester Business Journal*, 15 November 1996, 2.

Feitzinger, Edward, and Hau L. Lee. "Mass Customization at Hewlett-Packard: The Power of Postponement." *Harvard Business Review* 75, no. 1 (1997): 116.

Ferdows, Kasra. "Making the Most of Foreign Factories." *Harvard Business Review* 75, no. 2 (1997): 73–88.

"HP Launches Its First Locally Made Electronic Organiser." *Straits-Times Singapore*, 3 November 1995, 46.

"HP Targets the Growing Small-Business Market with New Products." *Business Wire*, 11 March 1996.

James, Geoffrey. "An Interview with Lewis Platt." *Upside* 8, no. 2 (1996): 66–67.

James, Kenneth. "HP Raises Internet Profile in Region." *Business Times*, 3 June 1996, 10.

Kraar, Louis. "How Americans Win in Asia." *Fortune*, 7 October 1991, 133.

Leonard-Barton, Dorothy, and George Thill. *Hewlett-Packard: Singapore (A, B, C)*. Cases 9-694-035, 9-694-036, and 9-694-037. Boston: Harvard Business School, 1993.

Sanger, David E. "Singapore Aim: High-Tech Future." *New York Times*, 15 May 1990.

Honda Motor Company

"Accent on Productivity." *Financial Times*, 7 January 1997.

"Even Apple Pie Isn't So American Anymore." *PR Newswire*, 8 April 1997.

"Japanese Cars Make New Inroads in US." *Financial Times*, 14 March 1997.

Taylor, Alex III. "The Man Who Put Honda Back on Track." *Fortune*, 9 September 1996, 92–100.

Intel

Berkowitz, Harry. "Intel's Aboutface Addresses Its Image." *Newsday*, 21 December 1994, A41.

Cogan, George, and Robert Burgelman. "Intel Corporation: The DRAM Decision." Case S-BP-256. Stanford, CA: Stanford Business School, 1989.

Grove, Andrew S. *Only the Paranoid Survive*. New York: Doubleday, 1996.

Hutheesing, Nikhil. "Excuse Me If I Invade Your Business." *Fortune*, 10 March 1997, 158–162.

Kirkpatrick, David. "Intel's Amazing Profit Machine." *Fortune*, 17 February 1997, 60–68.

Nanda, Ashish, and Christopher A. Bartlett. "Intel Corporation: Leveraging Capabilities for Strategic Renewal." Case 9-394-141. Boston: Harvard Business School, 1994.

Reinhardt, Andy. "Intel inside the Net." *Business Week*, 18 November 1996, 166–174.

Ristelhueber, Robert. "Microprocessor War: How Intel Did It." *Electronic Business Today* (October 1996): 38–46.

Laura Ashley

Ferry, Jeffrey. "The Flowers Bloom Anew: Laura Ashley Inc." *EuroBusiness* (September 1993): 24.

Flynn, Julia, and Christopher Power. "Giving Laura Ashley a Yank." *Business Week*, 27 May 1996, 147.

Nolan, Richard L., David C. Croson, and Christopher L. Marshall. "Laura Ashley (A): A New CEO Takes Charge." Case 9-194-142. Boston: Harvard Business School, 1994.

———. "Laura Ashley (B): Defining a Strategy." Case 9-194-143. Boston: Harvard Business School, 1994.

Nolan, Richard L., and Dr. Gloria Schuck. "Laura Ashley (C): Rebuilding and Transforming a Global Brand." Case 9-194-144. Boston: Harvard Business School, 1994.

Warnaby, Gail. "Laura Ashley—An International Retail Brand." *Management Decisions* 32, no. 3 (1994): 42–48.

McDonald's

"Battle of the Burgers Starts to Sizzle." *Financial Times*, 24 December 1996, 24.

Branch, Shelly. "McDonald's Strikes Out with Grownups." *Fortune*, 11 November 1996, 157–162.

Burns, Greg. "McDonald's: Now, It's Just Another Burger Joint." *Business Week*, 17 March 1997, 38.

———. "Fast-Food Fight." *Business Week*, 2 June 1997, 34–36.

"Canada's New Pizza Leader Opens 640 Restaurants Today!" *Canada Newswire*, 23 March 1992.

Commins, Patricia. "U.S. Fast-Food Chains Target Baby Boomers." *Reuters Financial Service*, 7 June 1996.

———. "U.S. Hamburger Chains Battle on into 1997." *Reuters Financial Service*, 18 December 1996.

"Expert Software Announces Licensing Agreement with McDonald's Corporation." *Business Wire*, 6 January 1997.

Gunn, Eileen P. "What's Eating McDonald's?" *Fortune*, 13 October 1997, 122–125.

"McDonald's Corporation Launches New Salads." *Reuters Financial Service*, 13 December 1996.

"McDonald's Introduces the McGrilled Chicken Sandwich: A Great New Chicken Choice." *PR Newswire*, 15 October 1993.

"McDonald's New 'California Cool Tastes' Warm Palates across the Southland." *PR Newswire*, 16 May 1995.

"McDonald's Testing Several New Products." *Reuters Financial Service*, 28 May 1993.

"Olympic Trials Set for McDonald's Arch Deluxe Sandwich on July 23." *PR Newswire*, 23 July 1996.

Samuels, Gary. "Golden Arches Galore." *Forbes*, 4 November 1996, 46–48.

Saporito, Bill. "Fallen Arches." *Time*, 9 June 1997.

Merck

"Merck & Co., Inc." *Med Ad News* (September 1996): 94.

"Merck's Top Officers Tell Stockholders How Company Is Dealing with Turbulent Environment." *Business Wire*, 27 April 1993.

Nichols, Nancy A. "Scientific Management at Merck: An Interview with CFO Judy Lewent." *Harvard Business Review* 72, no. 1 (1994): 89.

Spiegel, Francis H. Jr. "Strategic Alliances, with Care and Creativity." *Financial Executive*, March 1993, 28.

Weber, Joseph. "Mr. Nice Guy with a Mission." *Business Week*, 25 November 1996, 132.

Microsoft

Auerbach, Jon. "All Eyes Turn to Microsoft." *Boston Globe*, 7 December 1995, 48.

Baker, Sharon. "Microsoft's Internet Strategy May Encroach on Other Firms." *Puget Sound Business Journal* 16, no. 31 (1995): 6.

————. "Newsmaker of the Year: Bill Gates." *Puget Sound Business Journal* 16, no. 32 (1995): 8.

Bartholomew, Doug. "Bill Gates Envisions the Enterprise." *Industry Week* 245, no. 23 (1996): 8.

Carlson, Steven. "Looking Back on the Year of the Internet." *Budapest Business Journal*, 18 December 1995, 32.

Caruso, Denise. "Microsoft Morphs into a Media Company." *Wired* (June 1996): 128.

Coates, James. "Gates to Open Windows to the Internet Gospel." *Chicago Tribune*, 7 April 1994.

Cross, Michael. "Bill Gates' Bold Mission to Take Over Cyberspace." *Observer*, 10 December 1995, 1.

Eng, Paul, Amy Cortese, and Kathy Rebello. "Microsoft Plays the Net." *Business Week*, 1 January 1996, 41.

Einstein, David. "Microsoft Unveils Internet Strategy." *San Francisco Chronicle*, 8 December 1995.

Erickson, Jim. "Gates Gets Serious about the Internet." *Spokesman-Review*, 8 December 1995.

Flores, Michele Matassa. "Gates Casts Vision Across the 'Net." *Pittsburgh Post-Gazette*, 8 December 1995.

Gardner, Fran. "Jiving with Java." *Oregonian*, 8 December 1995.

Hof, Robert D., Kathy Rebello, and Amy Cortese. "Cyberspace Showdown." *Business Week*, 7 October 1996, 34.

Kehoe, Louise. "Engineer of the Electronic Era." *Financial Times*, 31 December 1994, 6.

Kehoe, Louise, and Paul Taylor. "Microsoft to Forge Internet Role with Rivals." *Financial Times*, 8 December 1995, 1.

————. "Microsoft Stakes a Claim in the Internet Goldrush." *Financial Times*, 11 December 1995, 25.

Lewis, Peter H. "Microsoft Seeks Internet Market; Netscape Slides." *New York Times*, 8 December 1995.

Poletti, Therese. "Microsoft Gets Boost to Internet Strategy." *Reuters Business Report*, 14 December 1995.

Rebello, Kathy. "After Win95, What Do You Do for an Encore?" *Business Week*, 16 October 1995, 68.

———. "Inside Microsoft." *Business Week*, 15 July 1996, 56.

Schlender, Brent. "Whose Internet Is It, Anyway?" *Fortune*, 11 December 1995, 120.

Wolk, Martin. "Microsoft Developing Online Service." *Reuters Business Report*, 13 September 1994.

———. "Interview—Microsoft Internet Plans." *Reuters Financial Service*, 14 November 1995.

Monsanto

Grant, Linda. "Monsanto's Bet: There's Gold in Going Green." *Fortune*, 14 April 1997, 116.

Lenzner, Robert, and Bruce Upbin. "Monsanto v. Malthus." *Forbes*, 10 March 1997, 58.

Stodghill, Ron, II. "So Shall Monsanto Reap?" *Business Week*, 1 April 1996, 66.

Motorola

Cane, Alan. "Markets Leave Motorola Alone with Its Troubles." *Financial Times*, 9 October 1996.

Chandrasekran, Rajiv. "Motorola's Next Page: The Cellular Giant and Onetime Stock Star Seeks Ways to Renew Its Growth." *Washington Post*, 29 September 1996.

Coy, Peter. "Is Motorola a Bit Too Patient?" *Business Week*, 5 February 1996, 150.

Elstrom, Peter. "Did Motorola Make the Wrong Call?" *Business Week*, 29 July 1996, 66.

Elstrom, Peter, Gail Edmondson, and Eric Schine. "Does this Galvin Have the Right Stuff?" *Business Week*, 17 March 1997, 102–105.

Melville, Richard. "Motorola's Twin Woes Seen as Unique." *Reuters Financial Service*, 11 September 1996.

Nadeau, Susan. "Motorola Passing Through Rough Patch, Seen Recovering." *Reuters Financial Service*, 12 September 1996.

Tetzeli, Rick. "And Now for Motorola's Next Trick." *Fortune*, 28 April 1997, 122–130.

NBC

Lesly, Elizabeth. "Seinfeld." *Business Week*, 2 June 1997, 116–121.

Nike

Condor, Bob. "Author Sees Nike Running on Sears' Path." *Chicago Tribune*, 26 June 1994.

Himelstein, Linda. "The Soul of a New Nike." *Business Week*, 17 June 1996, 70.

————. "The Swoosh Heard 'Round the World." *Business Week*, 12 May 1997, 76–80.

Jones-Yang, Dori. "Can Nike Just Do It?" *Business Week*, 18 April 1994, 86.

Krentzman, Jackie. "The Force Behind the Nike Empire." *Stanford Magazine* (January 1997): 63.

Willigan, Geraldine E. "High-Performance Marketing: An Interview with Nike's Phil Knight." *Harvard Business Review* 70, no. 4 (1992): 91.

————. "Why Networks May Fail." *Economist*, October 1992, 83.

Nintendo

Baird, Roger. "Video Games Market Falls Back on Speed." *Marketing Week*, 6 September 1996, 25.

Brandt, Richard. "Is Nintendo a Street Fighter Now?" *Business Week*, 29 August 1994, 35.

Britt, Russ. "Film Star Silicon Graphics Brings 3-D to Main Street." *Investor's Business Daily*, 12 November 1996.

Browder, Seanna, Steven Brull, and Andy Reinhardt. "Nintendo: At the Top of its Game." *Business Week*, 9 June 1997, 72–73.

Curtiss, Aaron. "Personal Technology." *Los Angeles Times*, 30 September 1996.

Erickson, Jim. "Holiday Hotshot." *Sacramento Bee*, 27 November 1996.

Everly, Steve. "Toy Story." *Kansas City Star*, 27 October 1996.

Greenstein, Jane. "News Analysis: Nintendo Keeps N64 in Tight Supply." *Video Business*, 10 March 1997, 14.

Mannes, George. "Will Mario Find Love at 64?" *New York Daily News*, 29 September 1996, 38.

McGann, Michael E. "Bill Sets Sights on Mario." *Dealerscope Consumer Electronics Marketplace*, November 1996, 28.

Miller, Cyndee. "Video Makers Brace for Yule Showdown." *Marketing News*, 7 October 1996, 12.

"SGI Pumps Up the Power." *UNIX News*, November 1996, 6.

"Sony to Cut Prices in Computer Games War." *Daily Telegraph*, 1 March 1997.

Steiner, Rupert. "British Hardware to Bail Out Sega." *London Sunday Times*, 30 March 1997.

Turner, Nick. "Hot Game Machine Brings Good Cheer to Nintendo." *Investor's Business Daily*, 24 December 1996.

"U.S. N64 Will Remain at $199." *Multimedia Daily*, 10 March 1997.

"Videogame Consoles and PCs Share Home Entertainment Limelight Globally." *PR Newswire*, 10 March 1997.

Nokia

Edmondson, Gail, Peter Elstrom, and Peter Burrows. "At Nokia, A Comeback—and Then Some." *Business Week*, 2 December 1996, 106.

Jacob, Rahul. "Nokia Fumbles, But Don't Count It Out." *Fortune*, 19 February 1996.

Jarvenpaa, Sirkka, and Ilkka Tuomi. "Nokia Telecommunications: Redesign of International Logistics." Case 9-996-006. Boston: Harvard Business School, 1995.

McIvor, Greg. "Markets Cool on Ericsson Rise." *Financial Times*, 12 February 1997.

Peachey, Damian. "Giants Rule the World." *Financial Times*, 25 November 1996.

"US Cellular Industry 1996 Growth Slowed." *Reuters Financial Service*, 30 January 1997.

Putnam

Fairley, Juliette. "Mutual Fund Mania." *Black Enterprise* (October 1996): 109.

Rohrer, Julie. "Empowering Putnam." *Institutional Investor*, March 1993.

Teitelbaum, Richard. "Look Who's Beating Fidelity: Putnam." *Fortune 500*, 10 June 1996, 75.

Quaker

Bagli, Charles V. "Snapple Is Just the Latest Case of Mismatched Reach and Grasp." *New York Times*, 29 March 1997.

Berkowitz, Harry. "Annoyed, Frustrated (and Very Rich) Snapple Co-Founder Sold the Company for Millions But Hates to See His Baby Mismanaged." *Newsday*, 25 November 1996.

———. "Quaker Cereal Sales Up but Snapple's Still Down." *Newsday*, 7 February 1997.

Burns, Greg. "What Price the Snapple Debacle?" *Business Week*, 14 April 1997.

Collins, Glenn. "Is the Quaker Oats Company Considering Another Fling with Wendy the Snapple Lady?" *New York Times*, 20 December 1996.

Commins, Patricia. "Quaker's Snapple Sale Raises Questions about Gatorade." *Reuters Financial Service*, 31 March 1997.

Dow Jones News Service. "Potential Sale of Snapple Lifts Quaker." *Newsday*, 30 November 1996.

Dugan, I. Jeanne. "Will Triarc Make Snapple Crackle?" *Business Week*, 28 April 1997, 64–65.

Feder, Barnaby J. "Quaker Oats and Iced Tea Just Won't Mix." *New York Times*, 7 August 1996.

————. "Quaker Waking Up to a Snapple Hangover." *New York Times*, 3 November 1996.

————. "Quaker to Sell Snapple for $300 Million." *New York Times*, 28 March 1997.

"Quaker Oats." *Financial Times*, 22 June 1995.

Sears

"American Retailing: Back to the Future." *Economist*, 9 October 1993, 74.

Berss, Marcia. "A Turnaround Is the Best Revenge." *Forbes*, 3 August 1992, 83.

————. "We Will Not Be in a National Chain." *Forbes*, 27 March 1995, 50.

Bremner, Brian. "Now Sears Has Everyday Low Profits, Too." *Business Week*, 21 August 1989, 28.

Caminiti, Susan. "Sears' Need: More Speed." *Fortune*, 15 July 1991, 88.

Chandler, Susan. "Sears' Turnaround Is for Real—For Now." *Business Week*, 15 August 1994, 102.

————. "Where Sears Wants America to Shop Now." *Business Week*, 12 June 1995, 39.

————. "An Endangered Species Makes a Comeback." *Business Week*, 27 November 1995, 96.

————. "Gloomy Days Are Here Again." *Business Week*, 8 January 1996, 103.

Dobrzynski, Judith H. "Yes, He's Revived Sears: But Can He Reinvent It?" *New York Times*, 7 January 1996.

"Downsizing. And Now, Upsizing." *Economist*, 8 June 1996, 72.

Dunkin, Amy. "It's a Lot Tougher to Mind the Store." *Business Week*, 8 January 1990, 85.

Ellis, James. "Will the Big Markdown Get the Big Store Moving Again?" *Business Week*, 13 March 1989, 110.

Eng, Paul. "War of the Web." *Business Week*, 4 March 1996, 71.

Flynn, Julia. "Smaller But Wiser." *Business Week*, 12 October 1992, 28.

Greenwald, John. "Reinventing Sears." *Time*, 23 December 1996, 53.

Heins, John. "Name Recognition." *Forbes*, 30 November 1987, 137.

"Home Shopping: Home Alone?" *Economist*, 12 October 1996, 67.

Kelly, Kevin. "At Sears, the More Things Change . . . ." *Forbes*, 12 November 1990, 66.

————. "How Did Sears Blow This Gasket?" *Business Week*, 29 June 1992, 38.

Klebnikow, Paul. "A Little Brother's Big Score." *Forbes*, 26 November 1990, 148.

Lesly, Elisabeth. "When Layoffs Alone Don't Turn the Tide." *Business Week*, 7 December 1992, 100.

Loomis, Carol J. "Dinosaurs?" *Fortune*, 3 May 1993, 36.

McWilliams, Gary. "Strategies for the New Mail Order." *Business Week*, 19 December 1994, 82.

O'Neal, Michael. "Sears: Trimming the Worst of the Corporate Fat." *Business Week*, 16 March 1987, 39.

Power, Christopher. "Sears Catches the Value Bug." *Business Week*, 11 November 1991, 140.

Saporito, Bill. "Markdowns at Sears Roebucks." *Fortune*, 10 September 1990, 16.

"Sears, Roebuck: Minding the Store." *Economist*, 3 October 1992, 75.

Sellers, Patricia. "Sears: In with the New . . . Out with the Old." *Fortune*, 16 October 1995, 96.

———. "Sears: The Turnaround Is Ending; The Revolution Has Begun." *Fortune*, 28 April 1997, 106.

Siler, Julia Flynn. "Are the Lights Dimming for Ed Brennan?" *Business Week*, 11 February 1991, 56.

"Third Time Lucky?" *Economist*, 5 November 1988, 78.

Weiner, Steve. "Don't Write Sears off." *Forbes*, 28 November 1988, 196.

Weitzel, William, and Ellen Jonsson. "Reversing the Downward Spiral: Lessons from W. T. Grant and Sears Roebuck." *Academy of Management Executive* (August 1991): 7.

Sony

Brull, Steven V. "Sony's New World." *Business Week International Editions*, 27 May 1996, 36.

Cooper, Robin. "Sony Corporation: The Walkman Line." Case 9-195-076. Boston: Harvard Business School, 1994.

Starbucks

Amery, Elizabeth. "Catch the Jolt." *Forbes*, 21 April 1997.

Browder, Seanna. "Starbucks Does Not Live by Coffee Alone." *Business Week*, 5 August 1996, 76.

"Green, as in Greenbacks." *Economist*, 1 February 1997, 42.

Hawn, Carleen. "Drunk on Coffee: How a Lofty Vision Became an Overhyped Stock." *Forbes*, 10 February 1997.

Henkoff, Ronald. "Growing Your Company: Five Ways to Do It Right." *Fortune*, 25 November 1996, 78–88.

Holland, Kelley, and Peter Coy. "Starbucks' Use of the Old Bean." *Business Week*, 31 March 1997.

Katz, Ian. "The Wrong Kind of Coffee Is King . . . But a Cold Snap Has Opened Eyes." *Business Week*, 17 March 1997, 4.

Leonhardt, David. "Grabbing Bargains—And a $2 Cup of Coffee." *Business Week*, 17 March 1997, 90.

Reese, Jennifer. "Starbucks: Inside the Coffee Cult." *Fortune*, 9 December 1996.

Waxler, Caroline. "Starcrossed?" *Forbes*, 19 May 1997, 276.

Sun Microsystems

Bottoms, David. "Technology of the Year." *Industry Week*, 18 December 1995, 36.

Hof, Robert D. "The New Sizzle at Sun." *Business Week*, 13 November 1996, 48.

"Java Industry Sets a New Agenda." *Business Wire*, 2 April 1997.

Markoff, John. "Staking Claim in Alternative Software on the Internet." *New York Times*, 25 September 1995.

Moukheiber, Zina. "Windows NT—Never!" *Forbes*, 23 September 1996, 42–43.

Schlender, Brent. "Sun's Java: The Threat to Microsoft Is Real." *Fortune*, 11 November 1996, 165–170.

———. "The Adventures of Scott McNealy—Javaman!" *Fortune*, 13 October 1997, 70–78.

"Sun Java Processors to Supercharge Next Generation of Java Powered Consumer Appliances." *PR Newswire*, 2 April 1997.

"Sun Microsystems Chief: A Mission against 'Dark Side.'" *San Jose Mercury News*, 27 January 1997.

Time Warner

Garvin, David, and Jonathan West. "Time Life Inc. (A)." Case 9-395-012. Boston: Harvard Business School, 1995.

Rothenberg, Randall. "Time Warner Marketing Its Synergy." *New York Times*, 15 February 1990.

"Ted Turner's Management Consultant." *Economist*, 22 March 1997.

"Time Life Names IVI Publishing Exclusive Publisher for Health and Medical Multimedia Products." *Business Wire*, 19 October 1994.

"Time Warner, Turner Agree to Merge." *Reuters Financial Service*, 22 September 1995.

Zimmerman, Susan. "Time Warner Unveils Online Service." *Reuters Financial Service*, 10 September 1996.

Toyota

Bardacke, Ted, and Michiyo Nakamoto. "New Entries in Asian Car Race." *Financial Times*, 11 February 1997, 30.

Bremmer, Brian, Larry Armstrong, Kathleen Kerwin, and Keith Naughton. "Toyota's Crusade." *Business Week*, 7 April 1997, 104.

Kerwin, Kathleen. "Can This Minivan Dent Detroit?" *Business Week*, 3 February 1997, 37.

Margrath, Allan J. "The Importance of Unlearning." *Across the Board* (February 1997): 39.

"On the March." *Economist*, 22 March 1997, 83–84.

Taylor, Alex III. "Toyota's Boss Stands Out in a Crowd." *Fortune*, 25 November 1996, 116–122.

Updike, Edith. "Toyota: The Lion Awakens." *Business Week*, 11 November 1996, 52.

Walt Disney Company

Dubrowski, Jerry. "Disney Posts Higher Profits on Growth in All Units." *Reuters*, 26 November 1996.

Grover, Ronald. "At Disney, There's Life after Toons." *Business Week*, 11 November 1996.

Handy, Bruce. "Miracle On 42nd Street." *Time*, 7 April 1997.

Harbison, Georgia, and Jeffrey Ressner. "Independent's Day." *Time*, 24 February 1997.

Koselka, Rita. "Mergermania in Medialand." *Forbes*, 23 October 1995.

"The Disney Publishing Group Names Jorgan Copland to Newly Created Position, Director of Business Development." *PR Newswire*, 26 August 1996.

INDEX

Monte Carlo simulation, 134
Montreal Canadiens, 223
Moore, Gordon, 163
"Moore's Law," 164, 166
Motorola, 5, 163
  bibliography of, 278
  Power PC microprocessor of, 164
  and rhythm, 181
Multiple business strategy
  at Galaxy, 77–78
  at Jupiter, 71
  at Tai-pan, 84
  at Time Life, 59–60
Mutations, 97, 111, 112, 119

NASA, 132, 134–135, 147, 148
  interplanetary exploration by, 133
Naskapi people, 95–98, 116, 118
National Semiconductor, 163
Natural selection, 14, 97, 98, 105, 113
Nautilus (pseudonym) case study, 42–45,
    48, 51, 53, 54, 55, 149, 154,
    156–158, 251
  business implications, 44, 146
  reacting to the future at, 144–147
NBC, 10, 64, 164
Neagle, Denny, 224
Netcom, 174
NetPC, 5
Netscape, 10, 11, 166, 193
  and use of time pacing, 166
Newton, 105
NewWave (pseudonym) case study, 105,
    106–110, 115, 116, 118,
    121–122, 251
  business implications, 108–109
New York Stock Exchange, 91
New York Yankees, 222, 225
Nexus of strategy and tactics, 80, 81
Nike, 25, 33, 56, 245
  ability of to compete for customers,
    27–28
  bibliography of, 278–279
  footwear
    Air, 27
    Air Jordan, 56
    Air Max, 27
    Air Zoom, 27
  and return on investment, 30

Nike Town, 27
Nintendo, 111
  bibliography of, 279
  N64 machine of, 111
Nissan, 193
No attention to future, 143, 145–146,
    147
Nokia, 64, 148, 154, 193, 237
  bibliography of, 279–280
"No one in charge" trait, 73, 74–76
No-sight trap, 141–147
  diagram of, 143
  traits of managers falling into, 143
  warning signals for, 146–147
Novelty
  critical to success, 97
  too little, 99, 100–101
  too much, 106, 107, 109
No vision about business in future, 143,
    144, 146
Noyce, Bob, 163
Nucor, 3, 193

Old and new
  blending, 111, 115–116
  chasm between, 106, 108, 110
  speeding the blend of, 114, 116–118,
    120
Old Navy Kids, 112–113, 117
Old Navy stores, 112–113, 117, 227,
    254
One market vision, 137, 138, 141
"Only the paranoid survive," 163, 165
Options, 134, 135, 151
Oracle, 5, 107, 239
Order, science behind, 209
"Organization chart" mindset, 226
Organizations
  change mechanisms of, 14
  rules of, 244–246
Overcollaboration, 65–72
  warning signals of, 71–72
Overconnect trap, 98–104

Pacing. *See* Time pacing
Past
  as critical, 97
  gaining advantages of the, 89–123
  ignoring the, 104–110

ABOUT THE AUTHORS

Shona L. Brown is a consultant with McKinsey & Company, where her work spans multiple technology-based and consumer-focused industries. Dr. Brown's expertise is in the management of innovation, strategy, and marketing in highly uncertain, rapidly changing markets. She received her Ph.D. in strategy and organizational theory from Stanford University. She also holds an M.A. in economics and philosophy from Oxford University, where she studied as a Rhodes scholar, and a B.Eng. in systems and computer engineering from Carleton University.

Kathleen M. Eisenhardt is a professor of strategy and organization at Stanford University, where her work focuses on management in fast-paced, highly competitive industries. Her awards include the Pacific Telesis Foundation Award for her ideas on fast strategic decision making, the Whittemore Prize for her writing on organizing global firms in rapidly changing markets, and the Stern Award for her work on strategic alliance formation in entrepreneurial companies. Professor Eisenhardt has consulted for a number of firms, including Hewlett-Packard and Intel. She earned her B.S. in mechanical engineering from Brown University and her Ph.D. from the Graduate School of Business at Stanford University.